Learn Japanese for Adult Beginners

Speak Japanese in 30 Days!

3 Books in 1

Explore to Win

THIS COLLECTION INCLUDES
THE FOLLOWING BOOKS:

Complete Japanese Workbook for Adult Beginners:
Hiragana & Katakana
Speak Japanese In 30 Days!

Japanese Phrasebook for Adult Beginners:
Common Japanese Words & Phrases For Everyday Conversation and Travel

Learn Japanese with Short Stories for Adult Beginners
Shortcut Your Japanese Fluency! (Fun & Easy Reads)

Table of Contents

$~~100+~~ FREE BONUSES

Japanese Video Lessons

Japanese Flashcards + 30-Day Study Plan

100 Japanese Audio Pronunciations

Japanese Stories Audiobook

Japanese Conversations Narrated

Premium Japanese Learning Software

Scan QR code to claim your bonuses

— OR —

visit bit.ly/3shFIJg

BOOK 1

Complete Japanese Workbook for Adult Beginners: Hiragana & Katakana

Speak Japanese In 30 Days!

Explore to Win

Introduction

「きこそもののなれ 」

"What you love to do, you will learn to do well."
- Japanese Proverb

Doki Doki! ("Thump Thump"). Your Japanese-learning journey will be eye-opening, self-discovering, and quietly mind-blowing. This might be your "Blue Pill/Red Pill" moment, just like in the movie "Matrix," and you will decide between the willingness to learn something life-changing or remaining in ordinary everyday life. The Japanese language is considered one of the most challenging languages in the world because the language is so different in many ways down to the ways of thinking, but what if you can understand and speak it fluently?

Learn Japanese Workbook for Adult Beginners: Hiragana & Katakana, Speak Japanese in 30 Days! is the ideal book to start the Japanese-learning journey.

You will learn what you need for the first step in basic Japanese. Learn Japanese for Adult Beginners: 3 Books in 1; in this book 1, you will learn basic writing systems and basic grammar. Learning how to write Hiragana and Katakana, and read basic Kanji is critical to understand how the Japanese syllabus works and the fundamental structure.

By the end of this book, you should be able to write and read Hiragana and Katakana and understand basic grammar for everyday communication. You will also learn how to word a sentence and how to use basic particles and vocabulary. The units consist of different conjugation forms.

The Japanese conjugation forms are demanding and require repetitive practice. However, if you achieve this challenge, you should be able to reach an A1 level and have a sufficient command of Japanese for starters in 30 days!

The first target will be the two basic writing systems. Spaghetti-like characters, Hiragana, seem easier for many international students to memorize than number-like characters, Katakana. We will practice stroke orders as well and the effective learning will be writing with reading aloud at the same time so your listening/pronunciation skills will be improved faster. This is the first critical moment to see if you are capable of Japanese dictation. If you can catch and write down what the speaker says it will be so much easier to build vocabulary and expressions. Also, it's going to be so much easier for Japanese internalization, to think in Japanese.

The authors of this book are native Japanese instructors who have taught English-speaking students who had no knowledge of Japanese and now work at Japanese corporations after several months of training. The instructors understand the fundamental differences from English and can give you excellent tips on how to write and pronounce natural-sounding Japanese in this book. The cultural background behind communication also plays a vital role to understand the language.

You will become the master of a neutral way of communication, so you don't sound rude or childish to strangers or elders. And we will give you simple examples to say in a formal way and a more casual/friendly manner as well. One of the most significant communication differences from American culture is politeness/casual friendliness. So, showing respect by being polite is more focused in Japan, while showing acceptance by being friendly in the US.

The conclusion will summarize all the content so you can review and check everything you learned in the chapter. Besides, you will also give easy drills to start practicing for real-life communication in each chapter. You can check the answer key to double-check your language.

As a motivational booster, we strongly recommend immersing yourself in Japanese Anime, Movies, TV Dramas, Martial Arts, or Games. You can pick one Anime or Drama and watch/listen to it repeatedly. So, you will understand the language and culture simultaneously.

Sukikoso monono jouzu nare 「きこそもののなれ」

When you love to do, you will learn to do well.

Be Waku Waku! (excited!)

For Starters

"Only you can fill in what's missing. It's not something another person can do for you."

- Haruki Murakami

There are three writing systems in Japanese: Hiragana, Katakana and Kanji. In the first two chapters, we will learn about Hiragana and Katakana.

In three writing systems, there are two writing directions. Vertically from Top to Bottom, and Lines go from Right to Left (1st Image). Also, Horizontally from Right to Left, and Lines go from Top to Bottom (2nd Image).

<table>
<tr>
<td>

↓こんにちは。はじめ
まして。どうぞよろし
くお願いします。

</td>
<td>

→こんにちは。はじめまして。どう
ぞよろしくお願いします。

</td>
</tr>
</table>

Hiragana (sounds "hear-uh-gah -na") is the most fundamental writing system in Japanese. It is a syllabary and consists of two English letters (Romanization) and shows one sound or syllable. For example, T+O=TO ： と. とis always と in any word or sentence.

Hiragana is used for particles and additional conjugation forms of verbs and adjectives, while kanji is used for the main verb, noun, and adjective parts and meaning. Hiragana writing can be interpreted in many ways because of many homophones. So, once kanji is written, it conveys meanings and definitions.

For example, the Japanese first name, Akira ： あきら, only shows three sounds (a-ki-ra) in Hiragana but doesn't convey any meaning. So once the kanji letter(s) are applied, the meaning will be clarified. Akira can be "Light," "Shining," "Clear," "Warm-hearted," "Smart" etc. depending on which kanji(s) you choose.

Spaghetti-shaped Hiragana is not difficult to master or write, however, the stroke order and direction of the strokes do matter because that makes it easier to read someone's hasty handwriting and figure out from the flow of characters.

Katakana is also a syllabify and is used mainly for foreign words such as sandwich and computer. Foreign words fit into the limited sets of Japanese consonants and vowel sounds; however, it sometimes sounds and looks very different from the original English and is difficult to understand for English speakers. So, the best way to learn Katakana words is to learn as Japanese words. Even for names, Mr. Daniel will turn into "Misuta Danielu."

The third writing system, Kanji, originated from the Chinese language and was used mainly by men in medieval Japan. Simplified and invented from Kanji, Hiragana promoted the literacy rate and provided opportunities for women to communicate. However, the first ever written novel in the world, "The Tale of Genji," was written by a woman, Murasaki Shikibu, early in the eleventh century. Even though Murasaki Shikibu was so talented and familiar with Kanji, Chinese poems, and Chinese writing, she pretended not to be able to write any kanji, even "one" (一), to be politically savvy and avoid envy. Her novel is considered the first "psychological novel."

Phonetic Writing System and Romanization

There are no upper/lower cases in Japanese writing systems. The period is this punctuation mark 。, the quotation mark is 「」, and the comma is 、. There are generally no spaces between words. In the beginning, for more clarification and understanding, we will add some spaces between words.

One character One Sound	T+O＝と, T+A=た
Upper/Lower Cases	No upper/lower cases
Period	. = 。
Quotation	"" = 「」
Comma	, = 、

The Roman letters (Romaji : ローマ) are used to spell out sounds and are written in signs and directions for foreign residents and visitors in Japan. Romaji is also used to type on the computer. Romaji sounds are based on the five vowels and the pronunciation is relatively simple.

For example, i (sounds like eeh) pronounces always the same in words and sentences, not like English words such as "light" and "little." To avoid confusion, we use lowercase for Romaji.

How To Type in Japanese

You should be able to add the Japanese language in the computer setting and choose "Romaji" input. Then you can use the alphabet keyboard to input Japanese. Once you learn Hiragana and Katakana, you can type Japanese in Romaji, and you can choose Hiragana, Katakana or Kanji selections by hitting the space bar.

For example, if you type 「かんじ(kanji)」 then hit the space bar, you can choose the right choice among many different かんじ in the popup window. To scroll down the selections, you can hit the space bar, and once you find the right one, you can press enter to input.

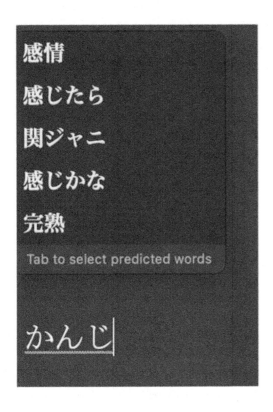

Question Marks

When a sentence ends with the particle か（ka）, that indicates the sentence is a question, even though you don't see any indication of a question sentence.

「こちらはダニエルです。(kochira wa Daniel desu)」 "This is Daniel."

「こちらはダニエルですか。(kochira wa Daniel desuka)」 "Is this Daniel?"

Normal Vowels

Here are the most important five basic vowels, and all words end with vowels.

Romaji	Pronunciation	Example
a（あ）	(Just like father)	Aki (Fall)：あき
i（い）	(Just like easy)	Ima (Now)：いま
u（う）	(Just like wood)	Umi (Sea)：うみ
e（え）	(Just like ten)	Ebi (Shrimp)：えび
o（お）	(Just like coat)	Otona (Adult)：おとな

Long Vowel Sound

Long vowels are extended vowel sounds for twice as long as short vowels by adding 「あ」(a)「い」(i)「う」(u).

1. 「ああ」 "aa" ex. おかあさん okaasan : Mother

2. 「いい」 "ii" ex. おじいさんojiisan : Grandfather

3. 「うう」 "uu" ex. くうき　kuuki : Air

4. 「ええ」 "ee" ex. おさんoneesanおねえさん : Older Sister

5. 「おお」 "oo" ex. きい ookii おおきい : Big

Furigana

Furigana is hiragana or katakana writing in small forms above kanji to show the pronunciation. Because each kanji character has a few ways of pronunciation, any formal forms require Furigana on top of the kanji name and addresses.

い（いたい, itai: Painful)

Double Consonant and Small 「っ」

In addition to lengthened sounds, another feature in Japanese pronunciation is the "Staccato" sound written in double consonants such as "kk," "pp," and "tt" in Romaji, this sound must be stressed and have a small space between syllabi such as "Mack" and "Mock."

In Hiragana, small っ(tsu)is written between two characters to represent a clogged sound and is called 小さな「つ」(chiisana "tsu"). When you add a small っfor example, between mo 「も」 and to 「と」 : もと moto （Former or Originally） becomes もっと motto(More) in a totally different meaning.

When you see the small っ at the end of a word, especially in Manga dialogue, not only it stresses the sound and rhythm but also shows highlighted emotions. For example, you might see in Manga comics, 「いたっ」(Ita tsu) shows the impactful shocking sensation of pain, "Ouch!"

Double Consonant (Small っ) Example

Single Consonant	Double Consonant
mata また(Again)	matta まった(Waited/Not yet)
oto おと(Sound)	otto おっと （Husband）
soto そと(Outside)	sotto そっと （quietly）

Japanese "R"

There is much discussions about Japanese "R" sounds. For many, it sounds close to "L." For example, "Lock" and "Rock" are the same in Japanese. When you pronounce Japanese "Ra" 「ら」 "Ri" 「り」 "Ru" 「る」 "Re" 「れ」 "Ro" 「ろ」 correctly, they are considered somewhere between La Li Lu Le Lo and Da Di Du De Do and so much easier for Spanish speakers to pronounce. So some pronunciations such as "Larry" "Relay" and "Laura" are in Japanese ラリー (rari-), リレー(rire-), and ローラ(ro-ra), and they are so confusing for English speakers.

Basic Numbers

Number	Japanese	Pronunciation
0	zero, rei, maru	dzeh-roh, ray, marooh
1	ichi 「いち」	ee-chee
2	ni 「に」	nee
3	san 「さん」	sahn
4	shi, yon 「し」「よん」	shee, yon
5	go 「ご」	goh
6	roku 「ろく」	roh-koo
7	shichi, nana 「しち」「なな」	see-chee, nahnah
8	hachi 「はち」	hah-chee
9	kyuu, ku 「きゅう」「く」	cue, koo
10	juu 「じゅう」	jooh
11	juu ichi 「じゅういち」	jooh-ee-chee
12	juu ni 「じゅういさん」	jooh-nee
13	juu san 「じゅういち」	jooh-san
14	juu yon, juu shi 「じゅうよん」「じゅうし」	jooh-yon, jooh-shee
15	juu go 「じゅうご」	jooh-goh

16	juu roku 「じゅうろく」	jooh-roh-koo
17	juu shichi , juu nana, 「じゅうしち」「じゅうなな」	jooh-sheechee, jooh-nahnah,
18	juu hachi 「じゅうはち」	jooh- hah-chee
19	juu kyuu, juu ku, 「じゅうきゅう」「じゅうく」	jooh-cue , jooh-koo
20	ni juu 「にじゅう」	nee-jooh
21	ni juu ichi 「にじゅういち」	nee-jooh -ee-chee
22	ni juu ni 「にじゅうに」	nee-jooh -nee
23	ni juu san 「にじゅうさん」	nee-jooh - sahn
24	ni juu yon, ni juu shi 「にじゅうよん」「にじゅうし」	nee-jooh- yon, nee-jooh-shee
25	ni juu go 「にじゅうご」	nee-jooh-goh
26	ni juu roku 「にじゅうろく」	nee-jooh- roh-koo
27	ni juu shichi , ni juu nana 「にじゅうしち」「にじゅうなな」	nee-jooh-sheechee, nee-jooh-nahnah,
28	ni juu hachi 「にじゅうはち」	nee-jooh-hah-chee
29	ni juu kyu , ni juu ku 「にじゅうきゅう」「にじゅうく」	nee-jooh-cue , nee-jooh-koo
30	san juu 「さんじゅう」	sahn-jooh
40	yon juu, shi juu 「よんじゅう」「しじゅう」	yon-jooh, shee-jooh
50	go juu 「ごじゅう」	goh-jooh
60	roku juu 「ろくじゅう」	roh-koo-jooh

70	nana juu「ななじゅう」	nahnah-jooh
80	hachi juu「はちじゅう」	hah-chee-jooh
90	kyuu juu「きゅうじゅう」	cue-jooh
100	hyaku「ひゃく」	hee-yaku

Two ways of pronunciation for 4,7, and 9

As you see in the three numbers of 4,7, and 9 there are two sounds. This is due to similarities in sounds with "back luck." One pronunciation of the number 4 (shi「し」) can be death(「死」し shi), although 7 (shichi「しち」)is also bad luck number because it can be 「死地」(shich, death place). Number 9 is ku or kyuu, ku is the same sound as ku (「苦」ku, suffering）.

Because of these "bad luck" similarities, the Japanese culture avoids using these numbers and added another sound.

Survival Japanese Words/Phrases

The following are very basic words/phrases in every Japanese. Those words are simple and easy to remember.

Greetings

おはようございます　ohayou gozaimasu	Good morning
こんにちは kon-nichiwa	Hello/Good afternoon
こんばんは konbanwa	Good evening
では、また dewa mata （じゃあ、また）jaa mata	See you later. See you later (casual)
ありがとうございますarigatou gozaimasu	Thank you
いただきます itadakimasu	I respectfully have this food (before a meal).
ごちそうさまでした gochisousamadeshita	Thank you for the food (at the end of a meal).
いってきます/いってらっしゃい itte kimasu/ Itte rasshai	I'll be back (This phrase is used when you leave your home/hotel/office.)/Have a good day (This phrase is only used in a situation when the person leaving will be back.)
ただいま/おかえりなさい	I'm home (I'm back)/Welcome back.

9

tadama/okaerinasai	

Everyday Phrases

すみません sumimasen	Sorry/Excuse me/Thank you
はい/いいえ hai/iie	Yes/No
そうです/ちがいます so desu/chigai masu	That's right/ That's wrong
わかりますか wakarimasu ka わかりません/わかります wakarimasen/wakarimasu	Do you understand? I don't understand/ I understand
だいじょうぶですか daijoubu desuka だいじょうぶです daijoubu desu	Are you all right? I'm all right.
いいですか iidesuka	May I...?/ It is okay?
どうぞ douzo すみません、ちょっと sumimasen, chotto	Please Sorry, but
もういちどおねがいします mouichido onegai shimasu	Could you say that again?

sumimasen: Sorry = Thank you??? How do they co-exist?

Arigatou: When you directly translate the word, it means "impossible" or "difficult." The underlying meaning is "you did something impossible/difficult for me and I am grateful for that" or "This situation is so rare like a miracle that I'm humbly thankful."

When they say "Sorry(sumimasen)" instead of "Thank you," the mindset behind it is something like "I'm sorry to have you do this extra work" or "I'm sorry to have you worry about me." So, the phrase is not about something bad you did and had to apologize for it, but the focus is more on the other person in the interaction.

Take-home message

The Japanese survival phrases and greetings are easy to pronounce and remember. There are only five vowels: a, i, u, e, and o. The only tricky sounds are long vowels and double consonants. "Mother" is "okaasan," "grandfather" is "ojiisan", and "more"is "motto."

Once you learned the Japanese numbers from 1-10, the teens and the tens are not difficult to remember. For teens, juu(10) first and add the single digit, 13 is juu-san and 15 is juu-go. The tens are in the same order as English, 20 is ni-juu, 30 is san-juu, and 35 is san-juu-go.

You may hear "sumimasen," from Japanese natives a lot once you travel to Japan. Most of the cases, it means more like "Thank you." When you interact with a person, the communication focus is more on the other person. Japan is a small country with a high population density. Politeness is part of the culture to keep peace and order on islands from the history lessons of civil wars.

Exercises

1. Name the following numbers in Japanese

5 _____

7 _____

10 _____

1 _____

27 _____

2 _____

4 _____

11 _____

50 _____

8 _____

12 _____

15 _____

13 _____

9 _____

16 _____

40 _____

19 _____

55 _____

18 _____

14 _____

2. Please answer the phrases.

"daijobu desuka?" _____

"okaeri nasai"_____

"wakarimasuka?" _____

3. Write the following numbers in figures:

san juu ni_____

juu yon_____

roku juu nana_____

juu ku _____

nijuu go_____

4. Please choose the right phrase.
"Good evening."
A. konnichiwa
B. konbanwa
C . jaa mata
"No"
A. ie
B. iie
C. iee

"Please"
A. douzo
B. doujo
C. doumo

"I don't understand."
A. wakarimasu.
B. wakarimasen.
C. wakariyasui.

"Thank you & sorry."
A. sumimasen
B. sumidagawa
C. arigatou

"That's right."
A. so desu
B. so desuka
C. chigaimasu

"I'm home (I'm back)."

A. tadaima

B. okaeri

C. ohayo

"May I...?/ It is okay?"

A. iyadesuka

B. iidesuka

C. imadesuka

5. Write the other pronunciation in Romaji

"yon(4)"
"nana(7)"
"ku(9)"

6. Change sentences to questions.

"daijoubu desu." _____

"so desu." _____

"chigai masu." _____

7. Choose the right phrase in the situation.

You ordered a cup of coffee and cheesecake, but a waiter brought iced tea and cheese sandwiches.

A. "arigatou gozaimasu"

B. "ohayo gozaimasu."

C. "sumimasen, chotto."

8. Choose the right phrase in the situation.

You're invited for a dinner at your friend's house. The food is all set, and everyone is at the table and ready to eat.

A. "arigatou gozaimasu"

B. "ittekimasu."

C. "itadakimasu."

Answer Keys

1. go, nana/shichi, juu, ichi, ni juu nana, ni, yon/shi, juu ichi, go juu, hachi, juu ni, juu go, juu san, kyu/ku, juu roku, yon/shi juu, juu kyu/ku, go juu go, juu hachi, and juu yon/shi.

2. "daijoubu desu"

"tadaima",

and "wakarimasu"

3. 32, 14, 67, 19, and 25

4. "Good evening," B (konbanwa)

"No," B (iie)

"Please," A(douzo)

"I don't know," B (wakarimasen)

"Thank you & sorry," A (sumimasen)

"That's right." A (so desu)

"I'm home." A (tadaima)

"May I...?/It is okay?" B (iidesuka)

5. 4 "shi," 7 "shichi," and 9 "kyu."

6. "daijoubu desuka"

"so desuka"

"chigai masuka"

7. C, "sumimasen, chotto."

8. C, "itadakimasu."

16

Hiragana-1

"There is more here than meet the eye."

- Murasaki Shikibu

Hiragana is the most fundamental wring system and phonetic script. You can technically write all the words in Japanese; however, because Japanese has so many homophones and is written with no space, it is difficult to understand the meaning of all hiragana writing.

Writing Hiragana in the correct order and direction is important because stroke direction is key to understanding handwriting. In the following Hiragana table, it's important not only to memorize how to write but also to match the script and the sound so reading aloud while writing is strongly recommended. All Japanese words are composed of the Hiragana sounds, and learning the correct pronunciation for a letter is critical for fluency.

Here is the instruction.

1. Basic hiragana-1: Read aloud with correct pronunciation

2. Basic hiragana-1: Trace the stroke order. One number has one stroke and the stroke includes a curbed line, 90-degree turn, U-turn and bounce fade (below in gray circle).

3. Basic hiragana-1: Write in the correct order. Continue Exercise A-B-C

4. Quiz A

5. Building Vocabulary

Basic hiragana-1

Read aloud from あ to お, then from the second line か to こ, to all the way down.

	A	I	U	E	O
	あ a ("ah")	い i ("ee")	う u("oo")	え e("eh")	お o("oh")
K	か ka("ca"r)	き ki("kee"p)	く ku("coo"l)	け ke("ke"n)	こ ko("co"t)
S	さ sa("sa"t)	し shi("she")	す su("sue")	せ se("se"t)	そ so ("so"le)
T	た ta("tah")	ち chi("chee")	つ tsu("tsu")	て te("tes")	と to("toh")
N	な na("nah")	に ni("knee")	ぬ nu("noo")	ね ne("ne"t)	の no("no"te)
H	は ha("ha"t)	ひ hi("hi"t)	ふ fu("fu")	へ he("hea"d)	ほ ho("ho"pe)
M	ま ma("ma"t)	み mi("me")	む mu("moo"n)	め me("me"xico)	も mo("mo"re)
Y	や ya("ya"cht)		ゆ yu("yew")		よ yo("yo"ga)
R	ら ra("ra"men)	り ri("ri"ck)	る ru("ru"by)	れ re("re"d)	ろ ro("ro"ck)
W	わ wa("wha"t)				を wo("wo"rry)
	ん n(li "n"k)				

18

HOW TO WRITE hiragana-1

BASIC RULE: Horizontal Line →(from Left to Right) & Vertical Line ↓(from Top to Bottom)
Each number is one stroke.

A	I	U	E	O
あ a ("ah")	い i ("ee")	う u ("oo")	え e("eh")	お o("oh")
か ka("ca"r)	き ki("kee"p)	く ku("coo"l)	け ke("ke"n)	こ ko("co"t)
さ sa("sa"t)	し shi("she")	す su("sue")	せ se("se"t)	そ so ("so"le)
た ta("tah")	ち chi("chee")	つ tsu("tsu")	て te("tes")	と to("toh")
な na("nah")	に ni("knee")	ぬ nu("noo")	ね ne("ne"t)	の no("no"te)
ほ ha("ha"t)	ひ hi("hi"t)	ふ fu("fu")	へ he("hea"d)	ほ ho("ho"pe)
ま ma("ma"t)	み mi("me")	む mu("moo"n)	め me("me"xico)	も mo("mo"re)
や ya("ya"cht)		ゆ yu("yew")		よ yo("yo"ga)
ら ra("ra"men)	り ri("ri"ck)	る ru("ru"by)	れ re("re"d)	ろ ro("ro"ck)
わ wa("wha"t)				を wo("wo"rry)
ん n(li "n"k)				

19

HOW TO WRITE hiragana-1
BASIC RULE: Horizontal Line →(from Left to Right) & Vertical Line ↓(from Top to Bottom)
Each number is one stroke.

	A	I	U	E	O
	あ a ("ah")	い i ("ee")	う u("oo")	え e("eh")	お o("oh")
K	か ka("ca"r)	き ki("kee"p)	く ku("coo"l)	け ke("ke"n)	こ ko("co"t)
S	さ sa("sa"t)	し shi("she")	す su("sue")	せ se("se"t)	そ so ("so"le)
T	た ta("tah")	ち chi("chee")	つ tsu("tsu")	て te("tes")	と to("toh")
N	な na("nah")	に ni("knee")	ぬ nu("noo")	ね ne("ne"t)	の no("no"te)
H	は ha("ha"t)	ひ hi("hi"t)	ふ fu("fu")	へ he("hea"d)	ほ ho("ho"pe)
M	ま ma("ma"t)	み mi("me")	む mu("moo"n)	め me("me"xico)	も mo("mo"re)
Y	や ya("ya"cht)		ゆ yu("yew")		よ yo("yo"ga)
R	ら ra("ra"men)	り ri("ri"ck)	る ru("ru"by)	れ re("re"d)	ろ ro("ro"ck)
W	わ wa("wha"t)				を wo("wo"rry)
S	ん n(li "n"k)				

20

Basic hiragana-1
Writing Exercise (■is the starting point) A
Please write in a pencil so you can correct/repeat.

	A	I	U	E	O
	a ("ah")	i ("ee")	u("oo")	e("eh")	o("oh")
K	ka("ca"r)	ki("kee"p)	ku("coo"l)	ke("ke"n)	ko("co"t)
S	sa("sa"t)	shi("she")	su("sue")	se("se"t)	so ("so"le)
T	ta("tah")	chi("chee")	tsu("tsu")	te("tes")	to("toh")
N	na("nah")	ni("knee")	nu("noo")	ne("ne"t)	no("no"te)
H	ha("ha"t)	hi("hi"t)	fu("fu")	he("hea"d)	ho("ho"pe)
M	ma("ma"t)	mi("me")	mu("moo"n)	me("me"xico)	mo("mo"re)
Y	ya("ya"cht)		yu("yew")		yo("yo"ga)
R	ra("ra"men)	ri("ri"ck)	ru("ru"by)	re("re"d)	ro("ro"ck)
W	wa("wha"t)				wo("wo"rry)
S	n(li "n"k)				

Writing Exercise B

Please write in a pencil so you can correct/repeat.

	A	I	U	E	O
	あ	い	う	え	お
	a ("ah")	i ("ee")	u("oo")	e("eh")	o("oh")
K	か	き	く	け	こ
	ka("ca"r)	ki("kee"p)	ku("coo"l)	ke("ke"n)	ko("co"t)
S	さ	し	す	せ	そ
	sa("sa"t)	shi("she")	su("sue")	se("se"t)	so ("so"le)
T	た	ち	つ	て	と
	ta("tah")	chi("chee")	tsu("tsu")	te("tes")	to("toh")
N	な	に	ぬ	ね	の
	na("nah")	ni("knee")	nu("noo")	ne("ne"t)	no("no"te)
H	は	ひ	ふ	へ	ほ
	ha("ha"t)	hi("hi"t)	fu("fu")	he("hea"d)	ho("ho"pe)
M	ま	み	む	め	も
	ma("ma"t)	mi("me")	mu("moo"n)	me("me"xico)	mo("mo"re)
Y	や		ゆ		よ
	ya("ya"cht)		yu("yew")		yo("yo"ga)
R	ら	り	る	れ	ろ
	ra("ra"men)	ri("ri"ck)	ru("ru"by)	re("re"d)	ro("ro"ck)
W	わ				を
	wa("wha"t)				wo("wo"rry)
	ん				
	n(li "n"k)				

Writing Exercise C (Final)

Please write in a pencil so you can correct/repeat.

	A	I	U	E	O
	a ("ah")	i ("ee")	u("oo")	e("eh")	o("oh")
K	ka("ca"r)	ki("kee"p)	ku("coo"l)	ke("ke"n)	ko("co"t)
S	sa("sa"t)	shi("she")	su("sue")	se("se"t)	so ("so"le)
T	ta("tah")	chi("chee")	tsu("tsu")	te("tes")	to("toh")
N	na("nah")	ni("knee")	nu("noo")	ne("ne"t)	no("no"te)
H	ha("ha"t)	hi("hi"t)	fu("fu")	he("hea"d)	ho("ho"pe)
M	ma("ma"t)	mi("me")	mu("moo"n)	me("me"xico)	mo("mo"re)
Y	ya("ya"cht)		yu("yew")		yo("yo"ga)
R	ra("ra"men)	ri("ri"ck)	ru("ru"by)	re("re"d)	ro("ro"ck)
W	wa("wha"t)				wo("wo"rry)
N	n(li "n"k)				

Basic hiragana-1
Vocabulary Building

	A	I	U	E	O
	め ame(rain)	ま ima (now)	み umi(sea)	き eki(station)	と oto(sound)
K	に kani(crab)	た kita(north)	に kuni(country)	が kega(injury)	え koe(voice)
S	け sake(liquor)	お shio(salt)	き suki(like)	ん sen(line)	ら sora (sky)
T	け take(bamboo)	ず chizu(map)	り tsuri(fishing)	ん ten(point)	り tori(bird)
N	か naka(inside/ middle)	し nishi(west)	い inu(dog)	こ neko(cat)	り nori(seaweed)
H	い hai(yes)	る hi("hi"t)	ゆ fuyu(winter)	や heya(room)	ん hon(book)
M	ち machi(town)	ず mizu(water)	ら mura(village)	ん men(noodle)	の mono(thing)
Y	ま yama(mountain)		か yuka(floor)		る yoru(night)
R	か kara(empty)	ゆう riyuu(reason)	す rusu(absence)	きし rekishi(history)	い iro(color)
W	たし watashi(I)				wo(only used in particle, sounds "o")
	か kan(inkling)				

Take-home message

Hiragana is a phonetic writing system. There are only five vowels and 46 Hiragana alphabets. Sounds are relatively simple and easy to remember. The alphabet is mainly used for grammatical functions such as particles. However, it's so important that it can impact the meaning and tone of the context.

Hiragana is believed to be invented from Kanji by a Buddhist monk in 8th century. Kanji was mainly used by men at that time but because of Hiragana, women started using the writing system to express themselves, and the world's first "psychological" novel was born.

The Shodo, Japanese calligraphy, the artistic writing was developed in 7th century among leaders and aristocrats. Handwriting has been respected since then, and it is often said that handwriting can express the person (personality, character, and intelligence) in preciseness, strokes, thick lines, thin lines, straight lines, curved lines, and bounce fades. It is important to remember the stroke orders and write Hiragana elegantly.

Exercises

Basic hiragana-1 Quiz A
(あいうえお/かきくけこ/さしすせそ)
Let's check if you can match the sound with the correct hiragana.

1. Pick and circle the right hiragana for underlined sounds.

ex.	<u>C</u>ar	あ	か (circled)	い
1	W<u>oo</u>l	う	お	こ
2	<u>I</u>taly	え	い	こ
3	<u>Ki</u>d	き	く	け
4	<u>Ca</u>re	か	え	け
5	<u>E</u>dit	お	け	え
6	<u>Coo</u>l	え	く	い
7	<u>Sa</u>turday	そ	き	さ
8	<u>Su</u>e	す	せ	こ
9	<u>She</u>	く	し	け
10	<u>Se</u>t	せ	さ	あ

2. Fill the hiragana to compete the word.

ex.	み <u>せ</u>	Romaji: mise	Meaning: Store
1	__ か	Roma-ji: aka	Meaning: Red
2	__ ら	Romaji: sora	Meaning: Sky
3	__ もの	Romaji: kimono	Meaning: Kimono(Traditional Japanese Clothes)
4	__ __ え	Romaji: iie	Meaning: No
5	__ み	Romaji: kami	Meaning: Paper/God
6	__ し み	Romaji: sashimi	Meaning: Raw Fish
7	__ し	Romaji: sushi	Meaning: Sushi
8	__ え	Romaji: ue	Meaning: Top/Up
9	__ お	Romaji: shio	Meaning: Salt
10	き __	Romaji: kiso	Meaning: Basic

Basic hiragana-1 Quiz B
(たちつてと/なにぬねの/はひふへほ)
Let's check if you can match the sound with the correct hiragana.

1. Pick and circle the right hiragana for underlined sounds.

ex.	<u>T</u>ap	に	(た)	へ
1	<u>Tsu</u>nami	つ	て	こ
2	<u>Ni</u>nja	ち	に	こ
3	<u>Ho</u>me	と	の	ほ
4	<u>To</u>dd	ち	と	に
5	<u>No</u>tice	の	と	に
6	<u>No</u>on	に	な	ぬ
7	<u>Chee</u>se	ち	ら	た
8	<u>Hea</u>d	つ	へ	こ
9	<u>Ha</u>t	は	ほ	た
10	<u>Na</u>p	さ	な	た

2. Fill the hiragana to compete the word.

ex.	つ <u>ち</u>	Romaji: Tsuchi	Meaning: dirt
1	__ り	Roma-ji: tori	Meaning: Bird
2	__ こ	Romaji: tako	Meaning: Octopus
3	__ る	Romaji: hiru	Meaning: Daytime
4	__ じ	Romaji: niji	Meaning: Rainbow
5	__ か	Romaji: chika	Meaning: Underground
6	__	Romaji: te	Meaning: Hand
7	__	Romaji: chi	Meaning: Blood
8	__ り	Romaji: nori	Meaning: Seaweed
9	__ か	Romaji: naka	Meaning: Inside/Middle
10	__ ろ	Romaji: furo	Meaning: Bath

Basic hiragana-1 Quiz C
(まみむめも/やゆよ/らりるれろ/わをん)
Let's check if you can match the sound with the correct hiragana.

1. Pick and circle the right hiragana for underlined sounds.

ex.	<u>Y</u>oung	さ	や	わ
1	<u>M</u>other	さ	ま	ゆ
2	L<u>ea</u>d (metal)	わ	れ	む
3	<u>M</u>oon	む	ゆ	み
4	<u>M</u>ore	と	も	を
5	<u>M</u>ean	ま	む	み
6	<u>L</u>eader	み	し	り
7	<u>M</u>ember	わ	め	ね
8	<u>L</u>oop	ろ	る	そ
9	<u>L</u>obby	る	ろ	も
10	<u>Y</u>outh	わ	ゆ	や

2. Fill the hiragana to compete the word.

ex.	また	Romaji: mata	Meaning: Again
1	＿ん	Roma-ji: men	Meaning: Noodle
2	＿り	Romaji: mori	Meaning: Forest
3	＿	Romaji: me	Meaning: Eye
4	＿り	Romaji: muri	Meaning: Impossible
5	そ＿	Romaji: sora	Meaning: Sky
6	＿ま	Romaji: yama	Meaning: Mountain
7	＿	Romaji: wa	Meaning: Wheel
8	そ＿	Romaji: sore	Meaning: It
9	＿か	Romaji: naka	Meaning: Inside/Middle
10	＿か	Romaji: yuka	Meaning: Floor

Answer Keys

Basic hiragana-1 Quiz A
(あいうえお/かきくけこ/さしすせそ)
Let's check if you can match the sound with the correct hiragana.

1. Pick and circle the right hiragana for underlined sounds.

ex.	<u>C</u>ar	あ	(か)	い
1	W<u>oo</u>l	(う)	お	こ
2	<u>I</u>taly	え	(い)	こ
3	<u>K</u>id	(き)	く	け
4	<u>C</u>are	か	え	(け)
5	<u>E</u>dit	お	け	(え)
6	<u>C</u>ool	え	(く)	い
7	<u>S</u>aturday	そ	き	(さ)
8	<u>S</u>ue	(す)	せ	こ
9	<u>Sh</u>e	く	(し)	け
10	<u>S</u>et	(せ)	さ	あ

2. Fill the hiragana to compete the word.

ex.	み<u>せ</u>	Romaji: mise	Meaning: Store
1	<u>あ</u>か	Roma-ji: aka	Meaning: Red
2	<u>そ</u>ら	Romaji: sora	Meaning: Sky
3	<u>き</u>もの	Romaji: kimono	Meaning: Kimono(Traditional Japanese Clothes)
4	<u>い</u>いえ	Romaji: iie	Meaning: No
5	<u>か</u>み	Romaji: kami	Meaning: Paper/God
6	<u>さ</u>しみ	Romaji: sashimi	Meaning: Raw Fish
7	<u>す</u>し	Romaji: sushi	Meaning: Sushi
8	<u>う</u>え	Romaji: ue	Meaning: Top/Up
9	<u>し</u>お	Romaji: shio	Meaning: Salt
10	き<u>そ</u>	Romaji: kiso	Meaning: Basic

Basic hiragana-1 Quiz B
(たちつてと/なにぬねの/はひふへほ)

Let's check if you can match the sound with the correct hiragana.

1. Pick and circle the right hiragana for underlined sounds.

ex.	<u>T</u>ap	に	(た)	へ
1	<u>Ts</u>unami	(つ)	て	こ
2	<u>Ni</u>nja	ち	(に)	こ
3	<u>Ho</u>me	と	の	(ほ)
4	<u>To</u>dd	ち	(と)	に
5	<u>No</u>tice	(の)	と	に
6	<u>N</u>oo<u>n</u>	に	な	(ぬ)
7	<u>Ch</u>eese	(ち)	ら	た
8	<u>He</u>ad	つ	(へ)	こ
9	<u>Ha</u>t	(は)	ほ	た
10	<u>Na</u>p	さ	(な)	た

2. Fill the hiragana to compete the word.

ex.	つ <u>ち</u>	Romaji: Tsuchi	Meaning: dirt
1	<u>と</u> り	Roma-ji: tori	Meaning: Bird
2	<u>た</u> こ	Romaji: tako	Meaning: Octopus
3	<u>ひ</u> る	Romaji: hiru	Meaning: Daytime
4	<u>に</u> じ	Romaji: niji	Meaning: Rainbow
5	<u>ち</u> か	Romaji: chika	Meaning: Underground
6	<u>て</u>	Romaji: te	Meaning: Hand
7	<u>ち</u>	Romaji: chi	Meaning: Blood
8	<u>の</u> り	Romaji: nori	Meaning: Seaweed
9	<u>な</u> か	Romaji: naka	Meaning: Inside/Middle
10	<u>ふ</u> ろ	Romaji: furo	Meaning: Bath

Basic hiragana-1 Quiz C
(まみむめも/やゆよ/らりるれろ/わをん)
Let's check if you can match the sound with the correct hiragana.

1. Pick and circle the right hiragana for underlined sounds.

ex.	<u>Y</u>oung	さ	(や)	わ
1	<u>Mo</u>ther	さ	(ま)	ゆ
2	<u>Le</u>ad (metal)	わ	(れ)	む
3	<u>Moo</u>n	(む)	ゆ	み
4	<u>Mo</u>re	と	(も)	を
5	<u>Me</u>an	ま	む	(み)
6	<u>L</u>eader	み	し	(り)
7	<u>Me</u>mber	わ	(め)	ね
8	<u>L</u>oop	ろ	(る)	そ
9	<u>L</u>obby	る	(ろ)	も
10	<u>Y</u>outh	わ	(ゆ)	や

2. Fill the hiragana to compete the word.

ex.	ま た	Romaji: mata	Meaning: Again
1	め ん	Roma-ji: men	Meaning: Noodle
2	も り	Romaji: mori	Meaning: Forest
3	め	Romaji: me	Meaning: Eye
4	む り	Romaji: muri	Meaning: Impossible
5	そ ら	Romaji: sora	Meaning: Sky
6	や ま	Romaji: yama	Meaning: Mountain
7	わ	Romaji: wa	Meaning: Wheel
8	そ れ	Romaji: sore	Meaning: It
9	な か	Romaji: naka	Meaning: Inside/Middle
10	ゆ か	Romaji: yuka	Meaning: Floor

Hiragana-2

"People who do not get into scrapes are a great deal less interesting than those who do."
- Murasaki Shikibu

Once you master all the characters in Hiragana, Hiragana-2 will cover some additional sounds. The consonant sounds with two small lines on upper right is called dakuten – 濁点 to represent muddied sounds and small circle on upper right is called handakuten, 半濁点to represent p-sounds. Daku (濁)from dakuten means muddy and those sounds are considered muddied sounds.

In addition, there are youon ("yoh-on")拗音 as well. Consonants have additional small (half-size)「や(ya)」「ゆ(yu)」「よ(yo)」on the lower right side such as きゃ(kya), ちゅ (chu) andしょ (sho) . You (拗) from youon means "twisted" and those consonants are considered twisted sounds.

Since Japanese "R" sounds is somewhere between R, L and D. Some of youon are very difficult to pronounce. For example, Dragon is りゅう ("ryu") in龍or 竜 (The first one is in the traditional kanji, the second one is simplified kanji). In Chinese, it's "龙Long." And their common family name 劉(liu) is very close to the pronunciation of りゅう ("ryu") 龍/竜.

hiragana-2 (dakuon: Muddied Sounds & handakuon: Half-muddied Sounds)

Dakuon with two dots on upper right, stressed/accented "ka" （か） becomes "ga" （が）
Handakuon with a small circle on upper right is "p" sounds such as "pa" （ぱ） and "pyo" （ぴょ）

	A	I	U	E	O
G	が ga("go"t)	ぎ gi("gi"g)	ぐ gu("goo"d)	げ ge("ge"t)	ご go("go")
Z·J	ざ za("za"mbia)	じ ji("ji"tter)	ず zu("zoo")	ぜ ze("zeh")	ぞ zo("zo"ne)
D·J	だ da("da"nce)	ぢ di(do "dge")	づ du(lan "ds")	で de("de"sk)	ど do("do"or)
B	ば ba("ba"t)	び bi("bee")	ぶ bu("bo" on)	べ be("be" n)	ぼ bo("bo"y)
P	ぱ pa("pa"ck)	ぴ pi("pi"cture)	ぷ pu("poo"l)	ぺ pe("pa"y)	ぽ po("po"int)
KY	きゃ kya("ca"rry)		きゅ kyu("cue")		きょ kyo("kee-ow")
SH	しゃ sha("sha"dow)		しゅ shu("shoo"t)		しょ sho ("sho"t)
CH	ちゃ cha("cha"nnel)		ちゅ chu("choo"se)		ちょ cho("cho"p)
NY	にゃ nya("Knee-ah")		にゅ nyu("ne"w)		にょ nyo("knee-oh")
HY	ひゃ hya("he-ah")		ひゅ hyu("hu"e)		ひょ hyo("he-yo")
MY	みゃ mya("mi-ah")		みゅ mu("mu"sic)		みょ myo("mi-yo")

33

HIRAGANA-2 (dakuon & handakuon) How To Write
BASIC RULE: Horizontal Line →(from Left to Right) & Vertical Line ↓(from Top to Bottom)
Each number is one stroke.

	A	I	U	E	O
G	が ga("go"t)	ぎ gi("gi"g)	ぐ gu("goo"d)	げ ge("ge"t)	ご go("go")
Z·J	ざ za("za"mbia)	ぢ ji("ji"tter)	ず zu("zoo")	ぜ ze("zeh")	ぞ zo("zo"ne)
D·J	だ da("da"nce)	じ di(do "dge")	づ du(lan "ds")	で de("de"sk)	ど do("do"or)
B	ば ba("ba"t)	び bi("bee")	ぶ bu("bo" on)	べ be("be" n)	ぼ bo("bo"y)
P	ぱ pa("pa"ck)	ぴ pi("pi"cture)	ぷ pu("poo"l)	ぺ pe("pa"y)	ぽ po("po"int)
KY	きや kya("ca"rry)		きゆ kyu("cue")		きよ kyo("kee-ow")
SH	しや sha("sha"dow)		しゆ shu("shoo"t)		しよ sho ("sho"t)
CH	ちや cha("cha"nnel)		ちゆ chu("choo"se)		ちよ cho("cho"p)
NY	にや nya("Knee-ah")		にゆ nyu("ne"w)		によ nyo("knee-oh")
HY	ひや hya("he-ah")		ひゆ hyu("hu"e)		ひよ hyo("he-yo")
MY	みや hya("he-ah")		みゆ hyu("hu"e)		みよ hyo("he-yo")

34

HIRAGANA-2 (dakuon & handakuon)
Writing Exercise (-is the starting point) A

	A	I	U	E	O
G	ga("go"t)	gi("gi"g)	gu("goo"d)	ge("ge"t)	go("go")
Z·J	za("za"mbia)	ji("ji"tter)	zu("zoo")	ze("zeh")	zo("zo"ne)
D·J	da("da"nce)	di(do "dge")	du(lan "ds")	de("de"sk)	do("do"or)
B	ba("ba"t)	bi("bee")	bu("bo" on)	be("be" n)	bo("bo"y)
P	pa("pa"ck)	pi("pi"cture)	pu("poo"l)	pe("pa"y)	po("po"int)
KY	kya("ca"rry)		kyu("cue")		kyo("kee-ow")
SH	sha("sha"dow)		shu("shoo"t)		sho ("sho"t)
CH	cha("cha"nnel)		chu("choo"se)		cho("cho"p)
NY	nya("Knee-ah")		nyu("ne"w)		nyo("knee-oh")
HY	hya("he-ah")		hyu("hu"e)		hyo("he-yo")
MY	mya("mi-ah")		mu("mu"sic)		myo("mi-yo")

HIRAGANA-2 (dakuon & handakuon)
Writing Exercise B

	A	I	U	E	O
G	が	ぎ	ぐ	げ	ご
	ga("go"t)	gi("gi"g)	gu("goo"d)	ge("ge"t)	go("go")
Z·J	ざ	じ	ず	ぜ	ぞ
	za("za"mbia)	ji("ji"tter)	zu("zoo")	ze("zeh")	zo("zo"ne)
D·J	だ	ぢ	づ	で	ど
	da("da"nce)	di(do "dge")	du(lan "ds")	de("de"sk)	do("do"or)
B	ば	び	ぶ	べ	ぼ
	ba("ba"t)	bi("bee")	bu("bo" on)	be("be" n)	bo("bo"y)
P	ぱ	ぴ	ぷ	ぺ	ぽ
	pa("pa"ck)	pi("pi"cture)	pu("poo"l)	pe("pa"y)	po("po"int)
KY	きゃ		きゅ		きょ
	kya("ca"rry)		kyu("cue")		kyo("kee-ow")
SH	しゃ		しゅ		しょ
	sha("sha"dow)		shu("shoo"t)		sho ("sho"t)
CH	ちゃ		ちゅ		ちょ
	cha("cha"nnel)		chu("choo"se)		cho("cho"p)
NY	にゃ		にゅ		にょ
	nya("Knee-ah")		nyu("ne"w)		nyo("knee-oh")
HY	ひゃ		ひゅ		ひょ
	hya("he-ah")		hyu("hu"e)		hyo("he-yo")
MY	みゃ		みゅ		みょ
	mya("mi-ah")		mu("mu"sic)		myo("mi-yo")

HIRAGANA-2 (dakuon & handakuon)
Writing Exercise C(Final)

	A	I	U	E	O
G	ga("go"t)	gi("gi"g)	gu("goo"d)	ge("ge"t)	go("go")
Z·J	za("za"mbia)	ji("ji"tter)	zu("zoo")	ze("zeh")	zo("zo"ne)
D·J	da("da"nce)	di(do "dge")	du(lan "ds")	de("de"sk)	do("do"or)
B	ba("ba"t)	bi("bee")	bu("bo" on)	be("be" n)	bo("bo"y)
P	pa("pa"ck)	pi("pi"cture)	pu("poo"l)	pe("pa"y)	po("po"int)
KY	kya("ca"rry)		kyu("cue")		kyo("kee-ow")
SH	sha("sha"dow)		shu("shoo"t)		sho ("sho"t)
CH	cha("cha"nnel)		chu("choo"se)		cho("cho"p)
NY	nya("Knee-ah")		nyu("ne"w)		nyo("knee-oh")
HY	hya("he-ah")		hyu("hu"e)		hyo("he-yo")
MY	mya("mi-ah")		mu("mu"sic)		myo("mi-yo")

HIRAGANA-2 (dakuon & handakuon)
Vocabulary Building

	A	I	U	E	O
G	っこう	み	まっす	んきん	
	gakko (school)	migi(right)	massugu(straight)	genkin(cash)	go(five)
Z·J		かん	み	んぶ	う
	zannen(disappointing)	jikan (time)	mizu(water)	zenbu(all)	zou(elephant)
D·J	とも　ち	はな	つ　き	も	こ
	tomodachi(friend)	hanadi(nose blood)	tsuduki(continuation)	demo(but)	doko(where)
B	しょ	ゆ	んか	つ　つ	き　う
	basho(place)	yubi(finger)	bunka(culture)	betsubetsu(separately)	kibou(hope)
P	いっ　い	か　か	てん　ら	かん　き	さん
	ippai(a lot)	pikapika(shiny)	tempura(Japanese food)	kanpeki(perfect)	sanpo(walk)
KY	べつ		うり		う
	kyabetsu(cabbage)		kyuuri(cucumber)		kyou(today)
SH	ぶ　ぶ		うまつ		うゆ
	shabushabu(Japanese food)		shuumatsu(weekend)		shouyu (soy sauce)
CH	ちゃ		うい		っと
	ocha(Japanese tea)		chuui(attention)		chotto(a little)
NY	はん		うめん		らい
	han nya(prajna in Buddhism)		nyumen (Japanese food)		nyorai(enlighted person)
HY	く		うが		うばん
	hyaku(hundred)		hyuga(Japanese city)		hyouban(reputation)
MY	く				うじ
	myaku(pulse)		myu(no specific word, only used to show a sound)		myouji(last name)

HIRAGANA-3 (youon)

youon (continued from Hiragana-2) consists of two Hiragana (right side letter is half-size and they are "ya," "yu," and "yo"), and R sounds technically L sounds.

	A	I	U	E	O
RY	りゃ rya("li-ya")		りゅ ryu("lee-oo")		りょ ryo("li-yo")
GY	ぎゃ gya("ga"g)		ぎゅ gyu("gew"gaw)		ぎょ gyo("gee-ow")
J	じゃ ja("ja"net)		じゅ ju("je"welry)		じょ jo("jo"in)
BY	びゃ bya("bee-ya")		びゅ byu("beau"ty)		びょ byo("byaw")
PY	ぴゃ pya("pee-ya")		ぴゅ pyu("pu"rity)		ぴょ pyo("pee-yo")

HIRAGANA-3 (youon) How To Write

	A	I	U	E	O
RY	りゃ rya("li-ya")		りゅ ryu("lee-oo")		りょ ryo("li-yo")
GY	ぎゃ gya("ga"g)		ぎゅ gyu("gew"gaw)		ぎょ gyo("gee-ow")
J	じゃ ja("ja"net)		じゅ ju("je"welry)		じょ jo("jo"in)
BY	びゃ ja("ja"net)		びゅ ju("je"welry)		びょ jo("jo"in)
PY	ぴゃ pya("pee-ya")		ぴゅ pyu("pu"rity)		ぴょ pyo("pee-yo")

39

HIRAGANA-3 (youon)
Writing Exercise (- is the starting point) A

	A	I	U	E	O
RY	りゃ		りゅ		りょ
	rya("li-ya")		ryu("lee-oo")		ryo("li-yo")
GY	ぎゃ		ぎゅ		ぎょ
	gya("ga"g)		gyu("gew"gaw)		gyo("gee-ow")
J	じゃ		じゅ		じょ
	ja("ja"net)		ju("je"welry)		jo("jo"in)
BY	びゃ		びゅ		びょ
	bya("bee-ya")		byu("beau"ty)		byo("byaw")
PY	ぴゃ		ぴゅ		ぴょ
	pya("pee-ya")		pyu("pu"rity)		pyo("pee-yo")

hiragana-3(youon)
Writing Exercise B

	A	I	U	E	O
RY	りゃ		りゅ		りょ
	rya("li-ya")		ryu("lee-oo")		ryo("li-yo")
GY	ぎゃ		ぎゅ		ぎょ
	gya("ga"g)		gyu("gew"gaw)		gyo("gee-ow")
J	じゃ		じゅ		じょ
	ja("ja"net)		ju("je"welry)		jo("jo"in)
BY	びゃ		びゅ		びょ
	bya("bee-ya")		byu("beau"ty)		byo("byaw")
PY	ぴゃ		ぴゅ		ぴょ
	pya("pee-ya")		pyu("pu"rity)		pyo("pee-yo")

40

hiragana-3(youon)
Writing Exercise C(Final)

	A	I	U	E	O
RY	rya("li-ya")		ryu("lee-oo")		ryo("li-yo")
GY	gya("ga"g)		gyu("gew"gaw)		gyo("gee-ow")
J	ja("ja"net)		ju("je"welry)		jo("jo"in)
BY	bya("bee-ya")		byu("beau"ty)		byo("byaw")
PY	pya("pee-ya")		pyu("pu"rity)		pyo("pee-yo")

hiragana-3 (youon)
Vocabulary Building

	A	I	U	E	O
RY	りゃく		りゅう		りょこう
	ryaku(abbreviation)		ryu(dragon)		ryokou(travel)
GY	ぎゃく		ぎゅうにく		ぎょかい
	gyaku(reverse)		gyuniku(beef)		gyokai(seafood)
J	じゃま		じゅう		じょうほう
	jama(obstacle)		juu(ten)		jouhou(information)
BY	さんびゃく		びゅ		びょうき
	sanbyaku(300)		byu(no specific word, only used to show a sound)		byouki(sick)
PY	ろっぴゃく		ぴゅ		はっぴょう
	roppyaku(600)		pyu(no specific word, only used to show a sound)		happyou(announ cement/ presentation)

いろは poetry to memorize Basic Hiragana from the 11th century poem (7 -5 Rhyming)

いろはにほへと　ちりぬるを

わかよたれそ　つねならむ

うゐのおくやま　けふこえて

あさきゆめみし　ゑひもせず

Note:

ゐ（old yi: obsolete and rarely used currently)

ゑ（old ye: obsolete and rarely used currently)

はえど　りぬるを (Even a beautiful fragrant flower will soon fall)

がそ　ならむ (Who can be permanent in this ever-changing world)

の　えて(If we go beyond this uncertainty and reach enlightenment)

きじ　いもせず(we don't have to have a shallow dream or indulge in drunkenness)

Take-home message

Beautiful hiranaga handwriting is well-balanced, smooth curved lines and powerful bounce fades. Some of the characters are difficult to pronounce, but compared with other languages, the number of sounds is very small and easy to master.

Once again, reading aloud while writing exercises are very effective in matching the character and sound. There are not many words using "youon" but as you probably see in manga or anime, it's often used for onomatopoeia and it can be very impactful. For example, 「びゅんびゅん」 (byun-byun) expresses speedy running/driving with a feeling of a mighty wind, 「ぎゅうぎゅう」 (gyu-gyu) represents a "close-packed" state at a place, 「ぎゃあぎゃあ」 (gya-gya) shows annoyingly loud/noisy (by people).

That onomatopoeia might be difficult to grasp at first but once you understand the feeling, you should be able to understand the Japanese and its culture. You can say that the Japanese language is emotional and sentimental rather than logical.

Exercises

1. Write the following words in hiragana.

For example, Kyoto　きょうと

Cooking (ryouri): _____

Travel (ryokou): _____

Study (benkyou): _____

Train (densha): _____

Beef (gyuuniku): _____

Hiragana-2 (dakuon & handakuon) Exercises

Let's check if you can match the sound with the correct hiragana.

1. Pick and circle the right hiragana for underlined sounds.

ex.	Potato	が	⦅ぽ⦆	ほ
1	Goal	ぎ	こ	ご
2	Zone	そ	ぞ	ど
3	Debit	で	び	べ
4	Pet	べ	ぺ	へ
5	Billy	ぷ	ぴ	び
6	Bed	べ	へ	ぺ
7	Member	わ	め	ね
8	Pat	ぱ	ば	は
9	Door	ぽ	ど	と
10	Zoom	す	ず	ぶ

2. Fill the hiragana to compete the word.

ex.	が まん	Romaji: gaman	Meaning: Patience
1	いっ＿い	Roma-ji: ippai	Meaning: A lot
2	き＿う	Romaji: kibou	Meaning: Hope
3	た＿もの	Romaji: tabemono	Meaning: Food
4	＿しょ	Romaji: basho	Meaning:Place
5	か＿く	Romaji: kazoku	Meaning: Family
6	まん＿	Romaji: manga	Meaning: Manga
7	な＿	Romaji: naze	Meaning: Why
8	み＿	Romaji: mizu	Meaning: Water
9	とも＿ち	Romaji: tomodachi	Meaning: Friend
10	み＿	Romaji: migi	Meaning: Right

45

katakana-3 (youon) Exercises
Let's check if you can match the sound with the correct hiragana.

1. Pick and circle the right hiragana for underlined sounds.

ex.	<u>Pu</u>re	ぷ	⟮ぴゅ⟯	び
1	<u>Kyo</u>to	ちょ	きょ	ぎゃ
2	<u>Ca</u>rry	きょ	きゃ	きゅ
3	<u>Ja</u>cket	じょ	じゅ	じゃ
4	<u>Cha</u>t	ちゃ	ぴゃ	ひゃ
5	<u>Mu</u>sical	みゃ	みゅ	ぴゅ
6	<u>Ne</u>ws	にょ	にゅ	にゃ
7	<u>Hou</u>ston	きゃ	ひゃ	ひゅ
8	<u>Sho</u>w	しゅ	しゃ	しょ
9	<u>Ga</u>g	が	ぎゃ	ぎ
10	<u>Jo</u>b	じょ	ぞ	じゅ

2. Fill the hiragana to compete the word.

ex.	ぎょうざ	Romaji: gyoza	Meaning: Dumpling
1	__く	Roma-ji: kyaku	Meaning: Customer
2	__う	Romaji: chuu	Meaning: Medium
3	い__	Romaji: isha	Meaning: Doctor
4	__う	Romaji: ryuu	Meaning: Dragon
5	__こう	Romaji: ryokou	Meaning: Travel
6	__く	Romaji: hyaku	Meaning: Hundred
7	__うにく	Romaji: gyuniku	Meaning: Beef
8	__うり	Romaji: kyuuri	Meaning: Cucumber
9	__っと	Romaji: chotto	Meaning: A little
10	__う	Romaji: kyou	Meaning: Today

6. Pick the right youon hiragana.

"pyo"	"gyo"	"Ja"
A. びょ	A. ぎゃ	A. じょ
B. ひょ	B. ぎょ	B. ちゃ
C. ぴょ	C. きょ	C. じゃ

7. Write the following sentence. "ganbatte kudasai." (good luck or do your best).

8. Write the following sentence. "nihongo wo benkyou shimasu." (I study Japanese).

Answer Keys

1. りょうり, りょこう, べんきょう, でんしゃ, ぎゅうにく

Hiragana-2 (dakuon & handakuon) Quiz

Let's check if you can match the sound with the correct hiragana.

1. Pick and circle the right hiragana for underlined sounds.

ex.	<u>Po</u>tato	が	(ぽ)	ほ
1	<u>Go</u>al	ぎ	こ	(ご)
2	<u>Zo</u>ne	そ	(ぞ)	ど
3	<u>De</u>bit	(で)	び	べ
4	<u>Pe</u>t	べ	(ぺ)	へ
5	<u>Bi</u>lly	ぷ	ぴ	(び)
6	<u>Be</u>d	(べ)	へ	ぺ
7	<u>Me</u>mber	わ	(め)	ね
8	<u>Pa</u>t	(ぱ)	ば	は
9	<u>Do</u>or	ぽ	(ど)	と
10	<u>Zo</u>om	す	(ず)	ぶ

2. Fill the hiragana to compete the word.

ex.	<u>が</u>まん	Romaji: gaman	Meaning: Patience
1	いっ<u>ぱ</u>い	Roma-ji: ippai	Meaning: A lot
2	き<u>ぼ</u>う	Romaji: kibou	Meaning: Hope
3	た<u>べ</u>もの	Romaji: tabemono	Meaning: Food
4	<u>ば</u>しょ	Romaji: basho	Meaning:Place
5	か<u>ぞ</u>く	Romaji: kazoku	Meaning: Family
6	まん<u>が</u>	Romaji: manga	Meaning: Manga
7	な<u>ぜ</u>	Romaji: naze	Meaning: Why
8	み<u>ず</u>	Romaji: mizu	Meaning: Water
9	とも<u>だ</u>ち	Romaji: tomodachi	Meaning: Friend
10	み<u>ぎ</u>	Romaji: migi	Meaning: Right

49

hiragana-3 (youon) Quiz

Let's check if you can match the sound with the correct hiragana.

1. Pick and circle the right hiragana for underlined sounds.

ex.	<u>P</u>ure	ぷ	(ぴゅ)	び
1	<u>Kyo</u>to	ちょ	(きょ)	ぎゃ
2	<u>Ca</u>rry	きょ	(きゃ)	きゅ
3	<u>J</u>acket	じょ	じゅ	(じゃ)
4	<u>Ch</u>at	(ちゃ)	ぴゃ	ひゃ
5	<u>Mu</u>sical	みゃ	(みゅ)	ぴゅ
6	<u>N</u>ews	にょ	(にゅ)	にゃ
7	<u>H</u>ouston	きゃ	ひゃ	(ひゅ)
8	<u>Sh</u>ow	(しゅ)	しゃ	しょ
9	<u>G</u>ag	が	(ぎゃ)	ぎ
10	<u>J</u>ob	(じょ)	ぞ	じゅ

2. Fill the hiragana to compete the word.

ex.	ぎ<u>ょ</u>うざ	Romaji: gyoza	Meaning: Dumpling
1	き<u>ゃ</u>く	Roma-ji: kyaku	Meaning: Customer
2	ち<u>ゅ</u>う	Romaji: chuu	Meaning: Medium
3	い<u>しゃ</u>	Romaji: isha	Meaning: Doctor
4	り<u>ゅ</u>う	Romaji: ryuu	Meaning: Dragon
5	り<u>ょ</u>こう	Romaji: ryokou	Meaning: Travel
6	ひ<u>ゃ</u>く	Romaji: hyaku	Meaning: Hundred
7	ぎ<u>ゅ</u>うにく	Romaji: gyuniku	Meaning: Beef
8	き<u>ゅ</u>うり	Romaji: kyuuri	Meaning: Cucumber
9	ち<u>ょ</u>っと	Romaji: chotto	Meaning: A little
10	き<u>ょ</u>う	Romaji: kyou	Meaning: Today

2.

6. C 「ぴょ」 B 「ぎょ」 C 「じゃ」

7. がんばってください。

8. にほんごをべんきょうします。

Katakana 1

"In the beginner's mind there are many possibilities, but in the expert's there are few."

- Shunryu Suzuki

Mastering Number-like Shaped Katakana

Katakana is another phonetic script simplified from Kanji. The alphabet comprises 46 letters beginning with the five vowels of a, i, u, e, and o, just like hiragana.

The reason why there is another script to show sounds is that there are many western words since the first western explorer came to Japan from Portugal in 1543. There are some Portuguese still used in Japan, such as "Pan(pão)" (Bread), "Tabaco" (Cigarette), and "Cartas" (Cards). Portuguese pronunciation is relatively close to Japanese, but other western languages, especially English, are not easy to show in hiragana because of the limited Japanese sounds.

So, katakana is mainly used for foreign origin words, technical terms, and onomatopoeia you can often see in Manga, and for the names of some animals, insects, plants, vegetables, and fruits.

Since there are no spaces between words in Japanese, 「・」 is used between words to avoid confusion, such as 「コンピューター・サイエンス」 (Computer Science) and 「コピー・アンド・ペースト」 (Copy and Paste），

Long Vowel Sounds

The long vowel sounds in katakana are written in a simple way as 「ー」, a longer dash, such as 「ジョージ(jo-ji」 "George"，「ジュディー(judi-)」 "Judy," and 「スーパー・コンピューター(su-pa-konpyu-ta-)」 "Super Computer."

Double Consonants with small tsu 「ッ」

Same from hiragana, double consonants such as kk, pp, ss, and tt are written in small tsu, 「ッ」 such as 「カット・アンド・ペースト(katto ando pe-suto)」

"Cut and Paste" and 「ヒットソング(hitto songu)」 "Hit Song."

Foreign Words for Small Vowels

Because hiragana sounds are limited, to represent foreign words some Katakana letters have been developed. "Di" for example, didn't exist in Japanese words and they used to say 「desuko」 for "Disco" and 「dezuni- lando」 for "Disney Land." By using small "a" "i" "u" "e," and "o" now more sounds can be written in katakana. "Violin" was mainly written as 「バイオリン(baiolin)」 but now can be also written 「ヴァイオリン(vaiolin)」.

Writing katakana in the correct order and direction is also important because of the stroke directions. In the following katakana table, it's important not only to memorize how to write but also to match the script and the sound, so reading aloud while writing is strongly recommended. All Japanese words are composed of those sounds, so learning correct pronunciation for a letter is critical for language fluency.

Here is the instruction.

1. Basic katakana-1: Read aloud with correct pronunciation

2. Basic katakana-1: Trace the stroke order. One number has one stroke and stroke includes curbed line, 90-degree turn, u-turn and はね(hane)bounce fade (below in gray circle).

3. Basic katakana-1: Writing in the correct order. Writing Exercise A-B-C

4. Exercise A

5. Building Vocabulary

Basic katakana-1

Read aloud from あ to お, then from the second line か to こ, to all the way down.

	A	I	U	E	O
	ア a ("ah")	イ i ("ee")	ウ u ("oo")	エ e("eh")	オ o("oh")
K	カ ka("ca"r)	キ ki("kee"p)	ク ku("coo"l)	ケ ke("ke"n)	コ ko("co"t)
S	サ sa("sa"t)	シ shi("she")	ス su("sue")	セ se("se"t)	ソ so ("so"le)
T	タ ta("tah")	チ chi("chee")	ツ tsu("tsu")	テ te("tes")	ト to("toh")
N	ナ na("nah")	ニ ni("knee")	ヌ nu("noo")	ネ ne("ne"t)	ノ no("no"te)
H	ハ ha("ha"t)	ヒ hi("hi"t)	フ fu("fu")	ヘ he("hea"d)	ホ ho("ho"pe)
M	マ ma("ma"t)	ミ mi("me")	ム mu("moo"n)	メ me("me"xico)	モ mo("mo"re)
Y	ヤ ya("ya"cht)		ユ yu("yew")		ヨ yo("yo"ga)
R	ラ ra("ra"men)	リ ri("ri"ck)	ル ru("ru"by)	レ re("re"d)	ロ ro("ro"ck)
W	ワ wa("wha"t)				ヲ wo("wo"rry)
S	ン n(li "n"k)				

HOW TO WRITE katakana

BASIC RULE: Horizontal Line →(from Left to Right) & Vertical Line ↓(from Top to Bottom) except for シ & ン. Each number is one stroke.

	A	I	U	E	O
	ア a ("ah")	イ i ("ee")	ウ u ("oo")	エ e("eh")	オ o("oh")
K	カ ka("ca"r)	キ ki("kee"p)	ク ku("coo"l)	ケ ke("ke"n)	コ ko("co"t)
S	サ sa("sa"t)	シ shi("she")	ス su("sue")	セ se("se"t)	ソ so ("so"le)
T	タ ta("tah")	チ chi("chee")	ツ tsu("tsu")	テ te("tes")	ト to("toh")
N	ナ na("nah")	ニ ni("knee")	ヌ nu("noo")	ネ ne("ne"t)	ノ no("no"te)
H	パ ha("ha"t)	ヒ hi("hi"t)	フ fu("fu")	ヘ he("hea"d)	ホ ho("ho"pe)
M	マ ma("ma"t)	ミ mi("me")	ム mu("moo"n)	メ me("me"xico)	モ mo("mo"re)
Y	ヤ ya("ya"cht)		ユ yu("yew")		ヨ yo("yo"ga)
R	ラ ra("ra"men)	リ ri("ri"ck)	ル ru("ru"by)	レ re("re"d)	ロ ro("ro"ck)
W	ワ wa("wha"t)				ヲ wo("wo"rry)
	ン n(li "n"k)				

Basic katakana-1
Writing Exercise (• is the starting point) A
Please write in a pencil so you can correct/repeat.

	A	I	U	E	O
	ア a ("ah")	イ i ("ee")	ウ u("oo")	エ e("eh")	オ o("oh")
K	カ ka("ca"r)	キ ki("kee"p)	ク ku("coo"l)	ケ ke("ke"n)	コ ko("co"t)
S	サ sa("sa"t)	シ shi("she")	ス su("sue")	セ se("se"t)	ソ so ("so"le)
T	タ ta("tah")	チ chi("chee")	ツ tsu("tsu")	テ te("tes")	ト to("toh")
N	ナ na("nah")	ニ ni("knee")	ヌ nu("noo")	ネ ne("ne"t)	ノ no("no"te)
H	ハ ha("ha"t)	ヒ hi("hi"t)	フ fu("fu")	ヘ he("hea"d)	ホ ho("ho"pe)
M	マ ma("ma"t)	ミ mi("me")	ム mu("moo"n)	メ me("me"xico)	モ mo("mo"re)
Y	ヤ ya("ya"cht)		ユ yu("yew")		ヨ yo("yo"ga)
R	ラ ra("ra"men)	リ ri("ri"ck)	ル ru("ru"by)	レ re("re"d)	ロ ro("ro"ck)
W	ワ wa("wha"t)				ヲ wo("wo"rry)
	ン n(li "n"k)				

56

Basic katakana-1
Writing Exercise B
Please write in a pencil so you can correct/repeat.

	A	I	U	E	O
	a ("ah")	i ("ee")	u("oo")	e("eh")	o("oh")
K	ka("ca"r)	ki("kee"p)	ku("coo"l)	ke("ke"n)	ko("co"t)
S	sa("sa"t)	shi("she")	su("sue")	se("se"t)	so ("so"le)
T	ta("tah")	chi("chee")	tsu("tsu")	te("tes")	to("toh")
N	na("nah")	ni("knee")	nu("noo")	ne("ne"t)	no("no"te)
H	ha("ha"t)	hi("hi"t)	fu("fu")	he("hea"d)	ho("ho"pe)
M	ma("ma"t)	mi("me")	mu("moo"n)	me("me"xico)	mo("mo"re)
Y	ya("ya"cht)		yu("yew")		yo("yo"ga)
R	ra("ra"men)	ri("ri"ck)	ru("ru"by)	re("re"d)	ro("ro"ck)
W	wa("wha"t)				wo("wo"rry)
	n(li "n"k)				

Basic katakana-1
Writing Exercise C

Please write in a pencil so you can correct/repeat.

	A	I	U	E	O
K	a ("ah")	i ("ee")	u("oo")	e("eh")	o("oh")
S	ka("ca"r)	ki("kee"p)	ku("coo"l)	ke("ke"n)	ko("co"t)
T	sa("sa"t)	shi("she")	su("sue")	se("se"t)	so ("so"le)
N	ta("tah")	chi("chee")	tsu("tsu")	te("tes")	to("toh")
H	na("nah")	ni("knee")	nu("noo")	ne("ne"t)	no("no"te)
M	ha("ha"t)	hi("hi"t)	fu("fu")	he("hea"d)	ho("ho"pe)
Y	ma("ma"t)	mi("me")	mu("moo"n)	me("me"xico)	mo("mo"re)
R	ya("ya"cht)		yu("yew")		yo("yo"ga)
W	ra("ra"men)	ri("ri"ck)	ru("ru"by)	re("re"d)	ro("ro"ck)
	wa("wha"t)				wo("wo"rry)
	n(li "n"k)				

Basic katakana-1
Vocabulary Building

	A	I	U	E	O
	ニメ anime (Anime)	ト レ toire (Toilet)	イルス uirusu(Virus)	ネルギー enerugi(Energy)	イル oiru (Oil)
K	ナダ kanada(Canada)	チ ン chikin(Chicken)	ピン pinku(Pink)	ース keesu(case)	メディ komedi (comedy)
S	ラダ sarada (Salad)	レ ピ reshipi (Recipe)	テーキ suteeki(Steak)	ット setto (set)	ファ sofa(sofa)
T	オル taoru (Towel)	キン chikin (Chicken)	スポー supootsu (Sports)	ーブル teeburu (Table)	イレ toire (Toilet)
N	バ banana(Banana)	テ tenisu (Tennis)	ードル nuudoru (Noodle)	ーム neemu(Name)	ピア Piano (Piano)
H	ート haato (Heart)	ーター hiitaa (Heater)	ロント furonto(Front)	ッド heddo (Head)	テル hoteru (Hotel)
M	スク masuku (Mask)	ニ mini(Mini)	アイテ aitemu (Item)	ール meeru (Email)	モリ memori (Memory)
Y	タイ taiya (Tire)		ーザー yuuzaa (User)		ット yotto (Yacht)
R	イン rain (Line)	セット risetto (Reset)	ファイ fairu (File)	ポート repooto(Report)	ッカー Rokkaa (Locker)
W	イン wain (Wine)				wo(rarely used in katakana)
	ラーメ raamen (Ramen)				

Take-home message

Katakana seems more challenging to remember since some characters are similar, but the good news is most of katakana words originated in English. Write first your name in katakana, then your country, your hometown, and your favorite western food in katakana.

According to some statistics, 60% of new words that have been added to Japanese dictionaries are katakana words. Especially in the IT industry, words like "install," "compliance," and "security" are used as is today in Japan. So, katakana is playing an important role in modern Japanese culture.

The difficult part to get used to is long vowels and double consonants, and the best way to master is reading. Manga comics are good ones since they often use onomatopoeia. Those words imitate the sounds of animals, humans, machines, and nature such as 「ニャー」 " mew," 「キラキラ」 "twinkle", and 「ガチャン」 "clash." It only represents sounds, but strangely stories and characters in manga stand out vividly with onomatopoeia.

Exercises

1. Write the following words in katakana.

For example, America   アメリカ

Anime("a ni me") _____, Karaoke("ka ra o ke")_____ ,

Canada ("ka na da")_____, Chiken ("chi ki n")_____ ,

Taxi ("ta ku shi-") _____ , Manga ("ma n ga") _____

Michael ("ma i ke ru")_____, Chris ("ku ri su")_____,

Tony ("to ni-")_____, Kelly ("ke ri-")_____,

Sara("sa ra") _____, Naomi (na o mi)_____.

Basic katakana-1 Quiz A

(アイウエオ/カキクケコ/サシスセソ)

Let's check if you can match the sound with the correct katakana.

1. Pick and circle the right katakana for underlined sounds.

ex.	<u>C</u>ar	ア	(カ)	イ
1	W<u>oo</u>l	ウ	オ	コ
2	<u>I</u>taly	エ	イ	コ
3	<u>K</u>id	キ	ク	ケ
4	<u>C</u>are	カ	エ	ケ
5	<u>E</u>dit	オ	ケ	エ
6	<u>C</u>ool	エ	ク	イ
7	<u>S</u>aturday	ソ	キ	サ
8	<u>S</u>ue	ス	セ	コ
9	<u>Sh</u>e	ク	シ	ケ
10	<u>S</u>et	セ	サ	ア

2. Fill the hiragana to compete the word.

ex.	<u>セ</u> ール	Romaji: se-ru	Meaning: Sale
1	__ メリカ	Roma-ji: amerika	Meaning: America
2	__ ックス	Romaji: sokkusu	Meaning: Socks
3	メ __ シコ	Romaji: mekishiko	Meaning: Mexico
4	__ タリア	Romaji: itaria	Meaning: Italy
5	__ ナダ	Romaji: kanada	Meaning: Canada
6	__ ッカー	Romaji: sakka-	Meaning: Soccer
7	__ ペイン	Romaji: supein	Meaning: Spain
8	__ コー	Romaji: eko-	Meaning: Echo
9	タク __ ー	Romaji: takushi-	Meaning: taxi
10	__ レンジ	Romaji: Orenji	Meaning: Orange

Basic katakana-1 Quiz B
(タチツテト / ナニヌネノ / ハヒフヘホ)
Let's check if you can match the sound with the correct katakana.

1. Pick and circle the right hiragana for underlined sounds.

ex.	Tap	ニ	タ	ヘ
1	Tsunami	ツ	テ	コ
2	Ninja	チ	ニ	コ
3	Home	ト	ノ	ホ
4	Todd	チ	ト	ニ
5	Notice	ノ	ト	ニ
6	Noon	ニ	ナ	ヌ
7	Cheese	チ	ラ	タ
8	Head	ツ	ヘ	コ
9	Hat	ハ	ホ	タ
10	Nap	サ	ナ	タ

2. Fill the katakana to compete the word.

ex.	チ リ	Romaji: Chiri	Meaning: Chile
1	__ ランス	Roma-ji: furansu	Meaning: France
2	__ クシー	Romaji: takushi-	Meaning: Taxi
3	__ ット	Romaji: hitto	Meaning: Hit
4	テ __ ス	Romaji: tenisu	Meaning: Tennis
5	__ ードル	Romaji: nu-doru	Meaning: Noodle
6	__ ルウェー	Romaji: noruwe-	Meaning: Norway
7	__ ルーツ	Romaji: Furu-tsu	Meaning: Fruit
8	__ ンガ	Romaji: manga	Meaning: Manga
9	チー __	Romaji: chi-mu	Meaning: Team
10	モー __	Romaji: mo-ru	Meaning: Mall

Basic katakana-1 Quiz C
(マミムメモ/ヤユヨ/ラリルレロ/ワヲン)
Let's check if you can match the sound with the correct katakana.

1. Pick and circle the right katakana for underlined sounds.

ex.	Young	サ	(ヤ)	ワ
1	Mother	サ	マ	ユ
2	Red	ワ	レ	ム
3	Moon	ム	ユ	ミ
4	More	ト	モ	ヲ
5	Mean	マ	ム	ミ
6	Leader	ミ	シ	リ
7	Member	ワ	メ	ネ
8	Loop	ワ	ル	ソ
9	Lobby	ル	ル	モ
10	Youth	ワ	ユ	ヤ

1. Fill the hiragana to compete the word.

ex.	マスク	Romaji: masuku	Meaning: Mask
1	__ックス	Roma-ji: mikkusu	Meaning: Mix
2	__ニュー	Romaji: menyu-	Meaning: menu
3	__	Romaji: me	Meaning: Eye
4	タイ__	Romaji: taiya	Meaning: Tire
5	__ーザー	Romaji: yu-za-	Meaning: User
6	__ング	Romaji: yangu	Meaning: Young
7	__ンク	Romaji: rinku	Meaning: Link
8	__ポート	Romaji: repo-to	Meaning: report
9	__ール	Romaji: ru-ru	Meaning: Rule
10	__ンドン	Romaji: rondon	Meaning: London

8. Fill the empty tables.

Center	senta-	センター
Rice	raisu	
	masuku	マスク
	shawa-	シャワー
Contact	kontakuto	
Italia	itaria	
Item		アイテム
Tire	taiya	

Answer Keys

1. アニメ（Anime）、カラオケ(Karaoke)、カナダ(Canada)、チキン(Chicken) 、タクシー(Taxi) 、マンガ（Manga）、 マイケル(Michael)、クリス(Chris)、トニー（Tony）、 ケリー（Kelly）、サラ (Sara) 、ナオミ(Naomi)

Basic katakana-1 Quiz A
(アイウエオ/カキクケコ/サシスセソ)
Let's check if you can match the sound with the correct katakana.

1. Pick and circle the right katakana for underlined sounds.

ex.	<u>C</u>ar	ア	(カ)	イ
1	W<u>oo</u>l	(ウ)	オ	コ
2	<u>I</u>taly	エ	(イ)	コ
3	<u>K</u>id	(キ)	ク	ケ
4	<u>C</u>are	カ	エ	(ケ)
5	<u>E</u>dit	オ	ケ	(エ)
6	<u>C</u>ool	エ	(ク)	イ
7	<u>Sa</u>turday	ソ	キ	(サ)
8	<u>Su</u>e	(ス)	セ	コ
9	<u>Sh</u>e	ク	(シ)	ケ
10	<u>Se</u>t	(セ)	サ	ア

2. Fill the hiragana to compete the word.

ex.	<u>セ</u> ール	Romaji: se-ru	Meaning: Sale
1	<u>ア</u> メリカ	Roma-ji: amerika	Meaning: America
2	<u>ソ</u> ックス	Romaji: sokkusu	Meaning: Socks
3	メ <u>キ</u> シコ	Romaji: mekishiko	Meaning: Mexico
4	<u>イ</u> タリア	Romaji: itaria	Meaning: Italy
5	<u>カ</u> ナダ	Romaji: kanada	Meaning: Canada
6	<u>サ</u> ッカー	Romaji: sakka-	Meaning: Soccer
7	<u>ス</u> ペイン	Romaji: supein	Meaning: Spain
8	<u>エ</u> コー	Romaji: eko-	Meaning: Echo
9	タク <u>シ</u> ー	Romaji: takushi-	Meaning: taxi
10	<u>オ</u> レンジ	Romaji: Orenji	Meaning: Orange

67

Basic katakana-1 Quiz B
(タチツテト/ナニヌネノ/ハヒフヘホ)
Let's check if you can match the sound with the correct katakana.

1. Pick and circle the right hiragana for underlined sounds.

ex.	<u>T</u>ap	ニ	(タ)	ヘ
1	<u>Ts</u>unami	(ツ)	テ	コ
2	<u>N</u>inja	チ	(ニ)	コ
3	<u>H</u>ome	ト	ノ	(ホ)
4	<u>T</u>odd	チ	(ト)	ニ
5	<u>N</u>otice	(ノ)	ト	ニ
6	<u>N</u>oon	ニ	ナ	(ヌ)
7	<u>Ch</u>eese	(チ)	ラ	タ
8	<u>H</u>ead	ツ	(ヘ)	コ
9	<u>H</u>at	(ハ)	ホ	タ
10	<u>N</u>ap	サ	(ナ)	タ

2. Fill the katakana to compete the word.

ex.	<u>チ</u> リ	Romaji: Chiri	Meaning: Chile
1	<u>フ</u>ランス	Roma-ji: furansu	Meaning: France
2	<u>タ</u>クシー	Romaji: takushi-	Meaning: Taxi
3	<u>ヒ</u>ット	Romaji: hitto	Meaning: Hit
4	テ<u>ニ</u>ス	Romaji: tenisu	Meaning: Tennis
5	<u>ヌ</u>ードル	Romaji: nu-doru	Meaning: Noodle
6	<u>ノ</u>ルウェー	Romaji: noruwe-	Meaning: Norway
7	<u>フ</u>ルーツ	Romaji: Furu-tsu	Meaning: Fruit
8	<u>マ</u>ンガ	Romaji: manga	Meaning: Manga
9	チー<u>ム</u>	Romaji: chi-mu	Meaning: Team
10	モー<u>ル</u>	Romaji: mo-ru	Meaning: Mall

Basic katakana-1 Quiz C

(マミムメモ/ヤユヨ/ラリルレロ/ワヲン)

Let's check if you can match the sound with the correct katakana.

1. Pick and circle the right katakana for underlined sounds.

ex.	Young	サ	(ヤ)	ワ
1	Mother	サ	(マ)	ユ
2	Red	ワ	(レ)	ム
3	Moon	(ム)	ユ	ミ
4	More	ト	(モ)	ヲ
5	Mean	マ	ム	(ミ)
6	Leader	ミ	シ	(リ)
7	Member	ワ	(メ)	ネ
8	Loop	ワ	(ル)	ソ
9	Lobby	(ロ)	ル	モ
10	Youth	ワ	(ユ)	ヤ

1. Fill the hiragana to compete the word.

ex.	マスク	Romaji: masuku	Meaning: Mask
1	ミックス	Roma-ji: mikkusu	Meaning: Mix
2	メニュー	Romaji: menyu-	Meaning: menu
3	メ	Romaji: me	Meaning: Eye
4	タイヤ	Romaji: taiya	Meaning: Tire
5	ユーザー	Romaji: yu-za-	Meaning: User
6	ヤング	Romaji: yangu	Meaning: Young
7	リンク	Romaji: rinku	Meaning: Link
8	レポート	Romaji: repo-to	Meaning: report
9	ルール	Romaji: ru-ru	Meaning: Rule
10	ロンドン	Romaji: rondon	Meaning: London

8.

69

Center	senta-	センター
Rice	raisu	ライス
Mask	masuku	マスク
Shower	shawa-	シャワー
Contact	kontakuto	コンタクト
Italia	itaria	イタリア
Item	aitemu	アイテム
Tire	taiya	タイヤ

Katakana 2 & Essential Kanji

"Learn how to listen as things speak for themselves."

- Matsuo Basho

Katakana 2 is going to cover dakuon (Muddie Sounds) and youon (Twisted Sounds) . Some of the sounds might be unfamiliar, but again, reading a loud while practicing writing is the key to master katakana faster.

In manga, you might see onomatopoeia such as 「ガーン」 "whang" or 「ギャー」 "gack."When you type in Japanese ギャー, you will see a bunch of emojis like the one below.

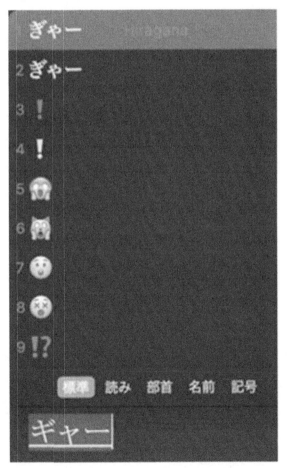

katakana-2 (dakuon & handakuon)

Dakuon with two dots on upper right, stressed/accented "ka" (カ) becomes "ga" (が)
Handakuon with a small circle on upper right is "p" sounds such as "pa" (パ) and "pyo" (ピョ)

	A	I	U	E	O
G	ガ ga("go"t)	ギ gi("gi"g)	グ gu("goo"d)	ゲ ge("ge"t)	ゴ go("go")
Z·J	ザ za("za"mbia)	ジ ji("ji"tter)	ズ zu("zoo")	ゼ ze("zeh")	ゾ zo("zo"ne)
D·J	ダ da("da"nce)	ヂ di(do "dge")	ズ du(lan "ds")	デ de("de"sk)	ド do("do"or)
B	バ ba("ba"t)	ビ bi("bee")	ブ bu("bo" on)	ベ be("be" n)	ボ bo("bo"y)
P	パ pa("pa"ck)	ピ pi("pi"cture)	プ pu("poo"l)	ペ pe("pa"y)	ポ po("po"int)
KY	キャ kya("ca"rry)		キュ kyu("cue")		キョ kyo("kee-ow")
SH	シャ sha("sha"dow)		シュ shu("shoo"t)		ショ sho ("sho"t)
CH	チャ cha("cha"nnel)		チュ chu("choo"se)		チョ cho("cho"p)
NY	ニャ nya("Knee-ah")		ニュ nyu("ne"w)		ニョ nyo("knee-oh")
HY	ヒャ hya("he-ah")		ヒュ hyu("hu"e)		ヒョ hyo("he-yo")
MY	ミャ mya("mi-ah")		ミュ mu("mu"sic)		ミョ myo("mi-yo")

katakana-2 (dakuon & handakuon) How to Write

BASIC RULE: Horizontal Line →(from Left to Right) & Vertical Line ↓(from Top to Bottom) except for シ＆ン. Each number is one stroke.

	A	I	U	E	O
G	ga("go"t)	gi("gi"g)	gu("goo"d)	ge("ge"t)	go("go")
Z·J	za("za"mbia)	ji("ji"tter)	zu("zoo")	ze("zeh")	zo("zo"ne)
D·J	da("da"nce)	di(do "dge")	du(lan "ds")	de("de"sk)	do("do"or)
B	ba("ba"t)	bi("bee")	bu("bo" on)	be("be" n)	bo("bo"y)
P	pa("pa"ck)	pi("pi"cture)	pu("poo"l)	pe("pa"y)	po("po"int)
KY	kya("ca"rry)		kyu("cue")		kyo("kee-ow")
SH	sha("sha"dow)		shu("shoo"t)		sho ("sho"t)
CH	cha("cha"nnel)		chu("choo"se)		cho("cho"p)
NY	nya("Knee-ah")		nyu("ne"w)		nyo("knee-oh")
HY	hya("he-ah")		hyu("hu"e)		hyo("he-yo")
MY	mya("mi-ah")		mu("mu"sic)		myo("mi-yo")

73

Basic katakana-2 (dakuon & handakuon)
Writing Exercise (• is the starting point) A

Please write in a pencil so you can correct/repeat.

	A	I	U	E	O
G	ガ	ギ	グ	ゲ	ゴ
	ga("go"t)	gi("gi"g)	gu("goo"d)	ge("ge"t)	go("go")
Z·J	ザ	ジ	ズ	ゼ	ゾ
	za("za"mbia)	ji("ji"tter)	zu("zoo")	ze("zeh")	zo("zo"ne)
D·J	ダ	チ	ズ	デ	ド
	da("da"nce)	di(do "dge")	du(lan "ds")	de("de"sk)	do("do"or)
B	バ	ビ	ブ	ベ	ボ
	ba("ba"t)	bi("bee")	bu("bo" on)	be("be" n)	bo("bo"y)
P	パ	ピ	プ	ペ	ポ
	pa("pa"ck)	pi("pi"cture)	pu("poo"l)	pe("pa"y)	po("po"int)
KY	キャ		キュ		キョ
	kya("ca"rry)		kyu("cue")		kyo("kee-ow")
SH	シャ		シュ		ショ
	sha("sha"dow)		shu("shoo"t)		sho ("sho"t)
CH	チャ		チュ		チョ
	cha("cha"nnel)		chu("choo"se)		cho("cho"p)
NY	ニャ		ニュ		ニョ
	nya("Knee-ah")		nyu("ne"w)		nyo("knee-oh")
HY	ヒャ		ヒュ		ヒョ
	hya("he-ah")		hyu("hu"e)		hyo("he-yo")
MY	ミャ		ミュ		ミョ
	mya("mi-ah")		mu("mu"sic)		myo("mi-yo")

74

Basic katakana-2 (dakuon & handakuon)
Writing Exercise B
Please write in a pencil so you can correct/repeat.

	A	I	U	E	O
G	ガ	ギ	グ	ゲ	ゴ
	ga("go"t)	gi("gi"g)	gu("goo"d)	ge("ge"t)	go("go")
Z·J	ザ	ジ	ズ	ゼ	ゾ
	za("za"mbia)	ji("ji'tter)	zu("zoo")	ze("zeh")	zo("zo"ne)
D·J	ダ	ヂ	ズ	デ	ド
	da("da"nce)	di(do "dge")	du(lan "ds")	de("de"sk)	do("do"or)
B	バ	ビ	ブ	ベ	ボ
	ba("ba"t)	bi("bee")	bu("bo" on)	be("be" n)	bo("bo"y)
P	パ	ピ	プ	ペ	ポ
	pa("pa"ck)	pi("pi"cture)	pu("poo"l)	pe("pa"y)	po("po"int)
KY	キャ		キュ		キョ
	kya("ca"rry)		kyu("cue")		kyo("kee-ow")
SH	シャ		シュ		ショ
	sha("sha"dow)		shu("shoo"t)		sho ("sho"t)
CH	チャ		チュ		チョ
	cha("cha"nnel)		chu("choo"se)		cho("cho"p)
NY	ニャ		ニュ		ニョ
	nya("Knee-ah")		nyu("ne"w)		nyo("knee-oh")
HY	ヒャ		ヒュ		ヒョ
	hya("he-ah")		hyu("hu"e)		hyo("he-yo")
MY	ミャ		ミュ		ミョ
	mya("mi-ah")		mu("mu"sic)		myo("mi-yo")

Basic katakana-2 (dakuon & handakuon)
Writing Exercise C
Please write in a pencil so you can correct/repeat.

	A	I	U	E	O
G					
	ga("go"t)	gi("gi"g)	gu("goo"d)	ge("ge"t)	go("go")
Z·J					
	za("za"mbia)	ji("ji"tter)	zu("zoo")	ze("zeh")	zo("zo"ne)
D·J					
	da("da"nce)	di(do "dge")	du(lan "ds")	de("de"sk)	do("do"or)
B					
	ba("ba"t)	bi("bee")	bu("bo" on)	be("be" n)	bo("bo"y)
P					
	pa("pa"ck)	pi("pi"cture)	pu("poo"l)	pe("pa"y)	po("po"int)
KY					
	kya("ca"rry)		kyu("cue")		kyo("kee-ow")
SH					
	sha("sha"dow)		shu("shoo"t)		sho ("sho"t)
CH					
	cha("cha"nnel)		chu("choo"se)		cho("cho"p)
NY					
	nya("Knee-ah")		nyu("ne"w)		nyo("knee-oh")
HY					
	hya("he-ah")		hyu("hu"e)		hyo("he-yo")
MY					
	mya("mi-ah")		mu("mu"sic)		myo("mi-yo")

katakana-2 (dakuon & handakuon)
Vocabulary Building

	A	I	U	E	O
G	イ ド gaido (Guide)	イ リス igirisu(England)	レ ー Gure-(Grey)	ー ト ge-to(Gate)	ールド go-rudo(Gold)
Z·J	デ ー ト deza-to(Dessert)	レ reji(Register)	サイ saizu(Size)	ッ ト zetto(Z)	ー ン Zo-n(Zone)
D·J	ン ス dansu(Dance)	Obsolete and rarely used	Obsolete and rarely used	ジタル dejitaru(Digital)	ライ dorai(Dry)
B	バ レ ー Bare-(valleyball)	タ ミ ン bitamin(Vitamin)	ラ ン ド burando(Brand)	ー コ ン be-kon(Bacon)	ト ル botoru(Bottle)
P	ー ト pa-to(Part Time)	コ Kopi-(Copy)	ロ puro(Professional)	ットボトル pettobotoru(Pet Bottle)	サ ー ト sapo-to(Support)
KY	ッ シ ュ kyasshu(Cash)		ウ リ kyuuri(cucumber)		kyo
SH	ー プ sha-pu(Sharp)		ー ト shu-to(Shoot)		ッ ピ ン グ shoppingu(Shopping)
CH	ン ス chansu(chance)		chu		コ レ ー ト chokore-to(Chocolate)
NY	nya		ー ス nyu-su(News)		Nyo
HY	hya		ー マ ン hyu-man(Human)		hyo
MY	mya		ー ジ カ ル myu-jikaru(Musica)		myo

katakana-3 (youon: Twisted Sounds)

youon (continued from Hiragana-2) consists of two Hiragana (right side letter is half-size and they are "ya," "yu," and "yo"), and R sounds technically L sounds.

	A	I	U	E	O
RY	リャ rya("ri-ya")		リュ ryu("ree-oo")		リョ ryo("ri-yo")
GY	ギャ gya("ga"g)		ギュ gyu("gew"gaw)		ギョ gyo("gee-ow")
J	ジャ ja("ja"net)		ジュ ju("je"welry)		ジョ jo("jo"in)
BY	ビャ bya("bee-ya")		ビュ byu("beau"ty)		ビョ byo("byaw")
PY	ピャ pya("pee-ya")		ピュ pyu("pu"rity)		ピョ pyo("pee-yo")

katakana-3 (youon) HOW TO WRITE

BASIC RULE: Horizontal Line →(from Left to Right) & Vertical Line ↓(from Top to Bottom)
Each number is one stroke.

	A	I	U	E	O
RY	リャ rya("ri-ya")		リュ ryu("ree-oo")		リョ ryo("ri-yo")
GY	ギャ gya("ga"g)		ギュ gyu("gew"gaw)		ギョ gyo("gee-ow")
J	ジャ ja("ja"net)		ジュ ju("je"welry)		ジョ jo("jo"in)
BY	ビャ bya("bee-ya")		ビュ byu("beau"ty)		ビョ byo("byaw")
PY	ピャ pya("pee-ya")		ピュ pyu("pu"rity)		ピョ pyo("pee-yo")

78

katakana-3 (youon)
Writing Exercise (• is the starting point) A

	A	I	U	E	O
RY	リャ rya("ri-ya")		リュ ryu("ree-oo")		リョ ryo("ri-yo")
GY	ギャ gya("ga"g)		ギュ gyu("gew"gaw)		ギョ gyo("gee-ow")
J	ジャ ja("ja"net)		ジュ ju("je"welry)		ジョ jo("jo"in)
BY	ビャ bya("bee-ya")		ビュ byu("beau"ty)		ビョ byo("byaw")
PY	ピャ pya("pee-ya")		ピュ pyu("pu"rity)		ピョ pyo("pee-yo")

katakana-3 (youon)
Writing Exercise B

	A	I	U	E	O
RY	リャ rya("ri-ya")		リュ ryu("ree-oo")		リョ ryo("ri-yo")
GY	ギャ gya("ga"g)		ギュ gyu("gew"gaw)		ギョ gyo("gee-ow")
J	ジャ ja("ja"net)		ジュ ju("je"welry)		ジョ jo("jo"in)
BY	ビャ bya("bee-ya")		ビュ byu("beau"ty)		ビョ byo("byaw")
PY	ピャ pya("pee-ya")		ピュ pyu("pu"rity)		ピョ pyo("pee-yo")

katakana-3 (youon)
Writing Exercise C

	A	I	U	E	O
RY					
	rya("ri-ya")		ryu("ree-oo")		ryo("ri-yo")
GY					
	gya("ga"g)		gyu("gew"gaw)		gyo("gee-ow")
J					
	ja("ja"net)		ju("je"welry)		jo("jo"in)
BY					
	bya("bee-ya")		byu("beau"ty)		byo("byaw")
PY					
	pya("pee-ya")		pyu("pu"rity)		pyo("pee-yo")

katakana-3 (youon)
Vocabulary Building

	A	I	U	E	O
RY	ク		ッ ク		
	ryaku (omitted)		ryukku(Rucksack)		ryo(rarely used)
GY	ッ プ		ウ　ウ		
	gyappu(gap)		gyugyu(packed)		gyo(rarely used)
J	ン プ		エ リ ー		ー ク
	janpu(jump)		jueri(jewelry)		jooku(joke)
BY			レ		
	bya(rarely used)		rebyu(review)		byo(rarely used)
PY			ー レ		ン ヤ ン
	pya(rarely used)		pyuure(puree)		pyon yan(Pyonyan)

Country & Nationality

Country in English	katakana	Romaji	Nationality
America	アメリカ	amerika	アメリカ
England	イギリス	igirisu	イギリス
Canada	カナダ	kanada	カナダ
Australia	オーストラリア	o-sutoraria	オーストラリア
Spain	スペイン	supein	スペイン
Germany	ドイツ	doitsu	ドイツ
Italy	イタリア	itaria	イタリア
France	フランス	furansu	フランス
Russia	ロシア	roshia	ロシア
China		chuugoku	
Japan		nihon	
Korea		kan koku	
India	インド	indo	インド
Singapore	シンガポール	shingapo-ru	シンガポール
Thailand	タイ	tai	タイ
Vietnam	ベトナム	betonamu	ベトナム
Indonesia	インドネシア	indoneshia	インドネシア

Philippines	フィリピン	firipin	フィリピン

Fundamental Kanji 100

Kanji is originally from China via Korea along with Buddhism around 4th century. Yamato kotoba was used in Japan at that time and there was no writing system in the language. Yamato Kotoba is applied to kanji and the writing system was mainly used by men. Then two kanas, Hiragana and Katakana, both are phonetic scripts, were invented by simplifying kanji in medieval era.

Kanji can be nouns, stems of verbs, adjectives, and adverbs so as to communicate descriptions, directions, ideas, opinions, feelings and emotions, kanji writing is necessary to convey meanings in every day life. We will be using the fundamental basic kanji so you will get to used to Kanji . We will add furigana on top of kanji so you understand how they are pronounced. Many learners are afraid of kanji just because it looks complicated but when you start learning about parts, meaning, and sounds you will enjoy not only the graphical aspects of script (be able to understand the meaning intuitively) but also the history and Eastern philosophical meanings.

The reason why Japanese kanji is tricky and difficult to master is that there are two types (sometimes more than two) of pronunciation. In Chinese, each character has only one pronunciation with a specific tone. When Japan adopted Chinese characters, each Chinese character already had a specific pronunciation. Japan had Yamato kotoba then. So, Japanese adopted their pronunciation, 訓読み"kun yomi", to kanji, also another pronunciation which is closer to the original Chinese pronunciations, 音読み"on yomi. "

For example, 「林(forest)」 is one of the common family names in Japan and China. In kun yomi, it's Hayashi. However, in on yomi, it's Lin which is almost the same pronunciation as Chinese. It can be either pronunciation depending on types of words and situations, so it is confusing especially the name of towns and places.

The Japanese language has a limited number of sounds (only five vowels and fourteen consonants) and simple tones. Korea also imported Chinese characters, and they also invented Hangul characters, eventually using only Hangul. However, the Japanese have many homophones that confuse meanings, so they continued to use Chinese characters.

Interestingly however, some of the Japanese kanji idioms were reimported to China in modern times. Vocabulary like Society （社会）, Culture （文化）, Market （市場）, International （国際）, and Economy（経済） was integrated in the 20th Century.

Here is the chart for most fundamental kanji list of 100. At this point, you don't need to write those kanjis but if you can remember the shapes, you should be able to notice the power of graphical script later in study and it will help you guess/imagine/understand what a sentence says.

Basic 100 Kanji

一	二	三	四	五
one	two	three	four	Five
六	七	八	九	十
six	seven	eight	nine	ten
百	千	万	水	火
hundred	thousand	ten thousand	water	fire
東	西	南	北	中
east	west	south	north	middle/center
日	月	木	金	土
day/sun	month/moon	tree/thursday	gold/friday	soil/earth/saturday
花	魚	空	山	川
flower	fish	sky/empty	mountain	river
女	男	子	大	小
woman	man	child	big	small
何	上	下	手	足
what	top/up	bottom/down	hand	foot
母	父	行	見	言
mother	father	going/execution/line	See/ideas/look/chances	saying/words
食	飲	来	会	学
eating/food	drinking	coming	meeting/seeing/gathering	Learning/studies

生	立	話	出	入
life/genuine/birth	stand	story/talk	exit/leave	enter/insert
前	後	読	聞	安
before/front	after/back	read	listen/hear	cheap/ease
新	古	多	少	高
new	old	many/frequent/much	few/little	high/expensive
長	白	分	時	間
long	white	minute/part	time/hour	between/during
週	年	今	先	午
week	year	Now	before/ahead	noon/sign of horse
半	店	外	電	道
half/middle	store	outside	electrical	course/road
毎	友	名	円	車
every	friend	name	circle/yen	car/wheel
駅	気	国	社	校
station	spirit/mind/air/mood	country	company	school
目	鼻	口	耳	雨
eye/class/look	nose	mouth	ear	Rain
買	右	左	休	天
buy	right	left	Rest/closed	sky/ceiling/heaven

Take-home message

More and more American vocabulary is becoming part of Japanese culture because of Technology and impactful American Culture. While Kanji is so graphical that you can instantly understand the meanings and tones, katakana English is more common in everyday life in Japan.

There are pros and cons to katakana English. While people are familiar with digital vocabulary, some differences in usage and pronunciation are more confusing. There are erroneous English as well such as 「ボリューミー」 (volumn +y = "volumny," meaning chunky) so you need to be careful with new katakana English.

100 Kanjis are recommended to be able to identify them. You don't need to practice writing at this point. Kanjis are graphical characters, so once you can identify them, everyday life in Japan will be so much easier.

Exercises

1. Please write the following words in katakana.

Juice ("ju-su")_____, Jouranlist ("ja-na ri su to)_____

News ("nyu-su")_____, Joke ("jo-ku")_____

Janet ("ja ne tto")_____, gap ("gya ppu")_____

Music ("my-ji kku)_____, Brooklyn ("bu ru kku rin")_____

2. Please circle your home country.

イギリス　フィンランド　アメリカ　カナダ　オーストラリア　オーストリア ドイツ

ニュージーランド　スリランカ　フィリピン　インド　アイルランド　タイ　スペイン

メキシコ　スウェーデン　デンマーク　フランス　スイス　オランダ　ベルギー　マレーシア　シン
ガポール　イタリア　ブラジル　ロシア　インドネシア　ベトナム

3 . How much is Iced Tea?
A.　コーヒー（アイス/ホット）　　350
B. アイスカフェオレ　　　　　　　450
C. アイスティー　　　　　　　　　400

katakana-2 Quiz A
(ガギグゲゴ/ザジズゼゾ/ダヂヅデゾ)
Let's check if you can match the sound with the correct katakana.

1. Pick and circle the right katakana for underlined sounds.

ex.	<u>G</u>et	ガ	ギ	（ゲ）
1	<u>Z</u>ombi	ゾ	ジョ	ショ
2	<u>Z</u>oo	ゾ	ズ	ソ
3	<u>Gui</u>tar	キ	ギ	ヂ
4	<u>Goo</u>ds	グ	ジ	ザ
5	<u>G</u>ene	ジ	ゲ	シ
6	<u>Z</u>en	エ	ゼ	ゲ
7	So<u>d</u>a	ジ	ダ	デ
8	<u>De</u>sign	ザ	デ	ヂ
9	<u>D</u>onut	ド	デ	ダ
10	<u>Gui</u>de	グ	ガ	ゲ

2. Fill the hiragana to compete the word.

ex.	ガラス	Romaji: garasu	Meaning: Glass
1	＿ループ	Roma-ji: guru-pu	Meaning: Group
2	＿ール	Romaji: go-ru	Meaning: Goal
3	＿ーンズ	Romaji: ji-nzu	Meaning: Jeans
4	サイ＿	Romaji: saizu	Meaning: Size
5	リ＿ート	Romaji: rizo-to	Meaning: Resort
6	＿ライブ	Romaji: doraibu	Meaning: Drive
7	＿ート	Romaji: de-to	Meaning: Date
8	＿イエット	Romaji: daietto	Meaning: Diet
9	チー＿	Romaji: chi-zu	Meaning: Cheese
10	ア＿ア	Romaji: ajia	Meaning: Asia

87

katakana-2 Quiz B

(バビブベボ/パピプペポ/キャキュキョ/シャシュショ)

Let's check if you can match the sound with the correct katakana.

1. Pick and circle the right katakana for underlined sounds.

ex.	Bubble	ガ	バ	ゲ
1	Pool	プ	ピ	ピョ
2	Potato	ポ	ペ	ボ
3	Cash	キャ	ギ	キュ
4	Show	シャ	シュ	ショ
5	Shadow	シャ	シュ	ショ
6	Bed	ベ	ペ	デ
7	Cue	キュ	キ	キャ
8	Boot	ボ	ブ	ビ
9	Building	ブ	ビ	デ
10	Bot	ブ	ボ	ポ

2. Fill the katakana to compete the word.

ex.	シュ ガー	Romaji: shuga-	Meaning: Sugar
1	＿ ルト	Romaji: beruto	Meaning: Belt
2	＿ スポート	Romaji: pasupo-to	Meaning: Passport
3	＿ リューム	Romaji: boryu-mu	Meaning: Volume
4	＿ レーク	Romaji: bure-ku	Meaning: Break
5	＿ ランス	Romaji: baransu	Meaning: Balance
6	＿ ンド	Romaji: bando	Meaning: Band
7	＿ アノ	Romaji: piano	Meaning: Piano
8	＿ リント	Romaji: purinto	Meaning: Print
9	＿ ット	Romaji: petto	Meaning: Pet
10	＿ ワー	Romaji: shawa-	Meaning: Shower

katakana-2 Quiz C

(チャチュチョ/ニャニュニョ/ヒャヒュヒョ/ミャミュミョ)

Let's check if you can match the sound with the correct katakana.

1. Pick and circle the right katakana for underlined sounds.

ex.	Chocolate	チャ	チョ	チ
1	New	ニャ	ニョ	ニュ
2	Hugo	ヒャ	ヒョ	ヒュ
3	Muse	ミ	ミュ	ム
4	Choose	チャ	チ	チュ
5	Chat	チャ	チュ	チェ
6	Gnocchi(Italian Food)	グ	ニョ	ニ
7	Check	チェ	チ	チャ
8	Menu	ニュ	ニョ	ヌ
9	Human	フ	ヒュ	ヒョ
10	Challenge	チャ	タ	チュ

2. Fill the katakana to compete the word.

ex.	ミュート	Romaji: myu-to	Meaning: Mute
1	ロー＿＿ン	Roma-ji: ro-shon	Meaning: Lotion
2	＿＿ンセル	Romaji: kyanseru	Meaning: Cancel
3	＿＿リー	Romaji: cheri-	Meaning: Cherry
4	＿＿ート	Romaji: cha-to	Meaning: Chart
5	＿＿ージーランド	Romaji: nyu-ji-ranndo	Meaning: New Zealand
6	＿＿ンス	Romaji: chansu	Meaning: Chance
7	＿＿ッキ	Romaji:nyokki	Meaning: Gnoochi (Italian Food)
8	＿＿ッチャー	Romaji: kyaccha-	Meaning: Catcher
9	＿＿ップ	Romaji: choppu	Meaning: Chop
10	＿＿ーストン	Romaji: hyu-suton	Meaning: Houston

Basic katakana-3 (youon) Quiz D

Let's check if you can match the sound with the correct katakana.

1. Pick and circle the right katakana for underlined sounds.

ex.	Vol<u>u</u>me	ル	(リュ)	リョ
1	Comp<u>u</u>ter	ピョ	ピャ	ピュ
2	<u>J</u>uice	ジ	ジュ	シュ
3	<u>Beau</u>ty	ピュ	ビュ	プ
4	Re<u>gu</u>lar	ギュ	グ	ギ
5	<u>Hu</u>man	ヒョ	ヒュ	ヒャ
6	<u>Ne</u>ws	ニュ	ネ	ニョ
7	M<u>u</u>sic	ミョ	ム	ミュ
8	<u>C</u>ash	ケ	キュ	キャ
9	Lo<u>ti</u>on	ショ	シャ	シュ
10	Re<u>vie</u>w	ビョ	ビュ	ビャ

2. Fill the katakana to compete the word.

ex.	ピュア	Romaji: pyua	Meaning: Pure
1	＿ンル	Roma-ji: janru	Meaning: Genre
2	＿ラリー	Romaji: gyarari	Meaning: Gallery
3	＿ート	Romaji: myuuto	Meaning: Mute
4	＿ース	Romaji: nyuusu	Meaning: News
5	＿ット	Romaji: chatto	Meaning: Chat
6	＿コレート	Romaji: chokoreeto	Meaning: Chocolate
7	＿ペル	Romaji: chaperu	Meaning: Chapel
8	マニ＿ア	Romaji: manikyua	Meaning: Manicure
9	＿ワー	Romaji: shawaa	Meaning: shower
10	＿ーストン	Romaji: hyuusuton	Meaning: Houston

Answer Keys

1. ジュース (Juice)、ジャーナリスト(Jouranlist)、ニュース(News)、ジョーク(Joke)、ジャネット (Janet)、ギャップ(Gap)、ミュージック(Music)、ブルックリン(Brooklyn)

2. イギリス(England)　フィンランド(Finland)　アメリカ(America)　カナダ(Canada)　オーストラリア(Australia)　オーストリア(Austria)　ドイツ(Germany)　ニュージーランド(New Zealand)　スリランカ(Sri Lanka)　フィリピン(The Phillipines)　インド(India)　アイルランド(Ireland)　タイ(Thailand)　スペイン(Spain)　メキシコ(Mexico)　スウェーデン(Sweden)　デンマーク(Denmark)　フランス(France)　スイス　　(Switzerland)　オランダ(Holland)　ベルギー(Belgium)　マレーシア(Malaysia)　シンガポール(Singapore)　イタリア(Italy)　ブラジル(Brazil)　ロシア(Russia)　インドネシア(Indonesia)　ベトナム(Vietnam)

3. C. アイスティー　400 (yon hyaku en)

katakana-2 Quiz A
(ガギグゲゴ/ザジズゼゾ/ダヂヅデゾ)
Let's check if you can match the sound with the correct katakana.

1. Pick and circle the right katakana for underlined sounds.

ex.	<u>Ge</u>t	ガ	ギ	(ゲ)
1	<u>Z</u>ombi	(ゾ)	ジョ	ショ
2	<u>Zoo</u>	ゾ	(ズ)	ソ
3	<u>Gui</u>tar	キ	(ギ)	ヂ
4	<u>Goo</u>ds	(グ)	ジ	ザ
5	<u>Ge</u>ne	(ジ)	ゲ	シ
6	<u>Ze</u>n	エ	(ゼ)	ゲ
7	So<u>da</u>	ジ	(ダ)	デ
8	<u>De</u>sign	ザ	(デ)	ヂ
9	<u>Do</u>nut	(ド)	デ	ダ
10	<u>Gui</u>de	グ	(ガ)	ゲ

2. Fill the hiragana to compete the word.

ex.	<u>ガ</u>ラス	Romaji: garasu	Meaning: Glass
1	<u>グ</u>ループ	Roma-ji: guru-pu	Meaning: Group
2	<u>ゴ</u>ール	Romaji: go-ru	Meaning: Goal
3	<u>ジ</u>ーンズ	Romaji: ji-nzu	Meaning: Jeans
4	サイ<u>ズ</u>	Romaji: saizu	Meaning: Size
5	リ<u>ゾ</u>ート	Romaji: rizo-to	Meaning: Resort
6	<u>ド</u>ライブ	Romaji: doraibu	Meaning: Drive
7	<u>デ</u>ート	Romaji: de-to	Meaning: Date
8	<u>ダ</u>イエット	Romaji: daietto	Meaning: Diet
9	チー<u>ズ</u>	Romaji: chi-zu	Meaning: Cheese
10	ア<u>ジ</u>ア	Romaji: ajia	Meaning: Asia

katakana-2 Quiz B
(バビブベボ/パピプペポ/キャキュキョ/シャシュショ)
Let's check if you can match the sound with the correct katakana.

1. Pick and circle the right katakana for underlined sounds.

ex.	<u>B</u>ubble	ガ	**(バ)**	ゲ
1	<u>P</u>ool	**(プ)**	ピ	ピョ
2	<u>P</u>otato	**(ポ)**	ペ	ボ
3	<u>C</u>ash	**(キャ)**	ギ	キュ
4	<u>Sh</u>ow	シャ	シュ	**(ショ)**
5	<u>Sh</u>adow	**(シャ)**	シュ	ショ
6	<u>B</u>ed	**(ベ)**	ペ	デ
7	<u>C</u>ue	**(キュ)**	キ	キャ
8	<u>B</u>oot	ボ	**(ブ)**	ビ
9	<u>B</u>uilding	ブ	**(ビ)**	デ
10	<u>B</u>ot	ブ	**(ボ)**	ポ

2. Fill the katakana to compete the word.

ex.	<u>シュ</u>ガー	Romaji: shuga-	Meaning: Sugar
1	<u>ベ</u>ルト	Romaji: beruto	Meaning: Belt
2	<u>パ</u>スポート	Romaji: pasupo-to	Meaning: Passport
3	<u>ボ</u>リューム	Romaji: boryu-mu	Meaning: Volume
4	<u>ブ</u>レーク	Romaji: bure-ku	Meaning: Break
5	<u>バ</u>ランス	Romaji: baransu	Meaning: Balance
6	<u>バ</u>ンド	Romaji: bando	Meaning: Band
7	<u>ピ</u>アノ	Romaji: piano	Meaning: Piano
8	<u>プ</u>リント	Romaji: purinto	Meaning: Print
9	<u>ペ</u>ット	Romaji: petto	Meaning: Pet
10	<u>シャ</u>ワー	Romaji: shawa-	Meaning: Shower

katakana-2 Quiz C

(チャチュチョ/ニャニュニョ/ヒャヒュヒョ/ミャミュミョ)

Let's check if you can match the sound with the correct katakana.

1. Pick and circle the right katakana for underlined sounds.

ex.	Chocolate	チャ	(チョ)	チ
1	New	ニャ	ニョ	(ニュ)
2	Hugo	ヒャ	ヒョ	(ヒュ)
3	Muse	ミ	(ミュ)	ム
4	Choose	チャ	チ	(チュ)
5	Chat	(チャ)	チュ	チェ
6	Gnocchi(Italian Food)	グ	ニョ	ニ
7	Check	(チェ)	チ	チャ
8	Menu	(ニュ)	ニョ	ヌ
9	Human	フ	(ヒュ)	ヒョ
10	Challenge	(チャ)	タ	チュ

2. Fill the katakana to compete the word.

ex.	ミュート	Romaji: myu-to	Meaning: Mute
1	ローション	Roma-ji: ro-shon	Meaning: Lotion
2	キャンセル	Romaji: kyanseru	Meaning: Cancel
3	チェリー	Romaji: cheri-	Meaning: Cherry
4	チャート	Romaji: cha-to	Meaning: Chart
5	ニュージーランド	Romaji: nyu-ji-ranndo	Meaning: New Zealand
6	チャンス	Romaji: chansu	Meaning: Chance
7	ニョッキ	Romaji:nyokki	Meaning: Gnoochi (Italian Food)
8	キャッチャー	Romaji: kyaccha-	Meaning: Catcher
9	チョップ	Romaji: choppu	Meaning: Chop
10	ヒュ ーストン	Romaji: hyu-suton	Meaning: Houston

Basic katakana-3 (youon) Quiz D

Let's check if you can match the sound with the correct katakana.

1. Pick and circle the right katakana for underlined sounds.

ex.	Vol<u>u</u>me	ル	リョ	リョ
1	Comp<u>u</u>ter	ピョ	ピャ	ピュ
2	<u>Ju</u>ice	ジ	ジュ	シュ
3	<u>Beau</u>ty	ピュ	ビュ	プ
4	Re<u>gu</u>lar	ギュ	グ	ギ
5	<u>Hu</u>man	ヒョ	ヒュ	ヒャ
6	<u>N</u>ews	ニュ	ネ	ニョ
7	M<u>u</u>sic	ミョ	ム	ミュ
8	<u>Ca</u>sh	ケ	キュ	キャ
9	Lo<u>ti</u>on	ショ	シャ	シュ
10	Re<u>vie</u>w	ビョ	ビュ	ビャ

2. Fill the katakana to compete the word.

ex.	ピュア	Romaji: pyua	Meaning: Pure
1	ジャンル	Roma-ji: janru	Meaning: Genre
2	ギャラリー	Romaji: gyarari	Meaning: Gallery
3	ミュート	Romaji: myuuto	Meaning: Mute
4	ニュース	Romaji: nyuusu	Meaning: News
5	チャット	Romaji: chatto	Meaning: Chat
6	チョコレート	Romaji: chokoreeto	Meaning: Chocolate
7	チャペル	Romaji: chaperu	Meaning: Chapel
8	マニキュア	Romaji: manikyua	Meaning: Manicure
9	シャワー	Romaji: shawaa	Meaning: shower
10	ヒューストン	Romaji: hyuusuton	Meaning: Houston

95

Basic Grammar

"There is no mistake in nature."

- Byron Katie

If you wanted to learn survival Japanese, you could do that by memorizing phrases and basic vocabulary. Many books offer functional and polite Japanese phrases and sentences to use right away. You might be able to do that easily by learning western languages that are similar to English. We understand they don't want to overwhelm learners with the three Japanese writing systems and nonidentical grammar systems and teach them how to say English phrases in Japanese.

Learning basic grammar is one of the solutions to understanding how the language works and develops internalization (think in Japanese). Internalization is vital to master foreign languages to communicate without depending completely on grammar rules or memories and the phrases and sentences you speak do make sense in Japanese.

Singular/Plural

This might be confusing, but the Japanese language doesn't have plurals. Even you have more than one, for example, め（eyes）you don't need to add articles or plural forms to the noun:「がきれい」(me ga kirei) "Your eyes are beautiful." So most of nouns mentioned can be singular or plural.

"Desu" & "Masu"

Most of the conversational Japanese textbook starts with sentences ending "です(desu)" or "ます (masu)." です and ます are polite form of "be" verbs. Before learning 「です」, we are going to learn the plain form of 「です」,「だ」(da). By learning first with 「だ」 it's going to be easier to master conjugation of verbs and adjectives.

Please keep in mind that this plain form of 「です」,「だ」 may sound very casual and assertive, not always appropriate to use in formal occasions or conversations with elders.

Topic Marker Particle 「は」 is pronounced "wa"

The most basic syntax in Japanese is the same as English, "A is B." One of the important elements is the particle for the subject is 「は」(wa) is always pronounced as "wa" not "ha." Other than the particle, はis always pronounced as "ha" such as 「はじめまして(hajimemashite)」「はっきり(hakkiri: clear)」.Usually the words before 「は」 is the subject or part of the subject. In 「こんにちは」 "hello," 「は」 is pronounced "wa" because originally the phrase came from "Today is…"「は」.

A is B. 「A はB だ。(A wa B da)」

「わたしはダニエルだ。Watasi wa Daniel da.」 "I am Daniel."

Without 「だ」 there will be no be-verb in a sentence that shows any "state-of-being." So the particle needs to complete the sentence.

それはだ」 (sore wa shiro da) "It's white."

「これはだ」 (kore wa aka da) "This is red."

「あれはダニエラだ」 (are wa Daniela da) "That's Daniela"

「あなたはケントだ」 (anata wa kent da) "You're Kent."

「はサラだ」 (kanojo wa Sarah da) "She's Sara."

Conversation Exercise: Answer the following question.

「あなたのおはですか」

(anata no onamae wa nan desuka) "What's your name?"

『わたしは ___your name です（だ）』

Question Form, Where is 「?」

You will see "?" in Japanese sentences in many places, especially in dialogues. To be precise, the Japanese language didn't use "?" that often instead, it usually adds 「か」 at the end of the sentence.

「か」 (ka) functions like the English question mark. To change a statement to a question, all you need is 「か」 at the end of the sentence.

「ダニエルさんですか」 (Daniel san desuka) "Are you Daniel?"

「それはしろですか」 (Sore wa shiro desuka) "Is it white?"

「さん」 can be used for Mr. , Ms., or Mrs. ?

「ダニエルさん」「ダニエラさん」、「さん」 (san) is gender-free in a polite manner but also a friendly way to call someone. In addition, 「さま」 (sama) is more polite way to call especially a customer. If you want something more friendly and casual, 「ちゃん」 (chan) can be used for close friends and younger friends.

In 「〜だ」 syntax, it shows "state-of-being" or "declaration."

「ダニエルだ」 (is Daniel)

「アメリカだ」 (is American)

「だ」 (is white)

「だ」 (is raining)

「だ」 (is fine)

However, In everyday conversation, not only pronouns/subjects but also 「だ」 is often omitted.

Conversation Scenario:

A: 「?」 (How are you?)

B: 「」 (I'm fine.)

A: 「ダニエルはアメリカ?」 ([Is] Daniel American?)

B: 「アメリカ」 ([I'm] American.)

The reason why we need to learn 「だ」 is because it's going to be very important later when you learn conjugations to the negative or the past tense. Conjugations are based on this 「だ」。

Conversation Scenario: In the negative "state-of-being" 「じゃない」

A: 「?」 (How are you?)

B: 「じゃない(genki janai)」 (I'm not fine.)

A: 「ダニエルはアメリカ?」 ([Is] Daniel American?)

B: 「アメリカじゃない」 ([I'm] not American.)

Now 「じゃない(janai)」 is added to the "state-of-being" part. Originally 「ではない(dewanai)」, replaced 「だ」 and the negative form 「ない(not)」 becomes 「ではない」 then more casually 「じゃない」.

「ダニエルじゃない」 (Daniel janai)" [I'm] not Daniel."

「ダニエラじゃない」 (Daniela janai) " [I'm] not Daniela."

「アメリカじゃない」 (Amerika jin janai) " [I'm] not American."

「じゃない」 (shiro janai) " [It's] not white."

「じゃない」 (ame janai) " [It's] not raining."

Exercise:

Conjuguate 「だ」 to the negative form

i.e. ダニエルだ →negative	ダニエルじゃない(Daniel janai)
アメリカだ →negative	アメリカじゃない
だ →negative	じゃない

だ →negative	じゃない
だ →negative	じゃない

The past form can be made by adding 「だ」 + 「った」.

The conjugation part comes at the end of sentences. That's the reason why you need to listen to the whole sentence until the end to understand the final meaning. In other words, you can change the meaning by conjugating the last part of sentences.

Conversation Scenario: In the Past Tense "state-of-being" 「だった」

A: 「だった?」 "Were ［you］ fine?"

B: 「だった(genki datta)」 " ［I］ was fine."

「だ」 in the Past Tense is 「だった(datta)」.

「ダニエルだった」 (Daniel datta) "［It］ was Daniel."

「アメリカだった」 (Amerika jin datta) "［It］ was American."

「だった」 (shiro datta) "［It］ was white."

「だった」 (ame datta) "［It］ was raining."

「だった」 (genki datta) "［I］ was fine."

Exercise:

i.e. だ →past	だった (aka datta)
カナダだ →past	カナダだった
ダニエラだ →past	ダニエラ
だ(snow) →past	だった
だ →past	だった

Now if it was negative in the past tense, 「じゃない(janai)」 conjugates 「じゃなかった(janakatta)」.

「ダニエルじゃなかった」 (Daniel janakatta) "［It］ was not Daniel."

「アメリカじゃなかった」 (Amerika jin janakatta) "［It］ was not American."

「じゃなかった」 (shiro janakatta) "［It］ was not white."

「じゃなかった」 (ame janakatta) "［It］ was not raining."

「じゃなかった」 (genki janakatta) "［I］ was not fine."

Negative/Past Negative Conjugation Exercise:

「だ」 Conjugation to the Past Tense then the Past Negative

i.e. ダニエルだ →Past	ダニエルだった→ Present Negative	ダニエルじゃない→ Past Negative	ダニエルじゃなかった
アメリカだ →Past	アメリカだった →Present Negative	アメリカじゃない → Past Negative	アメリカじゃなかった
だ →Past	だった →Present Negative	じゃない→ Past Negative	じゃなかった
だ →Past	だった →Present Negative	じゃない → Past Negative	じゃなかった
だ →Past	だった→Present Negative	じゃない→ Past Negative	じゃなかった

Fundamental Japanese Three Particles 「は」 「も」 「が」

The Japanese particles compose basic sentences and identify the functions of a word such as "subject" or "object" of the sentence. Japanese particles, , also serve as connectors to have a smooth transition and add clarity to the meaning. These three particles are "Topic Marker" particles that show the subject of the sentence.

To connect more than two nouns to make a sentence, you need to know these three particles. The Japanese particles are one or more than two Hiragana characters that bridge words to function grammatically in a sentence. Even though only one or two Hiragana of particles, it can change a meaning of a sentence completely. For example, "had fish" can be "Fish ate."

The most common "Topic Marker" 「は」 (wa)

The particle 「は」 is the topic marker that identifies what a sentence is about. If a person says, "not Daniel." That's the complete sentence in Japanese but not in English. It doesn't tell what the person is talking about. Now, while the character 「は」 is normally pronounced ha, but when it is used as a particle, pronunciation is always wa.

In general, everything that comes before 「は」 is the topic or part of the topic in the sentence. Everything else after 「は」 describe or ask a question about the topic.

「ダニエルはアメリカ人だ（です）」 (Daniel wa America jin da [desu]) "Daniel is American."

「はだ（です）」 (sora wa ao da [desu]) "The sky is blue."

Inclusive Topic Marker 「も」

Another subject particle is the "inclusive" topic marker which adds the meaning of "also" to the topic marker particle. So, this one syllabus 「も」 function as the subject and includes the meaning of "also."

Conversation Scenario: Inclusive Topic Marker

A: 「ダニエルもアメリカ?」 (Daniel mo America jin?) "Is Daniel American too?"

B: 「そう、ダニエルもアメリカ」 (So Daniel mo America jin) "Yeah, Daniel is American too."

In this scenario, if Daniel is not American, then use 「は」 as a topic marker.

「いいえ、ダニエルはアメリカじゃない」 (Nope, Daniel is not American.)

Conversation Scenario 2.

A: 「あなたもダニエル?」 (Anata mo Daniel ?) "Are you Daniel too?"

B: 「そう、ダニエルです」 (So Daniel desu) "Yeah, I'm Daniel."

A: 「のもダニエルです」 (Watashi no musuko mo Daniel desu) "My son is Daniel too."

Identifier Particle 「が」

The third important particle is 「が」 that can stress the topic/subject. For example, you just heard "Yeah, American." Then you want to ask about the subject, "Who is American?" In this case, "is" in the question is 「が」. Even though both of 「は」 and 「が」 can be used as the topic marker, 「が」 can highlight the subject.

Conversation Scenario: Identifier Particle

A: 「がアメリカ?」 (dare ga amerika jin?) "Who is the one that is American?"

B: 「ダニエルがアメリカ」 (danieru ga amerika jin) "Daniel is the one that is American."

In the answer, Daniel needs to be identified among other Americans.

The difference between 「が」 and 「は」.

「がアメリカ?」 (dare ga amerika jin?) "Who is the one that is American ?"

「あのはアメリカ?」 (ano hito wa amerika jin?) "Is that person American?"

The first question with 「が」 asks to identify a specific person regarding American. The second question is the additional question about the person, and you don't need to identify the person. Only one script of a particle can change the context and additional details.

「はアメリカだ」 (kare wa amerika jin da) "He is American."

「がアメリカだ。」 (watashi ga amerika jin da) "I am the one who is American."

The second sentence specifies the subject, who the 「」 is.

「がアメリカだ。」(I am the one who is American.)

Even though both 「は」 and 「が」 indicate the subject, two are quite different. 「が」 identifies specific information of something while 「は」 is only to bring up a new topic.

Take-home message

Learning basic grammar is the key to understanding how the Japanese language works and develops internalization (think in Japanese). In order to learn conjugation easily, by using 「だ」 ("to be" in English, casual/basic version of 「です」) you can conjugate the negative form and the past tense.

The negative form of 「だ」 is 「じゃない」, the past tense of 「だ」 is 「だった」, and the past negative is 「じゃなかった」.

There are three important Topic Marker Particles 「は」「も」「が」. The most common Topic Marker is 「は」 pronounced "wa," Inclusive Topic Marker is 「も」 and Identifier Topic Marker is 「が」。

Exercises

1. Conjugate the following sentences.

ダニエルだ。 →Past

だった。 →Present

ダニエラじゃなかった。 →Present

じゃない。 → Present Positive

だった。 →Present Negative

アメリカじゃなかった。 →Present Positive

2. Among 「は」「も」「が」, pick the correct particle in the sentences.

Scenario: Daniel, Daniela and John are from California, US.

A: 「ダニエルさんとダニエラさんはアメリカですか?」

B: 「そうです」

A: 「ジョンさんは?」

B: 「＿＿＿＿アメリカです」

3. Among 「は」「も」「が」, pick the correct particle in the sentences.

Scenario: Daniel is from the US. He went to his friend's party.

A: 「はアメリカがいるのですか」 ("I hear there are two Americans today.")

B: 「＿＿＿アメリカです」

4. Make a simple sentence, "I'm from San Diego too."

A: 「はサンディエゴからました」

B: 「＿＿＿＿＿＿＿＿＿＿＿＿＿＿＿＿＿＿＿＿＿」

5. Answer the question. You are from the US.

A: 「あなたはフランスですか」

B: 「＿＿＿＿＿＿＿＿＿＿＿＿＿＿＿＿＿＿＿＿＿」

6. Here are occupation list. Pick the right one and answer the question.

(Student)	(Doctor)	エンジニア(Engineer)
ITエンジニア(IT Engineer)	(Entrepreneur)	(Driver)
(Fire Fighter)	(Nurse)	シェフ （Chef）
（Singer）	パフォーマー(Performing Artist)	デザイナー(Designer)

A: 「あなたはですか」

B: 「_____」

7. There is one mistake in sentence B. Please correct one.

A: 「どのがダニエルですか」 ("Which one is Daniel?")

B: 「はい、私もダニエルです」

8. Here is the last week's weather report. Answer the question.

(Monday)	(Tuesday)	(Wednesday)	(Thursday)	(Friday)
(Rainy)	り(Cloudy)	れ(Sunny)	れ(Sunny)	(Snowy)

A: 「(Wed)と(Thus)はれました。(Fri)もれましたか」

B: 「_____」

Answer Keys

1.　　　ダニエルだ。→Pastダニエルだった　だった。→Present元気だ。　ダニエラじゃなかった。→Present　ダニエラだ。　じゃない。→ Present Positiveだ　だった。→Present Negativeじゃない。アメリカじゃなかった。→Present Positiveアメリカだ

2.「 もアメリカです」

3.「 がアメリカです」

4.「 もサンディエゴからました」

5.「 はフランスじゃない（です）。アメリカです」

6.「 はじゃない（です）。です」

7.「 はい、私もダニエルです」→が

8.「 はれじゃなかった（です）。だった（です）」

Basic Grammar 2

"Have good trust in yourself... not in the One that you think you should be, but in the One that you are."

- Maezumi Roshi

Properties of Adjectives

Now that you can connect two nouns together in various ways using particles, we want to describe our nouns with adjectives. An adjective can directly modify a noun that immediately follows it. It can also be connected in the same way we did with nouns using particles. All adjectives fall under two groups.

From this chapter there will be no supplementary romaji. I recommend to print out hiragana/katakana charts plus "100 Kanji" if you're not confident about two writing systems.

In Japanese, negative, and past tense are expressed in conjugation. This may be a bit hard to grasp at first but none of these state-of-being conjugations make anything declarative like 「だ」 does.

「な」 adjectives

「い」 adjectives

1. 「な」 adjectives

The 「な」 adjectives end with 「な」 and is very simple to learn because it basically acts like a noun. All the conjugation rules for both nouns and 「な」 adjectives are the same. One main difference is that a 「な」 adjective can directly modify a noun following it by sticking 「な」 between the adjective and noun: 「な」 adjectives.

きれいな: Beautiful Person

きな: Big House

さなもの: Small Thing

かな : Quiet River

な : Vivid Color

な : Weird Shape

Likes/Dislikes Expression

This is often used expression 「き」(like). However, 「き」 is not a verb in Japanese but an adjective. That's one of the reasons why Japanese people have a hard time learning the difference between be-verbs and regular verbs.

「ダニエルはアニメがきだ」 : Daniel likes Anime. (Present Positive)

「ダニエルはアニメがきじゃない」 : Daniel doesn't like Anime (Present Negative)

「ダニエルはアニメがきだった」: Daniel liked Anime. (Past Positive)

「ダニエルはアニメがきじゃなかった」 : Daniel didn't like Anime. (Past Negative)

Using adjectives to modify nouns:

アニメがきな : Person who likes Anime. (Present Positive)

アニメがきじゃない : Person who doesn't like Anime. (Present Negative)

アニメがきだった : Person who liked Anime. (Past Positive)

アニメがきじゃなかった : Person who didn't like Anime. (Past Negative)

Here, all clauses 「アニメがき」「アニメがきじゃない」 is modifying "person" to talk about people that like or dislike Anime. You can see why this type of sentence is useful because 「はアニメがきだ」 would mean "People like Anime," which isn't always the case. You can make the whole descriptive noun clause as a single noun. For instance, we can make the whole clause a topic like the following.

アニメがきじゃないはがきだ。

Person who doesn't like Anime likes books.

アニメがきなはもきだ。

Person who likes Anime also like movies.

アニメがきだったはこのがきだ。

People who liked Anime like this song.

アニメがきじゃなかったを知らない。

I don't know anyone who didn't like Anime.

「い」 adjectives

All 「い」 adjectives end in the hiragana 「い」. But if the word can be applied in Kanji and ends in 「い」 such as 「(Beauty)」 is 「な(Beautiful)」 is the adjective form so it's 「な」 adjective.

「い(dislike)」 oppose to 「き(like)」, is also exception for 「な」 adjective and the form is 「いな」 just like 「きな」. Typically 「い」 adjectives are 「い(High)」「い(A lot)」「い(Fast)」「い(Sweet)」.

い: Fast Car

い: High Mountain

いフルーツ: Sweet Fruits

すごいスキル: Awesome Skill

いコーヒー : Bitter Coffee

Now for the negative form, 「な」 adjective uses 「じゃない(janai)」 conjugation, however, 「い」 adjectives can't use 「じゃない」 form. Instead, different conjugation forms can be applied.

いof 「い」 adjective is replaced with 「くない(kunai)」.

い 　→ 高い　 →くない

い 　→い　 →くない

い 　→い　 →くない

い 　→い　 →くない

The Past Tens:

Then, the past tense is the following with 「かった」 instead of 「い」.

い 　→ 高い　 →かった

い 　→い　 →かった

い 　→い　 →かった

い 　→い　 →かった

い 　→い　 →かった

The Past Negative:

Lastly, the negative form in the past tense ends with 「くなかった」 from 「かった」.

かった 　→くなかった

かった 　→くなかった

かった 　→くなかった

かった 　→くなかった

かった 　→くなかった

Using adjectives to modify nouns:

い 　 High Mountain

くない　Not High Mountain

かった　Mountain that was high

くなかった　Mountain that was not high

There is one exception in 「い」 adjectives. "Good" is special and harder for beginners to clearly understand. 「い」 is the original form of "Good," however, 「いい(ii)」 is becoming more popularly used in conversations. For conjugation, you need to remember the original form. 「い」, here is why.

Positive to Negative

　　　いい　→よくない

　　　Good　→Not good

Present to Past

　　　いい　→よかった

　　　is good　→was good

Present Negative to Past negative

　　　よくない　→よくなかった

　　　is not good　→was not good

Verbs : Masu-verbs vs. Plain Form

We've now learned adjectives and how to describe things and people. This gives us quite a bit of expressive power. However, we still cannot express movements. We're now going to cover verbs. Verbs in Japanese always come at the end of clauses or sentences. We will now learn the three main categories of verbs, which will allow us to define conjugation rules. Before that, there is one important thing to keep in mind.

"Plain form" is also called "dictionary form" and it's a casual/informal version of ます"masu-form." It's present/future tense (keep in mind, the present/future tense is the same in Japanese) and is very important to learn "plain form" because this is the basis for conjugations for other forms and expressions.

Now we're going to learn three groups of verbs in plain forms and study verb conjugations.

ru-verb	u-verb	Irregular verb
る to see/look	す to speak/talk	する to do
べる to eat	く to listen	る to come

109

る to sleep	む to drink	

Here are "ru-verb" "u-verb," and "irregular" verbs in sentences.

ダニエルはよくべる（ru-verb）：Daniel eats a lot.

ダニエルはよくす（u-verb）：Daniel talks a lot.

ダニエラはよくく（u-verb）：Daniela listens well.

ダニエルはよくる（ru-verb）」"：Daniela sleeps a lot.

ダニエルはよくする（irregular）：Daniel does (it) a lot.

ダニエラはときどきる (irregular)：Daniela sometimes comes.

ダニエルはよくむ (u-verb)：Daniel drinks a lot.

1. U-verbs are verbs that end with "U" vowels.

Let's get into more detail about those three verbs. We're looking into with "u-verb."

1. U-verbs	
す	to speak/talk
く	to go
う	to wash
つ	to stand
む	to read
く	to write
う	to help

U-verbs: Conjugating to the negative

ぶ(play)　→ ぶ ＋「ば」ない　→ばない

Replacing the last syllabus of u-verb 「ぶ」to 「ば」(vowel is always "a" sound)＋「ない」

U-verbs Negative		
す to speak/talk	す　　negative→　さ	さない
く to go	く　　negative→　か	＋ない　→　かない
う to wash	う　　negative→　わ	＋ない　→　わない
つ to stand	つ　　negative→　た	＋ない　→　たない

む to read.	む negative→ ま	＋ない → まない
く to write	く negative→ か	＋ない → かない
う to help	う negative→ わ	＋ない → わない

U-verbs: Conjugating to the past

Conjugating U-verbs to the past tense is challenging because there are four sub-categories depending on the last syllabus of the verb. The basic past tense form ends 「た」 or 「だ」.

Present	Last Syllabus	Past	Conjugation Form
す	す →した	した	1. した
く	く →いた	いた	2. いた
ぐ	ぐ →いだ	いだ	いだ
む	む →んだ	んだ	3. んだ
ぶ	ぶ →んだ	んだ	
つ	つ →った	った	4. った
う	う →った	った	

Here is the conjugation table with the same verbs from the negative conjugation table.

U-verbs Past		
す to speak/talk	す past→ し	した
く to go	く past→ つ	った
う to wash	う past→ つ	った
つ to stand	つ past→ つ	った
む to read.	む past→ ん	んだ
く to write	く past→ い	いた
う to help	う past→ つ	った

Now, here is the past negative conjugation ending with 「なかった」.

U-verbs Past Negative	
した した Negative→さなかった	さなかった

った　っ た　 Negative→かなかった		かなかった
った　っ た　 Negative→わなかった		わなかった
った　っ た　 Negative→たなかった		たなかった
んだ　ん た　 Negative→まなかった		まなかった
いた　い た　 Negative→かなかった		かなかった
った　っ た　 Negative→わなかった		わなかった

2. Ru-verbs : Verbs that end with "る"

For example,

RU-VERB:べる ends with 「る」 and the one before 「る」 is 「べ」 vowel is "e."

Negative form is 「食べない」

U-VERB: る(fold) ends with 「る」 and the one before 「る」 is 「お」 vowel is "o."

Negative is 「らない」

U-VERB: る(ride) ends with 「る」 and the one before 「る」 is 「の」 vowel is "o."

Negative is 「らない」

2 Ru-verbs	
る	to come out
べる	to eat
る	to sleep
る	to see/look
いる	to exit

Ru-verb Past		
る	る → past	＋た → た
べる	る → past	＋た → べた
る	る → past	＋た → た
る	る → past	＋た → た
いる	る → past	＋た → いた

Ru-verb Past Negative		
た	た → past てない	てない
べた	た → past てない	べてない
た	た → past てない	てない
た	た → past てない	てない
いた	た → past なかった	いなかった *exceptional conjugation form

Lastly, there are only two "irregular" verbs.

3. Irregular Verbs	
する	to do
る	to come
ある	to exist (objects not life)

In order to conjugate to Negative or Past, you need to change the first syllabus and get rid of the 「る」.

する →Negative

1. す (change the first syllabus) →し（"i" vowel）、 2. る(get rid of the る) 3. add 「ない」
「しない」

する →Past

1. す (change the first syllabus) →し（"i" vowel）、 2. る(get rid of the る) 3. add 「た」
「した」

くる →Negative is an exceptional case, and conjugation will be "o" vowel.

1. く (change the first syllabus) →こ（"o" vowel）、 2. る(get rid of the る) 3. add 「ない」
「こない」

くる →Past takes "i" vowel.

1. く (change the first syllabus) →き（"i" vowel）、 2. る(get rid of the る) 3. add 「た」
「きた」

"Irregular Verbs" Nagative

する	"i" vowel +る	＋ない　→しない
くる	"o" vowel +る	＋ない　→こない
ある		ない

"Irregular Verbs" Past		
する	"i" vowel +る	＋た　→した
くる	"i" vowel +る	＋た　→きた
ある		＋た　→あった

"Irregular Verbs" Past Negative		
する	"i" vowel+る	＋なかった　→しなかった
くる	"o" vowel +る	＋なかった　→こなかった
ある		なかった

Let's go over once again for three kinds of verbs. "U-verb" "Ru-verb" and "Irregular."

Most of verbs are "U-verb" and for the negative form, conjugate with "a"vowel ＋「

ない」for the past tense, there are four types ending with 「た」or 「だ」. "Ru-verbs" conjugation is easier. For the negative form, get rid of 「る」and add 「ない」, for the past tense, get rid of 「た」and add 「た」.

Verb Types Tips

U-verb	Ends with "u-vowel"
Ru-verb	Ends with 「る」except the preceding syllabus is "a" "u," and "o."
Irregular	「する」「くる」「ある」

Classify those verbs into A: U-Verb, B: Ru-Verb, and C: Irregular Verbs. Remember that even though some verbs end with 「る」if the preceding vowel is "a" "o" or "u" that's a "U-verb."

i.e. まる	to start	A: ま "a" vowel prior to る

る	to enter	A
る	to ride	A
う	to meet	A
く	to write	A
う	to sing	A
る	to sleep	B
る	to go home/return	A
める	to collect	B
ある	to exist	C
きる	to wake, to occur	B
く	to draw	A
る	to wear	B
える	to teach	B
する	to do	C
る	to run	A
る	to know	A
る	to kick	A
ひねる	to twist	A
る	to decrease	A

Please read aloud. We're reviewing negative, past tense, and past negative once again.

"ru-verb"

1. 「ダニエラはべる」 : Daniela eats.

2. 「ダニエルはる」 : Daniel sleeps.

3. 「ダニエラはめる」 : Daniela collects.

"ru-verb" negative   (get rid of 「る」 and add 「ない」)

1. 「ダニエラはべない」

2. 「ダニエルはない」

3. 「ダニエラはめない」

"ru-verb" past tense   (get rid of 「る」 and add 「た」)

1. 「ダニエラはべた」

2. 「ダニエルはた」

3. 「ダニエラはめた」

"ru-verb" past negative   (change 「た」 to "e" vowel and add 「ない」)

1. 「ダニエラはべてない」

2. 「ダニエルはてない」

3. 「ダニエラはめてない」

"u-verb"

1. 「ダニエラはす」 : Daniela talks.

2. 「ダニエラはく」 : Daniela goes.

3. 「ダニエラはく」 : Daniela writes.

"u-verb" negative (Change 「the last character」 to "a" vowel and add 「ない」)

1. 「ダニエラはさない」

2. 「ダニエラはかない」

3. 「ダニエラはかない」

"u-verb" past tense (Four conjugation patterns and add 「た」)

1. 「ダニエラはした」

2. 「ダニエラはった」

3. 「ダニエラはいた」

"ru-verb" past negative   (change 「the last character」 to "a" vowel and add 「なかった」)

1. 「ダニエラはさなかった」

2. 「ダニエラはかなかった」

3. 「ダニエラはかなかった」

"irregular" verbs

1. 「ダニエラはする」: Daniela does.

2. 「ダニエラはくる」: Daniela comes.

"irregular" verbs negative

1. 「ダニエラはしない」

2. 「ダニエラはこない」

"irregular" verbs past tense

1. 「ダニエラはした」

2. 「ダニエラはきた」

"irregular" verbs past negative

1. 「ダニエラはしなかった」

2. 「ダニエラはこなかった」

Object Particles of 「を」「に」「へ」「で」

In addition to subject particles we learned, there are important object particles that we should be able to complete simple conversational sentences. We will learn how to specify the direct object of a verb and the location where a verb takes place whether it's physical or abstract.

「を」: Object Particle

This particle is simple to understand. The script 「を」 is basically only used for this function to indicate objects. 「を」 is added to the end of word to show the word is the object of the verb. The pronunciation was "wo" officially but in everyday conversation, it's more like "o."

Here are sample sentences including 「を」,

はをべた。 I had fish.

はビールをんだ。 He had a beer.

はスピーチをした。 She made a speech.

はをいた。 I drew a painting.

はをた。 She left the store.

はダニエラをた。 I saw Daniela.

「を」 is unlike English, used for places that are direct object of motion verbs such as 「る」 (run), 「く」 (walk), and 「む」 (proceed).

をる。 : Run through an expressway.

橋を歩いた。 : Walked on a bridge.

「に」 : Target Particle

「に」 can indicate a target of a verb. In 「を」, the verb does something to the direct object. A verb does something to the object with 「に」.

ダニエラはにった。 : Daniela went to Kyoto.

このバスはにかない。 : This bus doesn't go to Shibuya.

ダニエルはにった。 : Daniel went to the store.

If you want to add the original location to the destination, you can use 「から」.

ダニエルはここからにった。 : Daniel went to the store from here.

ダニエラはからにった。 : Daniela went to Kyoto from Shinagawa.

In Japanese, a target can be the location or time and doesn't have to be a moving object and 「に」 is used for those targets. The difference between verbs 「ある」 and 「いる」 to indicate the existence, 「ある」 is for an object such as the table or phone, 「いる」 is for life.

はリビングにいる。 : A puppy is in the living room.

はにあった。 : The wallet was in the kitchen.

ダニエラに３にった。 : Met Daniela at 3.

ダニエラはシェフになる。 Daniela will become a chef.

「へ」 Particles , toward

「へ」 is pronounced "e" when it's used as a particle. Other than that, 「へ」 is always 「へ"he"」 such as 「(Change)」 and 「へび(Snake)」,The difference between 「に」 and 「へ」 is that 「に」 expresses the final destination, while 「へ」 only indicates "toward" the target.

ダニエルはへった。: Daniel headed toward Japan.

ダニエルはにった。: Daniel went to Japan.

「で」 The contextual particle

「で」 can specify places, means of action or components. For example, if a person found a nice shoes, where did she find? If a person went to the concert, by what means did she go? With what will you eat the rice? All of these questions can be answered with 「で」

バスで帰る。: Go home by bus.

カフェでランチを食べた。: Had lunch at a café.

テレビで見た。: Watched on TV.

The word for "what" () is quite confusing because while it's usually pronunced as 「なに」 sometimes it is read as 「なん」 depending on how it's used.

「でた？」: How did you get here?

In this question form, the confusing part is 「で」 can be "why" same as 「どうして」 or 「なぜ」.

「でた?」: Why did you come?

Take-home message

In Japanese, negative, and past tense are expressed in conjugation. This may be a bit hard to grasp at first but none of these state-of-being conjugations make anything declarative like 「だ」 does. So evern though, this 「」 is not always as polite as 「です」 we learned this 「だ」, state-of-being conjugations, first for adjective conjugation.

There are two categories of adjectives: one ends with 「い」 another with 「な」. The two categories take different conjugation forms for the negative and the past tense, and 「だ」 played an important role. Likes/dislikes are adjectives in Japanese, and they are 「

な」 adjectives.

When it comes to verbs, there are three categories "u-verb," "ru-verb," and "irregular." Each category conjugates differently for the negative and past tense. To learn conjugation system better, we used 「

」 the plain form which is not as formal as 「ます」.

Also, we covered the basic four participles that are necessary to make a sentence. With

「を」「に」「へ」「で」 and we can make a simple sentence by combining a subject, verb, adjectives and nouns.

Exercises

1. Conjugate in those forms from the basic sentence/phrase.

ダニエルはアニメがきだ。

In the negative form _____

In the past tense _____

In the past negative _____

しい (Beautiful Person)

In the negative form _____

In the past tense _____

In the past negative _____

2. The adjective 「いい（よいoriginally）」(Good) conjugates in the special way. Change the adjective to the forms.

いい

In the negative form _____

In the past tense _____

In the past negative _____

2. Categorize those verbs into three: A "u-verb," B "ru-verb," C "irregular."

う(to meet)　りる(to go down)　く(to go)　る(to get angry)　ぶ(to call)　む(to rest)　る (to cut)　る (to wear)　る(to sleep)　す(to lend)　る(to enter)　つ(to wait)　る(to return)　いる(to exist)

A "u-verb"

_____

B "ru-verb"

_____

C "irregular."

_____

3. Conjugate the sentence to the following forms.

ダニエルはべる。

In the negative form _____

In the past tense _____

In the past negative _____

4. Conjugate the sentence to the following forms.

ダニエルはくる。

In the negative form _____

In the past tense _____

In the past negative _____

5. Conjugate the sentence to the following forms.

ダニエルはく。

In the negative form _____

In the past tense _____

In the past negative _____

6. Choose 「を」: Object Particle or 「に」 Target Particle

は＿＿る。(I run in the park.)

と3＿＿う。(I will meet my teacher at 3.)

、＿＿行く。(I will go to Osaka tomorrow.)

ダニエルはその＿＿＿んだ。(Daniel read the book.)

7. Choose 「へ」 Particles (toward) or 「で」 The contextual particle.

＿＿で＿＿く。 (I will go by car.)

ダニエルはから＿＿く。 （Daniel will go to Kyoto from Osaka.）

カフェ＿＿ランチを食べる。 (I will have lunch at a café.)

ネット＿＿＿ニュースを見た。 (I saw the news on internet.)

8. Pick the most appropriate answer.

「でにたの?」

A: でた。 (Came by plane)

B: 3にた。 (Came three days ago.)

C: がきだから。 (Because I like Japan.)

D: サンフランシスコからた。 (Came from San Francisco.)

Answer Keys

1. ダニエルはアニメがきだ。

In the negative form ダニエルはアニメがきじゃない。

In the past tense ダニエルはアニメがきだった。

In the past negative ダニエルはアニメがきじゃなかった。

しい (Beautiful Person)

In the negative form　しくない

In the past tense しかった

In the past negative しくなかった

2. いい

In the negative form　よくない

In the past tense よかった

In the past negative よくなかった

3. ダニエルはべる。

In the negative form ダニエルはべない。

In the past tense ダニエルはべた。

In the past negative ダニエルはべなかった。

4. ダニエルはくる。

In the negative form ダニエルはこない。

In the past tense ダニエルはきた。

In the past negative ダニエルはこなかった。

5. ダニエルはく。

In the negative form ダニエルはかない。

In the past tense ダニエルはった。

In the past negative ダニエルはかなかった。

6.

はをる。(I run in the park.)

と3にう。(I will meet my teacher at 3.)

、に行く。(I will go to Osaka tomorrow.)

ダニエルはそのをんだ。(Daniel read the book.)

7.

でく。(I will go by car.)

ダニエルはからへく。 (Daniel will go to Kyoto from Osaka.)

カフェでランチを食べる。(I will have lunch at a café.)

ネットでニュースを見た。(I saw the news on internet.)

8. C: がきだから。(Because I like Japan.)

で=why, で=how.

Masu-form & Desu-form

"Art is long, life is short."

- Ryuichi Sakamoto

Thank you for learning from to get familiar with adjective conjugation and verb conjugation. In everyday conversation in Japanese, you will hear more 「ます」「です」 at the end of sentences. Those are polite forms of communication in Japan.

Conjugation is something you need to learn repeatedly. In this chapter, we're going to practice changing forms and making sentences. If you're not confident with verbs and adjective basic conjugation, please go over the basic grammar chapters again.

We learned nouns, verbs, adjectives and particles to compose a sentence now and we should be able to move on to 「ます」 forms so you can start communicating verbally in Japanese. 「ます」 is used for regular verbs, and 「です」 is used for be verbs. 「ます」 must always come at the end of a sentence and never in relative clause. For the polite way of "to be" you can simply replace 「だ」 to 「です」. 「はダニエルです」「アメリカです」

u-verbs

(Plain Form)	ます (Masu-form)
う to help　　　　う　→ polite　い	＋ます　→　います
す to speak/talk　す　→ polite　し	＋ます　→　します
く to write　　　　き　→ polite　き	＋ます　→　きます
む to read　　　　む　→ polite　み	＋ます　→　みます
む to drink　　　　む　→ polite　み	＋ます　→みます
う to buy　　　　う　→ polite　み	＋ます　→います
ぐ to swim　　　　ぐ　→ polite　ぎ	＋ます　→ぎます
つ to wait　　　　つ　→ polite　ち	＋ます　→ちます
れてくる to bring someone　くる　→ polite　き	＋ます　→れてきます
ここにいる to stay here　　いる　→ polite　い	＋ます　→ここにいます

126

ru-verbs

(Plain Form)	ます　(Masu-form)
べるto eat　　　　　　　る　→ polite	＋ます　→　べます
るto sleep　　　　　　　る　→ polite	＋ます　→　べます
るto look/see　　　　　　る　→ polite	＋ます　→　ます
つけるto put/turn on　　　る　→ polite	＋ます　→　つけます
める to close　　　　　　る　→ polite	＋ます　→　めます
ける to open　　　　　　る　→ polite	＋ます　→　けます
ける to tidy up　　　　る　→ polite	＋ます　→　けます

Irregular -verbs

(Plain Form)	ます　(Masu-form)
するto do　　　　　　する　→ polite　し	＋ます　→　します
くるto come　　　　　くる　→ polite　き	＋ます　→　きます
あるto exist　　　　ある　→ polite　あり	＋ます　→　あります

「ます」conjugation uses "i" vowels in verbs. Now, conjugate back from ます to . Remember, we have "u-verb" "ru-verb" and "irregular" ones.

ます	
i.e. います　to meet	う
めます to collect	
にきます go to Kyoto	
ります to ride/ get on	
にります　to get in a bathtub	
ります　to return/go home	
います　to sing	

127

Answer

ます	
めます to collect	める
にきます go to Kyoto	にく
ります to ride/ get on	る
にります to get in a bathtub	にる
ります to return/go home	る
います to sing	う

Syntax 1. 「ゲームをするのがきです」 "I like to play games."

When you make a sentence with a verb ＋が好きです(I like), 「ゲームをします」 (I play games)＋「きです」 (I like) , add 「の」 to the plain form of the verb.

「ゲームをするのがきです」

「ります」＋「きです」 →Plain Form 「走る」＋の＋が好きです

＝「走るのが好きです」

「べます」＋「きです」＝「べるのがきです」

「ぎます」＋「きです」＝「ぐのがきです」

「います」＋「きです」＝「うのがきです」

「きます」＋「きです」＝「くのがきです」

By adding 「を」 Object Particle, you can convey more specific information.

「いもの (Something sweet)」＋「を」＋「べるのがきです」＝「いものをべるのがきです」 I like to eat sweets.

「クロール(Crawl)をぐのがきです」: I like to swim freestyle.

「カラオケをうのがきです」 : I like to sing Karaoke.

「をくのがきです」 : I like to walk in a park.

Practice: Make a sentence 「が好きです」 Syntax using the following verbs

「をます (I watch baseball)」 _____

「にります(I ride the shinkansen)」 _____

「アニメをます (I watch an Anime)」 _____

「ギターをきます (I play the guitar)」 _____

128

「マンガをみます (I read a manga)」 _____

「DJをします(I do DJ)」 _____

Answer:

をるのがきです。

にるのがきです。

アニメをるのがきです。

ギターをくのがきです。

マンガをむのがきです。

DJをするのがきです。

Syntax 2. 「にくつもりです」 "plan to go to Kyoto."

る＋つもりです

Used to express an intention or plan you have had for some time. Using ～つもりですか(do you plan to…) towards someone else gives an impression of being impolite, so it is best to avoid it in questions.

Remember, the future tense and present tense in Japanese are identical and if there is no time indication such as tomorrow, this afternoon, next week, you can't tell if it's the present tense or future tense. So, if yo use 「つもりです」 it's very similar to "going to."

「 、そのレストランにくつもりです」 "I'm going to the restaurant tomorrow."

ます → る＋つもりです （Plan to do~ ）

i.e. います to meet → 「う」	→うつもりです
めます to collect → 「める」	→
にきます go to Kyoto	→
ります to ride/ get on	→
にります to get in a bathtub	→
ります to return/go home	→
います to sing	→

Answer

めます to collect	→めるつもりです

にきます go to Kyoto	→にくつもりです
りJ ます to ride/ get on	→るつもりです
にります to get in a bathtub	→にるつもりです
J ます to return/go home	→るつもりです
います to sing	→うつもりです

Let's add some particles and information to complete a sentence.

ます→る＋つもりです +more information with particles

ex. います to meet Daniela tomorrow	→ダニエラにうつもりです
めます to collect Anime cards (this week)	→
にきます go to Kyoto (this weekend)	→
ります to ride/ get on Shinkansen（）	→
にります to get in (onsen)(next week)	→
ります to return/go (home)（at 6 6）	→
います to sing （Karaokeカラオケ）(tonight)	→

Answer

めます to collect Anime cards (this week)	→アニメカードをめるつもりです。
にきます go to Kyoto (this weekend)	→にくつもりです。
ります to ride/ get on Shinkansen（）	→にるつもりです。
にります to get in (onsen)(next week)	→にるつもりです。
ります to return/go (home)（at 6 6）	→6にるつもりです。
います to sing （Karaokeカラオケ）(tonight)	→カラオケをうつもりです。

Conversation Exercise

A: 「、をしますか」 "What are you going to do this weekend?"

B: 「に行くつもりです」 "I'm going to Kyoto ."

「、をしますか」

Your answer_____つもりです。

Time- related vocabulary

	Today
	Yesterday
	Tomorrow
（月 =Moon）	Monday
（火 =Fire）	Tuesday
（水 =Water）	Wednesday
（木 =Tree）	Thursday
（金 =Metal）	Friday
（土 =Earth）	Saturday
（日 =Sun）	Sunday
	Weekend
	This Weekend
	Next Weekend
	Next Month
	Last Month
	Last Week
の	Next Monday
の	Last Monday

Japanese Year has two formats. One is Western （）, the year of 2023, 2023 is called, "ni sen ni ju san" nen (two thousand twenty three year). Another is Japanese （）, each emperor has the name of the period. Currently it's called 5, the current emperor took over the predecessor five years ago.

At one last time to practice ます to be sure from . So when you talk with natives, you can talk to anyone on any occasion with the proper conjugation.

u-verbs

	ます	つもりです （going to…）
ex. う to help	います	うつもりです
す to speak/talk		

く to write →		
む to read →		
む to drink →		
う to buy →		
ぐ to swim →		
つ to wait →		
れてくる to bring someone →		
ここにいるto stay here→		

Answer:

u-verbs

	ます	つもりです （going to...)
す to speak/talk	します	すつもりです
く to write →	きます	くつもりです
む to read →	みます	むつもりです
む to drink →	みます	むつもりです
う to buy →	います	うつもりです
ぐ to swim →	ぎます	ぐつもりです
つ to wait →	ちます	つつもりです
れてくる to bring someone →	れてきます	れてくるつもりです
ここにいるto stay here→	ここにいます	ここにいるつもりです

Ru-verbs

	ます	つもりです （going to...)
ex. べる to eat	べます	べるつもりです
るto sleep →		
るto see/look →		

Answer

	ます	つもりです (going to...)
るto sleep →	ます	るつもりです
るto see/look →	ます	るつもりです

Irregular Verbs

	ます	つもりです (going to...)
するto do →		
くるto come →		

Answer

	ます	つもりです (going to...)
するto do →	します	するつもりです
くるto come →	きます	くるつもりです

Practice with Noun + Participle

	Meaning	ます
i.e. かばんをつ	Carry a bag	かばんをちます
をう	Help a friend	
をす	Lend an umbrella	
をわる	Change seats	
おをう	Pay money	
をむ	Drink water	
わさびをつける	Put Wasabi on	
えにく	Pick someone up	
をべる	Eat Sushi	
でぶ	Play in a park	
をける	Open a box	
する	Make a reservation	

ってくる	Go and buy	
をつける	Turn on the light	
をる	Puck up a phone	
する	Place an order	
ドアをめる	Close a door	
でる	Sleep on a Futon	

Answer

	Meaning	ます
をう	Help a friend	をいます
をす	Lend an umbrella	をします
をわる	Change seats	をわります
おをう	Pay money	おをいます
をむ	Drink water	をみます
わさびをつける	Put Wasabi on	わさびをつけます
えにく	Pick someone up	えにきます
をべる	Eat Sushi	をべます
でぶ	Play in a park	でびます
をける	Open a box	をけます
する	Make a reservation	します
ってくる	Go and buy	ってきます
をつける	Turn on the light	をつけます
をる	Puck up a phone	をります
する	Place an order	します
ドアをめる	Close a door	ドアをめます
でる	Sleep on a Futon	でます

ます Syntax 「かばんをちしましょうか」 "Shall I carry your bag?"

When you help, for example, "Do you want me to do something for you?" 「ましょうか」 conjugated from 「ます」 is used. Also, this expression can be used when you invite someone to do something, such as in "Would you have some coffee?"

Replace the 「ます」 かばんをちます　then add 「ましょうか」

A: 「かばんを持ちましょうか」 "Shall I carry your bag?"

B: 「すみません。おいします」 "Thank you(sorry), please."

A: 「をおししましょうか」 " Could I lend you an umbrella?"

B: 「すみません。かります」 "Thank you(sorry), that'll be helpful."

Please convert 「ます」 to 「ましょうか」

ex. かばんをつ	かばんをちましょうか
かう　(help with something)	
をってくる(bring some water)	
をける(open the window)	
ドアをめる(close the door)	
をつける(turn on the light)	
メールでる(send by email)	
をす(lend you an umbrella)	
をかわる(switch seats)	

Answer

かう　(help with something)	かいましょうか
をってくる(bring some water)	をってきましょうか
をける(open the window)	をけましょうか
ドアをめる(close the door)	ドアをめましょうか
をつける(turn on the light)	をつけましょうか
メールでる(send by email)	メールでりましょうか
をす(lend you an umbrella)	をしましょうか
をかわる(switch seats)	をかわりましょうか

ます Syntax 「にライブをにきます」 "I'll go to Shibuya to see a live performance."

「Vます」＋に行きます(will go to do ...). This expression can show the destination and the action.

For example,

A:「おでかけですか」Are you going out?

B:「ライブを見に行きます」I'm going to see a live performance.

「AにBしにきます」"I'm going to A to do B."

Compose a sentence using A and B vocabulary.

「Vます」＋にきます

A	B	Sentence
i.e. Kyoto	をる See cherry blossom	にをにきます
の A friend's house	ぶ Have fun	
Shibuya	をる Watch a movie	
コンビニ A convenience store	ランチを買う　Buy lunch	
A park	る Run	
A bookstore	をう Buy a magazine	
Sapporo	ラーメンをべる Have Ramen	
ネットカフェ Internet Cafe	リサーチをする　Do some research	
に Akihabara(in Tokyo)	ゲームをす Find a video game	
に The station	をえる Pick up a friend	

Answer

A	B	Sentence
の A friend's house	ぶ Have fun	のにびにきます
Shibuya	をる Watch a movie	にをにきます
コンビニ A convenience store	ランチをう　Buy lunch	コンビニにランチをいにきます
A park	る Run	をりにきます
A bookstore	をう Buy a magazine	にをいにきます
Sapporo	ラーメンをべる Have Ramen	にラーメンをべにきます
ネットカフェ Internet Cafe	リサーチをする　Do some research	ネットカフェにリサーチをしにきます

| に Akihabara(in Tokyo) | ゲームをす Find a video game | にゲームをしにきます |
| に The station | をえる Pick up a friend | にをえにきます |

ます Syntax 「ラーメンが食べたいです」 "I want to eat Sapporo ramen"

「Vます」＋たいです（want to）, to express wants and wishes. Conjugation is the same as い adjectives.

「Vます」＋たくないです(don't want to), 「Vます」＋たかったです （wanted to, Past Tense）, 「Vます」＋たくなかったです （didn't want to, Past-Negative）. The particle 「が」can be used instead of 「を」

「ラーメンをべます(I eat ramen.)」 → 「ラーメンがべたいです(I want to eat ramen.)」 The first sentence is "I eat food and ramen is one of them." In the second sentence, 「が」is the identifier particle that is highlighting ramen, no other food.

In the negative form, the particle 「を」often changes to 「は」.

「ラーメンをべます(I eat ramen.)」 → 「ラーメンはべたくないです(I don't want to eat ramen.)」

Conversation Example

A: 「ランチにがべたいですか」 (What do you feel like eating for lunch?)

B: 「ラーメンがべたいです」 (I want to have ramen.)

Conjugate to "wan to" and "don't wan to."

	Want to	Don't want to
ex.　みそラーメンをべる　eat miso ramen	みそラーメンがべたいです I want to eat miso ramen.	みそラーメンはべたくないです I don't want to eat miso ramen
にく go to an onsen		
にする travel to Okinawa		
でく work in Japan		
にる climb Mt. Fuji		
(Famous Pilgrimage) をく walk on Kumano Kodo		
にく　go to a Zen temple		
をする practice zazen		

Answer

	Want to	Don't want to

137

にく go to an onsen	にきたいです	にきたくないです
にする travel to Okinawa	にしたいです	にしたくないです
でく work in Japan	できたいです	できたくないです
にる climb Mt. Fuji	にりたいです	にりたくないです
をく walk on Kumano Kodo	をきたいです	をきたくないです
にく go to a Zen temple	にきたいです	にきたくないです
をする practice zazen	をしたいです	をしたくないです

Conversation Exercise

「(Japan)で(What)がしたいですか」

ex. 「でをしたいです」"I want to practice zazen in Kyoto."

_____がしたいです。

One last conjugation practice is "wanted to" and "didn't want to."

Want to	Wanted to
i.e. みそラーメンがべたいです (I want to eat miso ramen.)	みそラーメンがべたかったです。
にきたいです	
にしたいです	
できたいです	
にりたいです	
をきたいです	
にきたいです	
をしたいです	

Don't want to	Didn't want to
i.e. みそラーメンはべたくないです "I don't want to eat miso ramen."	みそラーメンはべたくなかったです
にきたくないです	

にしたくないです	
できたくないです	
にりたくないです	
をきたくないです	
にきたくないです	
をしたくないです	

Answer

Want to	Wanted to
にきたいです	にきたかったです
にしたいです	にしたかったです
できたいです	できたかったです
にりたいです	にりたかったです
をきたいです	をきたかったです
にきたいです	にきたかったです
をしたいです	をしたかったです

Don't want to	Didn't want to
にきたくないです	にきたくなかったです
にしたくないです	にしたくなかったです
できたくないです	できたくなかったです
にりたくないです	にりたくなかったです
をきたくないです	をきたくなかったです
にきたくないです	にきたくなかったです
をしたくないです	をしたくなかったです

Take-home message

We're now learned 「ます」「です」 forms that are more common in conversation and polite way to communicate. 「ます」 is used for regular verbs, and 「です」 is used for be verbs.You can start communicating using those phrases with Japanese natives.

In the meantime, is important as well since some syntax requires such as "I like to do…" and "I'm planning /going to." Then we should be able to expand expressions from ます such as "want to" and "not want to" to convey your opinions and feelings.

Conjugation might be the hardest part of learning a foreign language, and we came up with lots of drills and composition practice in this chapter. Some of the tips to learn effectively is 1. Reading aloud to let yourself hear to store sounds and rhythms in your brain, 2. Talking/mumbling to yourself in everyday situation in Japanese.

Exercises

1. Conjugate to ます.

うto buy	
ぐto swim	
つto wait	
れてくるto bring someone	
ここにいるto stay here	

えにく	Pick someone up	
をべる	Eat Sushi	
でぶ	Play in a park	
をける	Open a box	
する	Make a reservation	

2. Combine two to make a sentence.

「カラオケをう」 「きです」 →I like to sing Karaoke ＿＿＿＿＿＿＿＿＿＿＿＿＿

「京都をく」 「きです」 : I like to walk in Kyoto＿＿＿＿＿＿＿＿＿＿＿＿＿＿＿

3. Make a sentence of "I will go to A to do B."

A	B
Sapporo	ラーメンをべる Have Ramen

A	B
ネットカフェ Internet Cafe	リサーチをする Do some research

4. Conjugate the following to "want to" and "wanted to" form.

	"want to"
にる climb Mt. Fuji	
をく walk on Kumano Kodo	

にく go to a Zen temple	

	"wanted to"
にる climb Mt. Fuji	
をく walk on Kumano Kodo	
にく go to a Zen temple	

5. Conjugate to "Shall I ...?" form.

	"Shall I...?"
をける(open the window)	
ドアをめる(close the door)	
をつける(turn on the light)	

6. Correct the mistake in answer B.

A: 「、をしますか」"What are you going to do this weekend?"

B: 「ピザをべました」

7. Correct the grammatical error.

(Baseball) をますがきです。

(Bullet Train)でにきますつもりです。

8. Pick one food and answer the question.

A: 「ランチにがべたいですか」

　うどん　ピザ　サンドウィッチ　ハンバーガー

B:_____

Answer Keys

1. Conjugate to ます.

う to buy	います
ぐ to swim	ぎます
つ to wait	ちます
れてくる to bring someone	れてきます
ここにいる to stay here	ここにいます

えにく	Pick someone up	えにきます
をべる	Eat Sushi	をべます
でぶ	Play in a park	でびます
をける	Open a box	をけます
する	Make a reservation	します

2. カラオケをうのがきです

くのがきです

3. にラーメンをべにきます。

ネットカフェにリサーチをしにきます。

4.

	"want to"
にる climb Mt. Fuji	にりたいです
をく walk on Kumano Kodo	をきたいです
にく　go to a Zen temple	にきたいです

	"wanted to"
にる climb Mt. Fuji	にりたかったです
をく walk on Kumano Kodo	をきたかったです
にく　go to a Zen temple	にきたかったです

5.

	"Shall I...?"
をける(open the window)	をけましょうか
ドアをめる(close the door)	ドアをめましょうか
をつける(turn on the light)	をつけましょうか

6. 「ピザをべました」→べに行きます or べるつもりです

7. (Baseball) をますがきです。→るのがきです

(Bullet Train)でにきますつもりです。→ くつもりです

8. 　　(or うどんorピザorサンドウィッチorハンバーガー) がべたいです。

Conclusion

"Never regard study as a duty but as an enviable opportunity to learn."

\- Albert Einstein

Congratutation on finishing the book 1! おめでとう！ここまでがんばりました。This must have been a long and challenging path, but look at all the progress you made.

You're now able to write two Japanese writing systems, Hiragana and Katakana, in addition, to identifying basic Kanji. Also, you can make simple sentences in Japanese in the negative form and past tense. You learned the basic language structure, and vocabulary/kanji is your next target.

We have already learned adjective and verb conjugation. This must be practiced repeatedly, along with building vocabulary. Please go over 「な」 「い」 adjectives and 「う」 「る」 verbs conjugation. Continue to compose sentences to express your thoughts and feelings. We will see how you can keep working on the things you mastered in order to reinforce your knowledge and further investigate smaller aspects, such as particles and expressions for the natural Japanese.

Here is some advice on what we believe is the best way to keep on learning Japanese. In particular, we'll talk about what topics are best for you to take up next and what methods of study could bring the best results.

A: How to consolidate your new knowledge

You have built the basic Japanese skills that you can read (with furigana on kanji) and understand the basic sentences in Japanese. Your next targets are:

Vocabulary and Kanji

Practical expressions with precise grammar (particles and idioms)

Particles are challenging even for the natives, and this will be accomplished as Japanese internalization progresses. Grammar is something very helpful to understand the language but to improve language fluency, internalization (thinking in the language) is always the key. In other words, the usage of the right side of the brain will be very valuable. Besides, relying on your memory and thinking logically to communicate your thoughts and feelings can be exhausting and not always fun. Communication should be joyful and inspiring.

In order to consolidate your current knowledge, you should consider the various kinds of practical approach to the language (manga, anime, movies, podcasts, tv shows, language-exchange apps etc.).

Secondarily, you can keep practicing on the grammar topics we learned together. We've just started the basic grammar and continuously study grammar to communicate in the next books, in the Phrasebook for Adult Beginners.

If you struggled with some specific topics in this book, you should try and target these topics specifically online, you can find all the single grammar topics; there are various reliable websites that present the topic with different examples and visual material.

B: Next steps to communicate in Japanese

Again, we just started learning Japanese grammar, we will be continuously learning more grammar to be fluent and be able to communicate in Japanese. You don't need to be an expert on grammar but we learned the basics so we can communicate in natural Japanese.

In terms of communication skills, the most vital aspect of it is listening skills. Japanese pronunciation is relatively simple and easy to understand so you should be able to pick the sounds. However, if you don't understand the basic structure and grammar, it's impossible to understand the essence. In Japanese, verbs come at the end of sentences and the verb can be in the negative form or the past tense. You need to listen to the sentence all to the end, even in a simple sentence.

「はへ...」 "I to school..."

The second part of the sentence can be "went" " don't go" " didn't go" " want to go" "don't want to go"…. In Japanese comedy skits, this kind of trick in the grammatical structure is used to tease the audience. And most of cases, the subject is omitted so sentences can be unclear. So, listening skills require an extra open mind, guessing, and imagination.

Communication is fun, and we will learn grammar to communicate. In the Phrasebook for Adult Beginners, you will learn phrases and practical conversation, also cultural side stories of the phrases. The reason why communication is fun is that you can meet interesting people and understand them in communication. When you encounter a new culture or new person, you will discover new horizon, and the language is the vehicle for enhanced visibility.

BOOK 2

Japanese Phrasebook for Adult Beginners:

Common Japanese Words & Phrases
For Everyday Conversation and Travel

Explore to Win

Introduction

In communication, the most important skill is considered listening. Listening to your own voice as well. Reading is also another form of listening to what the writer/author says. The way the Japanese communicate, and think might differ from you or your culture, but as Jorge Luis Borges writes, "O joy of understanding, greater than the joy of imagining, greater than the joy of feeling!"

In this book, we will further cover basic grammar but mainly for practical communication. We will cover how we can build a sentence and use practical phrases. This workbook helps you communicate better in Japanese and understand the culture and people at different levels. Alongside learning, this book will provide a <u>collection of useful phrases and vocabulary for travelers and tourists</u>, giving this guide a handy instrument to experience Japan to the fullest.

2. MYTHBUSTERS

Are you comfortable pushing yourself harder and harder to go to the next chapter? This is not a learn-or-die type of boot camp. As the first quote says, 「好きこそものの上手なれ」 ("What you love to do, you will learn to do well.").When your interests and curiosity grow, you are just learning in a neutral mental state without getting shaken up. For many people, the more they push themselves, the more pressure and fear of failure they get...I'm one of them for sure. We ask good questions from time to time.

There are many precautions/advice/biases for learning a foreign language. We can be creatures of habits and live with inner dialogues. So, we will check your self-talk and emotional level as the workbook chapter continues and use paradoxes by asking questions. Paradoxes can be a great tool for MythBusters and Kaizen 改善 (good change) masters.

The bottom line is that no one forces you to study Japanese. It's not the end of the world if you don't speak Japanese. And we will check in with you on how you are doing and bring you back to a "neutral" mental state. "Beginner's mind." You have the freedom to choose your direction. In this neutral state, you would feel less pressure and hard feeling, and we will ask if you would carry on to the next level to be a better communicator from the moment of right here and now.

The truth is that the more knowledge and skills you have, the more confidence and self-esteem you will have. You will have something you like about the language, culture, and communication. When you feel good about yourself, you will find a way to communicate with Japanese culture and people. Maybe you are already planning to travel alone to Kyoto?

3. LOST IN TRANSLATION

Have you watched the 2003's movie "Lost in Translation"? Scarlett Johansen traveled to Kyoto alone and encountered the traditional wedding march at a temple. Visiting Japan can be a mind-opening experience and, at the same time, a self-discovery challenge.

You can watch many "first time in Japan" travel channels on YouTube, but it's not 360 views with smells and feelings. And how to communicate with the locals in big cities and small towns and villages? You would encounter real local people who see an American for the first time. That's a new experience that only you can witness.

As mentioned in the first introduction of the book, the priority of communication is different between Japan and US. Japan is a small country with a high population density. Politeness is the tool to communicate from the history lessons to keep peace on the small island without slaying each other all the time. And interactive focus highlights the other person in dialogue to show respect. In the meantime, in a big country like the US, friendliness is the key to communicating and building trust. Once you get to know each other, an open and friendly manner shows trust.

One of the Youtubers arrived in Osaka and got excited to be on the street and in a subway but was taken aback to see how quiet people were. Again, Japan is a small country with a high-density population, so speaking loudly is unnecessary. On the contrary, in Chinese, you must speak clearly to communicate the correct words with the correct intonations, so your voice must be loud.

The Experiences and communication with locals in Japan can become your life gem. It might take some time to notice, but your expanded consciousness can lift your life experience to the next level. Ultimately, this experience might be the best way to learn about different cultures and tolerance. And if you could understand the people and culture through communication, it would lead to something everyone in the world can benefit from.

Verb Conjugations to Four Expressions of 「て形」 (te-Form)

"Listen with curiosity. Speak with honesty. Act with integrity. The greatest problem with communication is we don't listen to understand. We listen to reply. When we listen with curiosity, we don't listen with the intent to reply. We listen for what's behind the words."

- Roy T. Bennet

Here comes Book 2 Chapter 1. Are you feeling pressure? Or Stress? Have you noticed how much you made progress? From this chapter, it's about communication and it's all about having fun.

In this lesson, you will be learning what is called the て形(te-form) of verbs. They are so called because mos of them end with the sound て. The way a verb て形is derived varies depending on the type of the verb, as seen in the following table:

With て形 we will be able to communicate

- Polite Request 「て」＋ください

「もう一度言ってください」

(Say again, please, 一度: One Time, もう一度:: one more time, 言う: Say)

- Actions in Sequence

「今から渋谷に行って映画を見ます」

(I'm going to Shibuya to watch a movie. 今: Now, 行く: Go, 映画: Movie, 見る: watch)

- Action in Progress　「て」＋います

「私は今、メールを書いています」

(I'm writing an email right now., メール: Email, 書く: Write)

- Resultant State　「て」＋います

「今日、ダニエルさんはかっこいい帽子をかぶっています」

(Daniel is wearing a cool hat(cap) today. かっこいい: Cool, 帽子(ぼうし): Hat/Cap, かぶる: Wear something over one's head)

- Habitual Action

「ダニエラさんはいつも６時に起(お)きています」

(Daniela always gets up at six. いつも: Always, 起(お)きる: Get up)

Kanji & Hiragana in the Right Mix

You are now familiar with basic sentences in hiragana, katakana, and kanji. Kanji communicates an idea or a concept of subject, action, and object.

「いってください」can be either

1. 「行(い)ってください」Go, please.

2. 「言(い)ってください」Say, please.

If you write in hiragana, the meaning can be either meaning, and it's confusing.

For example,

1. 「早(はや)く行(い)ってください」Go fast, please.   You might want to ask, "to where?"

2. 「早(はや)く言(い)ってください」Say fast, please. You might want to ask, "say what?"

Selecting the wrong kanji changes the sentence's meaning completely, and the accents are identical. Since many homophones exist, kanji is key in distinguishing them in writing.

Conjugation of て形 verbs

For U-verbs, there are three patterns for conjugation. Verbs ending with 「う」「つ」「る」will be added small つ before て. Verbs ending with 「む」「ぶ」「ぬ」will be 「ん」＋「で」, てbecomes dakuon "muddie sound." And the final pattern is verbs ending with 「く」「ぐ」will be either 「いて」「って」or 「いで」.

Verbs		普通形(ふつうけい) Plain Form	て形(けい) te-Form
Ru-verbs		食(た)べる　(to eat)　→る	て形(けい)→て　食(た)べて
		寝(ね)る　(to sleep)　→る	て形(けい)→て　寝(ね)て
		見(み)る　(to see/look)　→る	て形(けい)→て　見(み)て
U-verbs	Ending Sound		

152

う	買う (to buy)　→う	て形→っ　買って	
つ	立つ (to stand)　→つ	て形→っ　立って	
る	帰る (to return/go home)　　　　→る	て形→っ　帰って	
む	読む (to read)　→む	て形→ん　読んで	
ぶ	遊ぶ(to play)　→ぶ	て形→ん　遊んで	
ぬ	死ぬ (to die)　→ぬ	て形→ん　死んで	
く	書く(to write)　→く	て形→い　書いて	
	行く(to go)　→く	て形→い　行って	
ぐ	泳ぐ(to swim)　→ぐ	て形→い　泳いで	
Irregular Verbs	する　　　　　→する	て形　して	
	来る　　　　　→来る	て形　来て	

Conjugation Exercise: Conjugate 普通形 to て形

普通形 Plain Form	英語English	カテゴリ Categories	て形　te-form
座る	to sit	U-verbs	座って
飲む	to drink	U-verbs	飲んで
待つ	to wait	U-verbs	待って
送る	to send	U-verbs	送って
急ぐ	to hurry	U-verbs	急いで
言う	to say	U-verbs	言って

書く	to write	U-verbs	書いて
貸す	to lend	U-verbs	貸して
会う	to meet	U-verbs	会って
歯を磨く	to brush one's teeth	U-verbs	歯を磨いて
教える	to teach	Ru-verbs	教えて
取り替える	to replace	Ru-verbs	取り替えて
会議に出る	to attend a meeting	Ru-verbs	会議に出て
見せる	to show	Ru-verbs	見せて
来る	to come	Irregular	来て
連絡する	to contact	Irregular	連絡して
連れてくる	to bring someone	Irregular	連れてきて
たばこを吸う	to smoke a cigarette	U-verbs	たばこを吸って
卒業する	to graduate	Irregular	卒業して

1.Polite Request

「もう一度言ってください」

(Say again, please, 一度: One Time, もう一度:: Another time once, 言う: Say)

To make a simple request or instruct someone or encourage someone to do something.

Verbて＋ください

「ゆっくり話してください」

(Speak slowly, please. ゆっくり: Slowly, 話す（話します）: Speak)

Conversation Example:

A: 「わかりましたか」（"Did you understand?" わかる（わかります）: Understand）

B: 「すみません、ゆっくり話してください」 （Excuse me, please speak slowly.）

154

A: 「わかりました」

「Verbて＋ください」

Make a simple polite request using the following verbs.

普通形	て形Polite Request
ゆっくり話す（Speak slowly）	ゆっくり話してください
いっしょに行く(Go together)	いっしょに行ってください
ちょっと待つ(Wait a little)	ちょっと待ってください
名前を教える(tell one's name)	名前を教えてください
あとでメールする(Email me later)	あとでメールしてください
ちょっと急ぐ(Hurry a little)	ちょっと急いでください

2. Actions in Sequence

「今から渋谷に行って映画を見ます」

(I'm going to Shibuya to watch a movie. 今: Now, 行く: Go, 映画: Movie, 見る: Watch)

You can express multiple actions with て形 verbs. It is interpreted as consecutive actions. (I did A, then I did B, and I finally did C.) There are two forms: positive and negative. The tense is indicated at the end of the sentence with the verb.

Verbて、Verbます。

「今から渋谷に行って映画を見ます」

Conversation Example:

A: 「今週、何をしますか」（"What are you going to do this week?" 今週: This Week)

B: 「京都に桜を見に行って、大阪で友達とご飯を食べます」（"I'm going to see cherry blossom in Kyoto and meet a friend in Osaka to have some food." 桜: Cherry Blossom, 友達: a friend(s), ご飯: Food/Meal, 食べる：Eat)

A: 「いいですね」（"Sounds great."）

「Verbて、Verbます」

「Verbて、Verbました」 (Past Tense)

「渋谷に行って映画を見ました」 ("I went to Shibuya to watch a movie.")

Combine two sentences by using て形

1	2	Present/Future Tense	Past Tense
i.e. 渋谷に行く (go to Shibuya)	映画を見る (watch a movie)	渋谷に行って、映画を見る	渋谷に行って、映画を見た
日本に行く(go to Japan)	友達に会う (meet a friend)	日本に行って、友達に会う	日本に行って、友達に会った
鎌倉に行く(go to Kamakura)	坐禅をする(do zazen)	鎌倉に行って、坐禅をする	鎌倉に行って、坐禅をした
風呂に入る(take a bath)	寝る(sleep)	風呂に入って、寝る	風呂に入って、寝た
ケーキを買う (buy some cakes)	帰る (return/go home)	ケーキを買って、帰る	ケーキを買って、帰った

Exercise: Present/Future Tense

Answer as B by combining two verbs.

A:「ダニエルさん、これから何をしますか」 ("Daniel-san, what are you going to do now?")

B:「Verbて、Verbます」 ("I'm going to do Verb and Verb.")

A:「そうですか」 ("I see.")

1.	友達を迎えに行く(go pick up a friend)	ご飯を食べる(to have some food)
2.	家に帰る(go home)	パッキングをする(pack)
3.	公園に行く(go to a park)	走る(run)

1._____

2._____

3._____

1. 友達を迎えに行って、ご飯を食べます

2. 家に帰って、パッキングをします

156

3. 公園に行って、走ります
こうえん　い　　　　　　はし

Exercise: Past Tense

Answer as B by combining two verbs.

A: 「ダニエルさん、 週末、何をしましたか」 ("Daniel-san, what did you over the weekend" 週末:
しゅうまつ　なに　　　しゅうまつ
Weekend)

B: 「Verbて、Verbしました」 ("I did Verb and Verb.")

A: 「いいですね」 ("That's great.")

1.	新宿に行く(go to Shinjuku) しんじゅく　い	レコードを買う(buy records) か
2.	友達の家に行く(go to a friend's ともだち　いえ　い house)	食事をする(have some food) しょくじ
3.	電車に乗る(take a train) でんしゃ　の	日光まで行く(go to Nikko) にっこう　い

1._____

2._____

3._____

1. 新宿に行って、レコードを買いました
しんじゅく　い　　　　　　　　　か

2. 友達の家に行って、食事をしました
ともだち　いえ　い　　　　しょくじ

3. 電車に乗って、日光まで行きました
でんしゃ　の　　にっこう　い

3. Action in Progress 「ています」 "be-Verb ing"

The meaning of 「ています」 varies depending on verbs. Continuous verbs show the action that is ongoing at a point in time. Also used to express repeated activities. 「毎日走っています」("I go running
まいにちはし
every day.")

「私は今、メールを書いています」
わたし　いま　　　　　　か

(I'm writing an email right now., メール: Email, 書く: Write)
か

Verb＋ています

157

「 私 は今、メールを書いています」

書く → く → て形　いています

Conjugate　普通形 to 「ています」

普通形	英語	カテゴリ	て形
聞く	ask/listen	U-verb	聞いています
持つ	have/carry/hold	U-verb	持っています
頼む	ask/request	U-verb	頼んでいます
洗う	Wash	U-verb	洗っています
働く	Work	U-verb	働いています
住む	Live	U-verb	住んでいます
知る	Know	U-verb	知っています
ご飯を作る	cook a meal	U-verb	ご飯を作っています
待つ	Wait	U-verb	待っています
買う	Buy	U-verb	買っています
話す	speak/talk	U-verb	話しています
読む	Read	U-verb	読んでいます
風呂に入る	Take a bath	U-verb	風呂に入っています
食べる	Eat	Ru-verb	食べています
決める	Decide	Ru-verb	決めています
結婚する	get marry	Irregular	結婚しています
電話する	Call	Irregular	電話しています
来る	Come	Irregular	来ます

Exercise: Add 今 in the beginning of the sentence and conjugate the present tense to 「ています」.

158

i.e. テレビを見る	今、テレビを見ています
本を読む	今、　　　　　本を読んでいます
日本語を勉強する	今、　　　　　日本語を勉強しています
友達を待つ	今、　　　　　友達を待っています
友達と話す	今、　　　　　友達と話しています

「ています」can indicate a situation or status such as place, marital status, or working status.

Conversation Example:

A: 「どこで働いていますか」("Where are you working?"　働く（働いています）: work)

B: 「渋谷で働いています」（"I'm working in Shibuya."）

Conjugate the present tense to ていますto show the status or the situation.

i.e. 渋谷で働く （work in Shibuya）	渋谷で働いています
IT会社に勤める (work at an IT firm)	IT会社に勤めています
プログラマーをする (work as a programmer)	プログラマーをしています
渋谷に住む (live in Shibuya)	渋谷に住んでいます
結婚する (be married)	結婚しています

Answer the following questions.

1. 「仕事は何ですか」 （What's your occupation?）＿＿＿＿＿＿＿＿＿＿＿＿＿

2. 「車を持っていますか」 （Do you have a car?）＿＿＿＿＿＿＿＿＿＿＿＿＿

3. 「このレストランを知っていますか」 （Do you know this restaurant?）

＿＿＿＿＿＿＿＿＿＿＿＿＿

1. 英語を教えています　 (I teach English.)

2. はい、持っています。Or いいえ、持っていません。(Yes, I do, or No, I don't)

159

3. はい、知っています。Or いいえ、知りません。(Yes, I do, or No, I don't)

「まだ＋Verbて＋いません」can be used to communicate "haven't...yet." The action that is planned is not yet complete. When it's completed, 「もう＋Verbました」

(I already did).

Conversation Example:

A:「ダニエルさん、もうランチ食べましたか」("Daniel-san, did you have lunch yet?)

B:「いいえ、まだ食べていません」("No, I haven't eaten yet.")

A:「ラーメンを食べに行きませんか」("Why don't we have some ramen?")

Conjugate the present tense to 「まだ＋Verbて＋いません」and 「もう＋Verbました」

i.e.ランチを食べる(have lunch)	まだランチを食べていません	もうランチを食べました
レストランを予約する(reserve a restaurant)	まだレストランを予約していません	もうレストランを予約しました
チケットを買う(buy a ticket)	まだチケットを買っていません	もうチケットを買いました
予約をキャンセルする(cancel a reservation)	まだ予約をキャンセルしていません	もう予約をキャンセルしました
ウニを食べる(have some sea urchin)	まだウニを食べていません	もうウニを食べました

3. Resultant State 「しています」

When a verb represents an action that signifies an instantaneous change and has no duration, such as marriage, death, and learning, 「ています」can express the remaining state of the verb.

「今日、ダニエルさんはかっこいい帽子をかぶっています」

(Daniel is wearing a cool hat(cap) today. かっこいい: Cool, 帽子: Hat/Cap, かぶる: Wear something over one's head)

Conversation Example:

A:「ダニエラさんはどこですか」("Where is Daniela-san?")

160

B:「リビングの赤いソファに座っていますよ」（ "She's sitting on the red sofa in the living room." ）

Exercise: Pick One right answer.

1.「田中さんはどこですか」

A. 外で待っています（外: Outside）

B. 食べています

C.もうすぐきます（もうすぐ : Soon）

2.「ダニエルさんはどの人ですか」

A. アメリカ人です

B. 黒いシャツを着ている人です。(黒:Black)

C.今、ご飯を作っています

1. A

2. B

Take-home message

With て形verbs, you can conjugate verbs with four expressions. The first one is the polite request 「てください」such as 「ゆっくり話してください」（ "Please speak slowly." ）

The second one is Action in sequence. You can communicate more than one action with て形, and your story is going to be more detailed chronologically. The third expression is the Action in progress, which enables you to indicate a situation or status such as place, marital status, or working status. Lastly, て形 represents an action that an instantaneous change such as "Verb-ed," "Verb-ing," and be adjective.

"Request," "Action in sequence," "Actuion in progress," and "Resultant State." て形 is used in important grammatical and communicational expressions in verbs, please remember to conjugation and how they are used correctly.

Vocabulary List for Review

今	Now

映画	Movie
もう一度	One More Time
メール	email
書く	Write
かっこいい	Cool
帽子	Hat/Cap
被る	Wear Over One's Head
起きる	Get Up
いつも	Always
行く	Go
早く	Fast/Early
食べる	Eat
寝る	Sleep
見る	See/Look
買う	Buy
立つ	Stand
読む	Read
遊ぶ	Play
死ぬ	Die
泳ぐ	Swim
する	Do
来る	Come
座る	Sit
飲む	Drink

待つ	Wait
送る	Send
急ぐ	Hurry
言う	Say/Tell
貸す	Lend
会う	Meet
歯を磨く	Brush One's Teeth
教える	Teach
取り替える	Replace
会議に出る	Go To a Meeting
見せる	Show
連絡する	Contact
連れてくる	Bring
たばこを吸う	Smoking
卒業する	Graduate
ゆっくり	Slowly
わかる	Understand
いっしょに	Together
ちょっと	A little
名前	Name
あとで	Later
今から	From Now On
今週	This Week
桜	Cherry Blossom

163

友達	Friend
ご飯	Meal/Food
食べる	Eat
いいですね	Sounds good/Looks Good/Seems Good
風呂に入る	Take A Bath
ケーキ	Cake
迎えに行く	Pick Up
帰る	Return/Go Home
公園	Park
走る	Run
週末	Weekend
電車	Train
毎日	Every Day
聞く	Listen/Hear
待つ	Wait
頼む	Ask
洗う	Wash
働く	Work
住む	Live
知る	Know
決める	Decide
結婚する	Marry
電話する	Call
テレビを見る	Watch TV

本_{ほん}を読_よむ	Read books
日本語_{にほんご}を勉強_{べんきょう}する	Study Japanese
会社_{かいしゃ}に勤_{つと}める	Work for a company
プログラマー	Programmer
仕事_{しごと}	Job
車_{くるま}	Car
レストラン	Restaurant
黒_{くろ}い	Black (adj)
白_{しろ}い	White (adj)
赤_{あか}い	Red (adj)
黄色_{きいろ}い	Yellow (adj)
青_{あお}い	Blue (adj)
緑色_{みどりいろ}の	Green (adj)
外_{そと}	Outside

Exercises

1. Conjugate 普通形 to て形

1. 見る→	2. 寝る→	3. 買う→	4. 帰る→
5. 読む→	6. 遊ぶ→	7. 話す→	8. 聞く→
9. 行く→	10. 泳ぐ→	11. する	12. 来る

2. Correct the underlined phrase to complete the conversation.

A: 「すみません、<u>もう一度言う</u>」 _____

B: 「はい、わかりました」

A: 「すみません、<u>ちょっと待つ</u>」 _____

B: 「はい、わかりました」

3. Combine two sentences by using て形

1.　カフェに行く	友達に会う	
2. アメリカの大学を卒業する	会社で１年間働いた	

4. Conjugate to しています

風呂に入る	Take a bath	U-verb	
食べる	eat	Ru-verb	
決める	decide	Ru-verb	
結婚する	get marry	Irregular	
電話する	call	Irregular	
来る	come	Irregular	

5. Choose ONE correct answer to the question.

「今、何をしていますか」

1. 電話をしました

2. 電話をしています

3. 電話をします

＊電話（Phone）

6. Conjugate to ています

日本に住む→	
エンジニアをする→	

7. Please read the passage and answer the question.

私の兄はシカゴの大学でコンピューターを勉強しています。車を持っています。結婚していません。

あなたの兄は大学でコンピューターを教えていますか

はい、＿＿＿＿＿＿＿＿

いいえ、＿＿＿＿＿＿＿＿

＊兄: Older Brother、大学: University、勉強: Study、車: Car、結婚: Marriage、教える: Teach

8. Choose the right answer.

「もうランチを食べましたか?」

A. まだ食べていません。

B. ハンバーガーを食べます

C. もう食べていません

9. Combine two sentences for Daniel's plan this Friday.

友達と会う(meet a friend)	コンサートに行く(go to a concert)	

10. Someone at a party is looking for Daniela. Daniela is sitting （Sit: 座^{すわ}る）on the sofa and having a cake. Answer the question.

「ダニエラさんはどの人^{ひと}ですか」

_____

Answer Keys

1.

1. 見る→見て	2. 寝る→寝て	3. 買う→買って	4. 帰る→帰って
5. 読む→読んで	6. 遊ぶ→遊んで	7. 話す→話して	8. 聞く→聞いて
9. 行く→行って	10. 泳ぐ→泳いで	11. する→して	12. 来る→来て

2. もう一度言ってください

ちょっと待ってください

3.

1.　カフェに行く	友達に会う	カフェに行って、友達に会います
2. アメリカの大学を卒業する	会社で1年間働いた	アメリカの大学を卒業して、会社で1年間働きました

4.

風呂に入る	Take a bath	U-verb	風呂に入っています
食べる	eat	Ru-verb	食べています
決める	decide	Ru-verb	決めています
結婚する	get marry	Irregular	結婚しています
電話する	call	Irregular	電話しています
来る	come	Irregular	来ます

5. 2 「電話をしています」

6.

日本に住む→	日本に住んでいます
エンジニアをする→	エンジニアをしています

7. Please read the passage and answer the question.

私の兄はシカゴの大学でコンピューターを勉強しています。車を持っています。結婚していません。

あなたの兄は大学でコンピューターを教えていますか

いいえ、教えていません。

8. B「まだ食べていません」

9.

友達に会う(meet a friend)	コンサートに行く(go to a concert)	（金曜日:Friday）、友達に会ってコンサートに行きます

10. ダニエラさんはソファに座って、ケーキを食べています。

Verb Conjugations of 「た形」 (ta-Form) & 「ない形」 (nai-Form)

"Mental Clarity is the child of courage, not the other way around."

\- Nassim Nicolas Taleb

Here is another important grammar chapter for communication. On a scale of 1-10, what's your excitement point vs. not-so-excitement point? And are you open for another chapter, or you need to take a short break? Most importantly, you're the decision maker and no one is forcing you to do anything. If your mental attitude or emotion is neutralized, you're ready for the next journey.

There are many forms of verb conjugation function similar to i-adjectives. た形 or the plain past form of verbs, enables you to communicate what you did in the past and what something was like in the past.

You can directly modify the noun with the clause of た形 just like a regular adjective, and express the noun in more detail.

「東京タワーを見たことがあります」 ("I have seen Tokyo Tower.")

Here are typical verb conjugation from 普通形 to て形 then た形

カテゴリ	普通形	て形	た形
Ru-verbs	食べる	食べて	食べた
Ru-verbs	寝る	寝て	寝た
Ru-verbs	見る	見て	見た
U-verbs (pattern 1) 「った」	待つ	待って	待った
U-verbs (pattern 1) 「った」	帰る	帰って	帰った
U-verbs (pattern 1)	手伝う	手伝って	手伝った

「った」			
U-verbs (pattern 2) 「んだ」	読^よむ	読^よんで	読^よんだ
U-verbs (pattern 2) 「んだ」	遊^{あそ}ぶ	遊^{あそ}んで	遊^{あそ}んだ
U-verbs (pattern 2) 「んだ」	死^しぬ	死^しんで	死^しんだ
U-verbs (pattern 3) 「した」「いた」「いだ」「った」	話^{はな}す	話^{はな}して	話^{はな}した
U-verbs (pattern 3) 「した」「いた」「いだ」「った」	急^{いそ}ぐ	急^{いそ}いで	急^{いそ}いだ
U-verbs (pattern 3) 「した」「いた」「いだ」「った」	書^かく	書^かいて	書^かいた
U-verbs (pattern 3) 「した」「いた」「いだ」「った」	行^いく	行^いって	行^いった
Irregular-verbs	する	して	した
Irregular-verbs	来^くる	来^きて	来^きた

Conjugation Exercise: Conjugate 普通形^{ふつうけい} to た形^{けい}

普通形^{ふつうけい}	英語^{えいご}	カテゴリ	た形^{けい}
謝^{あやま}る	to apologize	U-verbs	謝^{あやま}った
習^{なら}う	to learn	U-verbs	習^{なら}った
急^{いそ}ぐ	to hurry	U-verbs	急^{いそ}いだ
登^{のぼ}る	to climb	U-verbs	登^{のぼ}った

172

泊まる	to stay over	U-verbs	泊まった
道に迷う	to get lost	U-verbs	道に迷った
風邪をひく	to catch a cold	U-verbs	風邪をひいた
見つかる	to be found	U-verbs	見つかった
熱を測る	to check one's temperature	U-verbs	熱を測った
飲みに行く	to go for a drink	U-verbs	飲みに行った
準備ができる	to get ready	U-verbs	準備ができた
寝る	to sleep	Ru-verbs	寝た
友達が来る	a friend comes	Irregular verbs	友達が来た
町をぶらぶらする	to promenad around town	Irregular verbs	町をぶらぶらした
仕事を辞める	to quit one's job	Ru-verbs	仕事を辞めた

1. Expressing Experiences. 「Verb＋た＋ことがあります」: "I have done…" &

「Verb＋た」ことがありません: "I have never done…"

「新幹線に乗ったことがあります」（"I have taken a Shinkansen.": 新幹線: Bullet Train, 乗る: Ride/Take）

Conversation Example:

A: 「新幹線に乗ったことがありますか」（"Have you taken a Shinkansen?"）

B: いいえ、ありません/はい、あります（"No, I haven't./Yes, I have."）

「Verbた＋ことがあります」「Verbた＋ことがありません」

Make a simple polite request using the following verbs.

普通形	た形	た形Negative
i.e. 日本酒を飲む（Drink Sake）	日本酒を飲んだことがあります	日本酒を飲んだことがありません

温泉に入る(Bathe in a hot spring)	温泉に入ったことがあります	温泉に入ったことがありません
納豆を食べる (Eat Natto)	納豆を食べたことがあります	納豆を食べたことがありません
着物を着る(Wear Kimono)	着物を着たことがあります	着物を着たことがありません
抹茶を飲む(Drink Maccha)	抹茶を飲んだことがあります	抹茶を飲んだことがありません
日本食を作る(Cook Japanese Food)	日本食を作ったことがあります	日本食を作ったことがありません

Answer the question.

「日本で運転したことがありますか」

Yes: _____

No: _____

「日本で（車を）運転したことがありますか」 (Have you driven a car in Japan?)

Yes: 「はい、あります」

No: 「いいえ、ありません」

2. Giving advice. 「Verb＋た＋ほうがいいです」: "It's better to…"

When you recommend or suggest some opinion or advice strongly, た形 verbs express the suggested action.

「傘を持って行ったほうがいいです」 (It's better to take an umbrella with you. 傘: an Umbrella, ほう: a way)

Make a simple polite request using the following verbs.

普通形	た形
i.e. バスで行く (Go by bus)	バスで行ったほうがいいです
店の人に聞く(Ask a store staff)	店の人に聞いたほうがいいです
友達に相談する(Consult with a friend)	友達に相談したほうがいいです
少し休む(Take a short break)	少し休んだほうがいいです

174

朝ごはんを食べる(Eat breakfast)	朝ごはんを食べたほうがいいです
すこし急ぐ(Hurry a little)	すこし急いだほうがいいです

3. Non-definite listing of actions. 「Verb＋たり、Verb＋たりする」 "Do things like Verb ing, and Verb ing…"

「鎌倉でお寺を見<u>たり</u>、サーフィンをし<u>たり</u>しました」 ("In Kamakura, I did things like visiting temples and surfing.")

You can list up multiple actions using the structure 「たり、たりする」. This structure implies that the subject also did or will do other things than the actions stated. For example, in the sentence above, this person did other things besides visiting temples and surfing, something like having local foods and shopping.

「休みの日には本を読ん<u>だり</u>、ゲームをし<u>たり</u>します」 ("On my days off, I do things like reading books and playing video games.")

Combine two sentences and make a 「たり、たりします」 sentence.

1	2	「たり、たりします」
i.e. 映画を見る (Watch a movie)	買い物をする (Go shopping)	映画を見<u>たり</u>、買い物をし<u>たり</u>します
日本語を勉強する(Study Japanese)	料理をする(Cook)	日本語を勉強したり、料理をたりすます
ジムに行く(Go to the gym)	洗濯する(Do the laundry)	ジムに行ったり、洗濯したりします
自転車に乗る(Ride one's bike)	動画を撮る(Shoot a video)	自転車に乗ったり、動画を撮ったりします
友達とゲームをする(Play a video game with a friend)	ネットを見る(Browse internet)	友達とゲームをしたり、ネットを見たりします

4. Subjunctive Mood. 「Verb＋たら」 "If…or when…"

た形 also expresses the condition of an assumption, where once the "if…" condition is fulfilled, then what follows is what will happen. Or when doing something after a specific action has been done

「お金があっ<u>たら</u>、日本中を旅行します」 ("If I had the money, I would travel all around Japan.")

175

「日本に着いたら、メールしてください」("When you arrive in Japan, please email me.")

Combine two sentences and make a 「たら、します」 sentence.

1	2	「たら、します」
i.e. 仕事が終わる (Work is finished)	ジムに行く (Go to the gym)	仕事が終わったら、ジムに行きます
大学を卒業する(Finish the college)	北海道にスキーに行く (Go skiing in Hokkaido)	大学を卒業したら、北海道にスキーに行きます
準備ができる(Get ready)	メールする(Email)	準備ができたら、メールします
授業が終わる(A class ends)	ご飯を食べに行く(Go have a meal)	授業が終ったら、ご飯を食べに行きます
テストに合格する(Pass the test)	しばらくゆっくりする (Take it easy for a while)	テストに合格したら、しばらくゆっくりします

Making a suggestion/invitation with 「Verb＋たら」 using 「しませんか」

「しませんか」 is "why don't we...?"

1	2	"Why don't we...?"
i.e. 春になる (Becoming spring/spring comes)	お花見をする(Go see the cherry blossoms)	春になったら、お花見をしませんか
大阪に行く(Go to Osaka)	たこ焼きを食べる(Eat takoyaki)	大阪に行ったら、たこ焼きを食べませんか
カリフォルニアから友達が来る(A friend comes from California)	鎌倉に行く(Go to Kamakura)	カリフォルニアから友達が来たら、鎌倉に行きませんか
2月になる(February comes)	箱根に温泉に行く(Go to an Onsen in Hakone)	2月になったら、箱根に温泉に行きませんか

元気になる(Fully recover from)	カラオケに行く(Go out to karaoke)	元気になったら、カラオケに行きませんか

ない形

In Book 1, we covered the negative form of "state-of-art" だ is 「じゃない」. For example, the negative form of i-adjective 「きれい(beautiful)」 is 「きれいじゃない」.

However, as we learned 「です」「ます」 polite form later in the book as well. 「きれいじゃない」 is neutral way but not always polite form. 「きれいじゃありません」 is more polite way of the negative form. 「ありません」 is the negative form of 「ある」 (exist for non-living things). And the negative form of 「ある」 is 「ない」 and with ない形.

There are four expression forms with ない形.

- Caution/Encouragement:「時間に遅れないでください」 ("Please don't be late.")

- Necessity/Obligation:「今日は早めに帰らないといけません」 ("I have to leave early today.")

- Suggestion not to:「あまり食べすぎないほうがいいです」 ("It's better not to overeat.")

- Advice:「日本語で書かなくてもいいです」 ("You don't have to write in Japanese.")

The following chart is how you can conjugate from 普通形 to ない形

普通形	英語	カテゴリ	ない形
手伝う	to help	U-verbs	手伝わない
書く	to write	U-verbs	書かない
急ぐ	to hurry	U-verbs	急がない
話す	to speak/Talk	U-verbs	話さない
死ぬ	to die	U-verbs	死なない
読む	to read	U-verbs	読まない
帰る	to return/go Home	U-verbs	帰らない

食_たべる	to eat	Ru-verbs	食_たべない
寝_ねる	to sleep	Ru-verbs	寝_ねない
見_みる	to see/look	Ru-verbs	見_みない
する	to do	Irregular verbs	しない
来_くる	to come	Irregular verbs	来_こない

Conjugate 普通形_{ふつうけい} to ない形_{けい}

普通形_{ふつうけい}	英語_{えいご}	カテゴリ	ない形_{けい}
話_{はな}す	to speak/talk	U-verbs	話_{はな}さない
払_{はら}う	to pay	U-verbs	払_{はら}わない
迎_{むか}えに行_いく	to go pick up	U-verbs	迎_{むか}えに行_いかない
置_おく	to put	U-verbs	置_おかない
座_{すわ}る	to sit	U-verbs	座_{すわ}らない
騒_{さわ}ぐ	to make a noise	U-verbs	騒_{さわ}がない
足_{あし}を組_くむ	to cross one's legs	U-verbs	足_{あし}を組_くまない
急_{いそ}ぐ	to hurry	U-verbs	急_{いそ}がない
脱_ぬぐ	to take a clothe off	U-verbs	脱_ぬがない
会員_{かいいん}になる	to become a member	U-verbs	会員_{かいいん}にならない
遅_{おく}れる	to get late	U-verbs	遅_{おく}らない
決_きめる	to decide	Ru-verbs	決_きめない
捨_すてる	to throw away	Ru-verbs	捨_すてない
覚_{おぼ}える	to memorize	Ru-verbs	覚_{おぼ}えない
いる	to stay	Ru-verbs	いない

わす 忘れる	to forget	Ru-verbs	わす 忘れない
も 持ってくる	to bring	Irregular verbs	も 持ってこない
き 気にする	to mind/worry	Irregular verbs	き 気にしない
む り 無理する	to take it too far	Irregular verbs	む り 無理しない

1. Caution/Encouragement. 「Verb＋ない＋でください」

This ない形(けい) expresses to ask someone not to do something, also to warn or encourage.

「時間に遅れないでください」 ("Please don't be late." 時間:)

Conjugate the following sentence to 「ないでください」 form.

i.e. じ かん おく 時間に遅れる	じ かん おく 時間に遅れないでください
すわ ここに座る	すわ ここに座らないでください
き 気にする	き 気にしないでください
しんぱい 心配する	しんぱい 心配しないでください
む り 無理する	む り 無理しないでください
なか はい 中に入る	なか はい 中に入らないでください
しゃしん と 写真を撮る	しゃしん と 写真を撮らないでください
けいたい でん わ つか 携帯（電話）を使う	けいたい でん わ つか 携帯（電話）を使わないでください

Conversation Example:

A: 「ここにものを置かないでください」 ("Please don't put anything here")

B: 「すみません」 ("I'm sorry.")

Exercise: Pick ONE answer in the following situation.

At a store, the cashier gave you the wrong amount of change.

"I'm sorry, my math was wrong. I must give you an additional fifty yen. My apologies."

A: き
気をつけてください

B: わす
忘れないでください

C: 気^きにしないでください

Answer: C 「気^きにしないでください」 (A's 「気^きをつけてください」 is "be careful, please.")

2. Necessity/Obligation: 「今日^{きょう}は早^{はや}めに帰^{かえ}らないといけません」 ("I have to leave early today.")

Conversation Example:

A: 「このあと、時間^{じかん}ありますか」 ("Do you have time after this?")

B: 「すみません、今日^{きょう}は早^{はや}めに帰^{かえ}らないといけません」 ("I'm sorry, but I have to leave early today")

Conjugate the following sentence to 「ないといけません」 form.

i.e. 早^{はや}めに帰^{かえ}る(Leave early)	早^{はや}めに帰^{かえ}らないといけません
友達^{ともだち}を迎^{むか}えに行^いく(Pick up a friend)	友達^{ともだち}を迎^{むか}えに行^いかないといけません
明日^{あす}のミーティングに出^でる(Attend a meeting tomorrow)	明日^{あす}のミーティングに出^でないといけません
9時^じの電車^{でんしゃ}に乗^のる (Catch a train at 9)	9時^じの電車^{でんしゃ}に乗^のらないといけません
明日早^{あしたはや}く起^おきる(Get up early tomorrow)	明日早^{あしたはや}く起^おきないといけません
10時^じまで待^まつ(Wait until 10)	10時^じまで待^またないといけません
ご飯^{はん}を作^{つく}る(Cook a meal)	ご飯^{はん}を作^{つく}らないといけません
予約^{よやく}をキャンセルする(Cancel the appoitment)	予約^{よやく}をキャンセルしないといけません

3. Suggestion not to: 「Verb＋ない＋ほうがいいです」

This ない形^{けい} form can suggest against doing something to give a general opinion or advice.

「あまり食^たべすぎないほうがいいです」 ("It's better not to overeat.")

Conversation Example:

A: 「昨日^{きのう}はとんかつと、天丼^{てんどん}と、焼肉^{やきにく}を食^たべました。胃^いが少^{すこ}し痛^{いた}いです」 ("I had Tonkatsu, Tendon and Yakiniku yesterday. I have some pain in stomach")

B: 「無理^{むり}しないほうがいいです」 ("It's better not to take it too much")

Conjugate the following sentence to 「しないほうがいいです」 form.

i.e. 食べすぎる(Overeat)	食べすぎないほうがいいです
時間に遅れる(Run late)	時間に遅れないほうがいいです
無理する(Take it too far)	無理しないほうがいいです
飲みすぎる (Drink too much)	飲みすぎないほうがいいです
気にする(Mind)	気にしないほうがいいです
心配する (Worry)	心配しないほうがいいです

4. Advice:「Verb＋ない」→「Verb＋なく＋てもいいです」("You don't have to...)

「日本語で書かなくてもいいです」("You don't have to write in Japanese.")

Conversation Example:

A:「髪を切りたいのですが、予約が必要ですか」("I want to have a haircut but do I have to make a reservation?")

B:「いいえ、予約しなくてもいいです」("No, you don't have to make a reservation")

A:「そうですか。よかったです」("Oh, that's great.")

Conjugate the following sentence to 「なくてもいいです」 form.

i.e. 書く(Write)	書かなくてもいいです
明日会社に行く(Go to work tomorrow)	明日会社に行かなくてもいいです
急ぐ(Hurry)	急がなくてもいいです
早く起きる(Get up early)	早く起きなくていいです
くつを脱ぐ(Take off the shoes)	くつを脱がなくてもいいです
今、決める (Decide now)	今、決めなくてもいいです
チップを払う(Tip)	チップを払わなくてもいいです

Vocabulary List for Review

謝る	Apologize

習う	Learn
登る	Climb
道に迷う	Get lost
風邪をひく	Catch a cold
見つかる	Be found
熱を測る	Take temperature
飲みに行く	Go for a drink
準備ができる	Get ready
町をぶらぶらする	Promenade around town
仕事を辞める	Quit a job
新幹線	Bullet train
日本酒を飲む	Drink sake
温泉に入る	Bathe in a hot spring
納豆	Natto (fermented beans)
着物	Kimono
抹茶を飲む	Drink Maccha
日本食を作る	Cook Japanese Food
運転する	Drive
傘	Umbrella
店	Store
相談する	Consult/Ask
休む	Rest
朝ごはん	Breakfast

少し	A little
お寺	Temple
休みの日	Days off
買い物	Shopping
料理する	Cook
洗濯する	Do the laundry
自転車	Bicycle
動画を撮る	Shoot a video
ネットを見る	Browse internet
お金	Money
着く	Arrive
終わる	End(Verb)
卒業する	Graduate
メールする	Send an Email
授業	A class
しばらく	For a while
ゆっくりする	Take it easy
合格する	Pass a test
春	Spring
夏	Summer
秋	Fall
冬	Winter
お花見	See cherry bloosom
元気	Fine/Healthy

早めに	Soon/Early
食べすぎる	Overeat
払う	Pay
騒ぐ	Make a noise
足を組む	Cross one's legs
脱ぐ	Take a cloth off
持ってくる	Bring
気にする	Mind
無理する	Take it too far
ここ	Here
心配する	Worry
中に入る	Enter inside
写真を撮る	Take a photo
携帯電話	Cell phone
使う	Use(Verb)
置く	Put
忘れる	Forget
キャンセルする	Cancel(Verb)
胃	Stomach
痛い	Painful
髪を切る	Have a haircut
予約	Reservagtion
必要	Necessity

明日 あす	Tomorrow
昨日 きのう	Yesterday
今日 きょう	Today
一昨日 おととい	A day before yesterday
明後日 あさって	A day after tomorrow
くつ	Shoes

Take-home message

With た形verbs, you can conjugate verbs with four expressions. The first one is to express experiences 「Verb＋た＋ことがあります」．For example「日本に行ったことがあります」("I have been to Japan.")

The second one is to give some advice with the form of 「Verb ＋た＋ほうがいいです」，「タクシーで行ったほうがいいです」("It's better to take a taxi there."). The third expression is used for non-exhaustive listing of actions, 「Verb＋たり、Verb＋たりする」like 「京都でお寺を見たり、買い物をしたりします」("I will do things like visiting temples and shopping in Kyoto.").「て形」specifies listing of actions but 「た形」implies some other actions besides listed ones.

The last form of た形 is used for Subjunctive Mood, 「Verb＋たら、します」．「お金があったら、世界旅行をします」("If I had the money, I will travel around the world."). And 「駅に着いたら、電話します」("When I arrive at the station, I will call you.")

ない形 Conjugation also has four expressions. The first one is for caution/encouragement, 「Verb ＋ない＋でください」．For example、「時間に遅れないでください」("Please don't be late."). The second expression is for necessity/obligation, 「Verb ＋ない＋といけません」．「早く行かないといけません」("I have to leave early.")

The third expression suggests no to, 「Verb ＋ない＋ほうがいいです」. 「食べすぎないほうがいいです」 ("It's better not to overeat.") Lastly, this ない形 gives some advice, "you don't have to do …." 「Verb ＋なく＋ていいです」. For example, 「予約しなくていいです」 ("You don't have to make a reservation."). なし形 is the negative form but when you translate every single words from English to Japanese to compose a sentence, it would take long and confuse the meaning. So the best way to master this is to use the syntax and practice with different verbs in various situations.

Exercises

1. Conjugate 普通形 to た形

1. 見る→	2. 寝る→	3. 買う→	4. 帰る→
5. 読む→	6. 遊ぶ→	7. 話す→	8. 聞く→
9. 行く→	10. 泳ぐ→	11. する	12. 来る

2. Correct the underlined phrase to complete the conversation.

A:「京都に行ったことがありますか」

B:「はい、<u>ありません</u>」＿＿＿＿＿＿＿＿＿

A:「日本酒を飲んだことがありますか」

B:「いいえ、<u>飲みました</u>」＿＿＿＿＿＿＿＿

3. Combine two sentences by using た形「たり、たりしました」

1.　ゲームをする	友達とカフェに行く	
2. 公園で走る	友達とサッカーをする	

4. Conjugate to した and ない

普通形	英語	た形	ない形
風呂に入る	Take a bath		
食べる	Eat		
決める	Decide		
結婚する	Get married		
電話する	Call		
来る	Come		

5. Choose ONE to complete the sentence.

「お金<small>かね</small>があったら」

1. 日本<small>にほん</small>に行<small>い</small>きます

2. 日本<small>にほん</small>から来<small>き</small>ました

3. 日本<small>にほん</small>が好<small>す</small>きです

6. Conjugate to 「ないでください」 to express caution/encouragement.

彼<small>かれ</small>の言葉<small>ことば</small>を気<small>き</small>にする→ *彼: His, 言葉: Words	
全部<small>ぜんぶ</small>食<small>た</small>べる→ *全部: All	

7. Please read the passage and correct the answer.

アメリカではレストランでチップを払<small>はら</small>います。15パーセントから20パーセントをチップで払<small>はら</small>います。日本<small>にほん</small>ではチップを払<small>はら</small>いますか。

日本<small>にほん</small>はチップを払<small>はら</small>いません。

8. Conjugate to 「ないといけません」

電車<small>でんしゃ</small>を新宿<small>しんじゅく</small>で乗<small>の</small>り換<small>か</small>える→ *電車*: Train 、乗り換える: Transfer/Change	
5時<small>じ</small>までに家<small>いえ</small>に帰<small>かえ</small>る→	

9. Correct B's last dialogue and recommend A to visit the place.

A: 「ダニエルさんの出身はどこですか」

B: 「アメリカです」

A: 「アメリカのどこですか」

B: 「ネバタです」

A: 「おすすめの 場所はありますか」 *おすすめ: Recommended　場所: Place

B: 「グランドキャニオンは行かないほうがいいです」

10. You and your friend will visit Fukuoka to have Tonkotsu ramen and other local specialties. There are three choices to stay. Your friend picked Ryokan. Please find the disadvantage and make a sentence using 「ないといけません」.

1. 家具付きアパート Furnished Apartment

・福岡の中心部にある　Located in Central Fukuoka

・ワンルーム　Studio Apartment

2.旅館 Japanese Traditional Inn

・露天温泉がある Open-air hot spring bath

・福岡までバスで45分 Requires 45-min bus ride to Central Fukuoka

3. カプセルホテル　Capsule Hotel

・福岡駅から徒歩1分 Only 1-min walk from Fukuoka Station

・チェックアウトは9時半 Check-out by 9:30AM

Answer Keys

1.

1. 見る→見た	2. 寝る→寝た	3. 買う→買った	4. 帰る→帰った
5. 読む→読んだ	6. 遊ぶ→遊んだ	7. 話す→話した	8. 聞く→聞いた
9. 行く→行った	10. 泳ぐ→泳いだ	11. する→した	12. 来る→来た

2.

B: 「はい、あります」

B: 「いいえ、飲んだことがありません」

3.

1. ゲームをする	友達とカフェに行く	ゲームをしたり、友達とカフェに行ったりしました
2. 公園で走る	友達とサッカーをする	公園で走ったり、友達とサッカーをしたりしました

4.

普通形	英語	た形	ない形
風呂に入る	Take a bath	風呂に入った	風呂に入らない
食べる	eat	食べた	食べない
決める	decide	決めた	決めない
結婚する	get marry	結婚した	結婚しない
電話する	call	電話した	電話しない
来る	come	来た	来ない

5. 1.「日本に行きます」(2. "I come from Japan." 3. "I like Japan.")

6.

彼の言葉を気にしないでください

全部食べないでください

7. 日本はチップを払いません(Meaning "Japan doesn't pay tips.")。→日本ではチップを払わなくていいです。

8.

電車を新宿で乗り換える→ *乗り換える: Transfer/Change	電車を新宿で乗り換えないといけません
5時までに家に帰る→	5時までに家に帰らないといけません

9.「グランドキャニオンに行ったほうがいいです」

10. 福岡まで45分バスに乗らないといけません。

ふ つうけい
普通形

Verb /Adjective Expressions for Opinions and Possibilities

"Maturity is not when we start speaking big things. It is when we start understanding small things."

- Anonymous

Are you open for the next grammar chapter? If you feel stressed or pressure, you might be resisting or defensive against something. You might hear some mental chatting about your progress or memories. What would you do if the chatting is removed? When you are ready, let's start.

In Book 1, we covered the Plain Form to understand conjugation before learning Masu/Desu Forms which are more polite forms that are commonly used in daily conversation. In this section, we go further the Plain Form of verbs and adjectives to express opinions, possibilities and guessing so your communication in Japanese will be more elaborated and simply natural.

「ダニエルさんは 京 都にいると思います」 ("I think Daniel is in Kyoto.")

「このアニメの 曲 はアメリカで人気が高いみたいです」 ("This Anime song seems popular in the US.")

Verbs

Let's review how we can conjugate ます形 verb to 普通形.

U-verbs

ます形	Negative	普通形	Negative
行きます	行きません	行く	行かない
座ります	座りません	座る	座わらない
払います	払いません	払う	払わない

Ru-verbs

ます形	Negative	普通形	Negative
食べます	食べません	食べる	食べない
寝ます	寝ません	寝る	寝ない
見ます	見ません	見る	見ない

Irregular verbs

ます形	Negative	普通形	Negative
します	しません	する	しない
来ます	来ません	来る	来ない

Exercise: Change them to 普通形

雨が降ります→	雨が降る
英語が通じません→ *通じる(be able to communicate)	英語が通じない
東京に住みます→	東京に住む
少し遅れます→	少し遅れる
もうすぐ結婚します→	もうすぐ結婚する

Adjectives

There are I-adjectives ending with 「い」 and Na-adjectives ending with 「な」. 「美しい」 (beautiful) is an I-adjective and 「素敵な」 is a na-adjective.

I-adjectives

です形	Negative	普通形	Negative

高(たか)いです (High/Expensive)	高(たか)くないです	高(たか)い	高(たか)くない
低(ひく)いです(Low)	低(ひく)くないです	低(ひく)い	低(ひく)くない
安(やす)いです(Inexpensive)	安(やす)くないです	安(やす)い	安(やす)くない

Na-adjectives

です形(けい)	Negative	普通形(ふつうけい)	Negative
元気(げんき)です(Fine/Healthy)	元気(げんき)じゃないです	元気(げんき)だ	元気(げんき)じゃない
大変(たいへん)です (Tough/Troublesoume)	大変(たいへん)じゃないです	大変(たいへん)だ	大変(たいへん)じゃない
静(しず)かです(Quiet)	静(しず)かじゃないです	静(しず)かだ	静(しず)かじゃない

Nouns

です形(けい)	Negative	普通形(ふつうけい)	Negative
学生(がくせい)です(Student)	学生(がくせい)じゃないです	学生(がくせい)だ	学生(がくせい)じゃない
アメリカ人(じん)です (American)	アメリカ人(じん)じゃないです	アメリカ人(じん)だ	アメリカ人(じん)じゃない

Exercise: Change them to 普通形(ふつうけい)

とても忙(いそが)しいです→ *とても(In a big way), 忙(いそが)しい(Busy)	とても忙(いそが)しい
おもしろくないです→ *おもしろい(Interesting)	おもしろくない
体(からだ)によくないです→ *体(からだ)(Body), 体(からだ)によくない(Unhealthy)	体(からだ)によくない
上手(じょうず)じゃないです→	上手(じょうず)じゃない

* 上手 じょうず (Excellent)	
危険 き けんじゃないです→ *危険 き けん (Dangerous)	危険 き けんじゃない

1. 普通形
ふ つうけいを使ったSyntax 1.　「Verb普通形
ふ つうけい＋と思
おもいます」("I think …")

「ダニエラはカフェに<u>いる</u>と思
おもいます」("I think Daniela is at the café.")

「と思
おもいます」can communicate supposition or opinions of the speaker. The subject 「私は」is usually omitted. For negative form, the conjugation is applied to the plain form verb. Instead of being like English, "I don't think…" the structure is "I think that … doesn't/don't or isn't/aren't.

Conversation Example:

「ダニエルは家
いえにいると思
おもいますか」("Do you think Daniel is home?")

「はい、いると思
おもいます」("Yes, I think so.")

「と思
おもいます」form composition practice.

i.e. ダニエラはカフェにいます(Daniela is at the café.)→	ダニエラはカフェにいると思 おもいます("I　　　think Daniela is at the café.)
ミカさんは家 いえにいます(Mika-san is at home.)	ミカさんは家 いえにいると思 おもいます
ジョンさんは忙 いろがしいです(John-san is busy)	ジョンさんは忙 いろがしいと思 おもいます
あの映画 えい がはおもしろくないです(That movie is not interesting)	あの映画 えい がはおもしろくないと思 おもいます
このゲームは楽 たのしいです(This game is fun).	このゲームは楽 たのしいと思 おもいます
彼 かれは日本人 に ほんじんじゃないです(He is not Japanese)	彼 かれは日本人 に ほんじんじゃないと思 おもいます

Questions and Answers Patterns

Question	Yes	No

195

i.e. 明日、雨が降ると思いますか("Is it going to rain tomorrow?")	はい、降ると思います("Yes, I think it will rain.")	いいえ、降らないと思います ("No, I don't think it will rain.")
今週末は暑いと思いますか ("Is it going to be hot this weekend?")	はい、暑いと思います("Yes, I think it will be hot.")	いいえ、暑くないと思います ("No, I don't think it will be hot.")
試験に合格すると思いますか ("Do you think you will pass the test?")	はい、合格すると思います ("Yes, I think I will pass.")	いいえ、合格しないと思います ("No, I don't think I will pass.")
駅にトイレがあると思いますか ("Do you think there is a bathroom in the station?")	はい、あると思います("Yes, I think there is one.")	いいえ、ないと思います("No, I don't think there is one.")
あの二人は結婚すると思いますか("Do you think those two are getting married?")	はい、結婚すると思います ("Yes, I think they will.")	いいえ、結婚しないと思います ("No, I don't think they will.")
札幌は寒いと思いますか("Do you think Sapporo is cold?")	はい、寒いと思います("Yes, I think so.")	いいえ、寒くないと思います ("No, I don't think so.")

2. 普通形を使ったSyntax 2. 「Verb 普通形＋かもしれません」 ("It might ...")

「Verb普通形＋かもしれません」 can indicate the possibility, though it's not 100% certain. The chance is smaller, you can add 「もしかしたら」 (Might be).

「京都行きの新幹線は遅れるかもしれません」 (The Shinkansen bound for Kyoto might be running late.)

Conversation Example.

A:「バスは遅れるかもしれません」 ("The bus might be running late.")

B:「何か起こったのですか」 ("Something happened?")

A:「道が混んでいます」 ("A lot of traffic.")

Change the sentence to 普通形and add かもしれません.

	Might...

i.e. 明日は雨が降ります→	明日は雨が降るかもしれません
ちょっと遅れます(Be a little late)	ちょっと遅れるかもしれません
今年は雪が多いです(There is a lot of snow this year)	今年は雪が多いかもしれません
ダニエラさんはもうすぐ引っ越します(Daniela-san will move soon)	ダニエラさんはもうすぐ引っ越しするかもしれません
ベサニーさんはビーガンです (Bethany is a Vegan)	ベサニーさんはビーガンかもしれません
来月、沖縄に旅行に行きます(will travel to Okinawa next month)	来月、沖縄に旅行に行くかもしれません
日本でビジネスを始めます(will start a Business in Japan)	日本でビジネスを始めるかもしれません
来年、京都に住みます(will live in Kyoto next year)	来年、京都に住むかもしれません
4月はもっと忙しくなります(will be busier in April)	4月はもっと忙しくなるかもしれません
自転車で日本を一周します(will travel all over Japan by bicycle)	自転車で日本を一周するかもしれません

3. 普通形を使ったSyntax 2. 「Verb 普通形＋みたいです」("seems like ...")

For 「Verb 普通形＋みたいです」 you can express the information, thoughts, and feelings based on the information you heard.

「このアニメはカナダで人気があるみたいです」("This Anime seems to be popular in Canada."

Change the sentence to 普通形 and add みたいです.

	Seems...
i.e. この映画は人気があります→	この映画は人気があるみたいです
入口は向こうにあります(The entrance is over there)	入口は向こうにあるみたいです

ダニエラさんは魚が苦手です(Daniela-san doesn't seem to like fish)	ダニエラさんは魚が苦手みたいです
ここのレストランには有名なシェフがいます (There is a well-known chef at this restaurant)	ここのレストランには有名なシェフがいるみたいです
ダニエルさんは人気のミュージシャンです (Daniel is a popular musician)	ダニエルさんは人気のミュージシャンみたいです
ダニエラさんは日本の大学に留学しります (Daniela-san will study at a Japanese University)	ダニエラさんは日本の大学に留学するみたいです
この新しいゲームはおもしろいです(This new game is intreesting)	この新しいゲームはおもしろいみたいです
ジョンさんは京都でレストランを開きます (John-san will open a restaurant in Kyoto)	ジョンさんは京都でレストランを開くみたいです
日本茶は体にいいです(Green tea is good for your health)	日本茶は体にいいみたいです
新しいバージョンが出ます(A new version will be released)	新しいバージョンが出るみたいです

Expressions using 普通形 Past form

By using 普通形 Past form, you can communicate your opinions and assumption from the past, indicate that something in the past might have happened and talk about something seems to have been happened.

To refresh our memories, let's cover the past tense conjugation for verbs and adjectives.

U-verbs

ます形 Past	Past Negative	普通形 Past	Past Negative
行きました	行きませんでした	行った	行かなかった
座りました	座りませんでした	座った	座らなかった
払いました	払いませんでした	払った	払わなかった

Ru-verbs

ます形 Past	Past Negative	普通形 Past	Past Negative
食べました	食べませんでした	食べた	食べなかった
寝ました	寝ませんでした	寝た	寝なかった
見ました	見ませんでした	見た	見なかった

Irregular verbs

ます形 Past	Past Negative	普通形 Past	Past Negative
しました	しませんでした	した	しなかった
来ました	来ませんでした	来た	来なかった

Exercise: Change those ます形 Past sentences to 普通形

わかりませんでした(Didn't understand)→	わかった
戻ってきませんでした(Didn't return)→	戻ってきた
鍵をなくしました(Lost the key)→	鍵をなくした
セーブしませんでした(Didn't save)→	セーブしなかった
トラブルがありました(There was trouble)→	トラブルがあった

Adjective 普通形 Past Tense

I-adjectives

です形 Past	Past Negative	普通形 Past	Past Negative
高かったです (High/Expensive)	高くなかったです	高かった	高くなかった
低かったです(Low)	低くなかったです	低かった	低くなかった
安かったです (Inexpensive)	安くなかったです	安かった	安くなかった

Na-adjectives

です形 Past	Past Negative	普通形 Past	Past Negative
元気でした (Fine/Healthy)	元気じゃなかったです	元気だった	元気じゃなかった
大変でした (Tough/Hard Time)	大変じゃなかったです	大変だった	大変じゃなかった
静かでした(Quiet)	静かじゃなかったです	静かだった	静かじゃなかった

Nouns

です形Past	Past Negative	普通形Past	Past Negative
学生でした(Student)	学生じゃなかったです	学生でした	学生じゃなかった
アメリカ人でした (American)	アメリカ人じゃなかったです	アメリカ人でした	アメリカ人じゃなかった

Exercise: Change those です形Past sentences to 普通形

雨でした(It was rainy)→	雨だった
具合が悪かったです(Didn't feel well)→	具合が悪かった
忙しくなかったです(It wasn't busy)→	忙しくなかった
かっこよかったです (It was cool) →	かっこよかった
ひまでした(It was slow)→	ひまだ

1. 普通形 Past Tense Syntax 1.「普通形 Past Tense＋と思います」

「ダニエラさんはもう帰ったと思います」("I think Daniela-san already went home.")

Conversation Example:

A:「ダニエラさんはいますか」("Is Daniela—san here?")

B:「ダニエラさんはもう帰ったと思います」("I think Daniela-san already went home.")

Exercise: Change ます形 to 普通形 Past ＋と思います

i.e.彼女はもう帰りました(She already went home)→	彼女はもう帰ったと思います
先週の日曜日は雨でした(Last Sunday was rainy)→	先週の日曜日は雨だったと思います
ダニエルさんはパーティーに行きませんでした(Daniel-san didn't go to the party)→	ダニエルさんはパーティーに行かなかったと思います
バンドの演奏はかっこよかったです(The band's performance was cool)→	バンドの演奏はかっこよかったと思います
先週はひまでした(It was slow last week)→	先週はひまだったと思います
この辺に駅がありました(There was a station around here)→	この辺に駅があったと思います
ファイルをメールしました(Emailed the file)→	ファイルをメールしたと思います
あのカフェは月曜日休みです(That café was closed on Monday)→	あのカフェは月曜日休みだったと思います
ダニエルさんは学生の時、まじめでした(Daniel-san was diligent when he was a student)→	ダニエルさんは学生の時、まじめだったと思います

2. 普通形 Past Tense Syntax 2. 「普通形 Past Tense＋かもしれません」

普通形 Past Tense＋かもしれません to express something might have happened.

「ワークショップは先週だったかもしれません」("The workshop might have been last week.")

Change です形 to 普通形 to compose a sentence, "might have ..."

i.e.彼女はもう帰りました(She already went home)→	彼女はもう帰ったかもしれません

先週の日曜日は雨でした(Last Sunday was rainy)→	先週の日曜日は雨だったかもしれません
ダニエルさんはパーティーに行きませんでした(Daniel-san didn't go to the party)→	ダニエルさんはパーティーに行かなかったかもしれません
バンドの演奏はかっこよかったです(The band's performance was cool)→	バンドの演奏はかっこよかったかもしれません
先週はひまでした(It was slow last week)→	先週はひまだったかもしれません
この辺に駅がありました(There was a station around here)→	この辺に駅があったかもしれません
ファイルをメールしました(Emailed the file)→	ファイルをメールしたかもしれません
あのカフェは月曜日休みでした(That café was closed on Monday)→	あのカフェは月曜日休みだったかもしれません
ダニエルさんは学生の時、まじめでした(Daniel-san was diligent when he was a student)→	ダニエルさんは学生の時、まじめだったかもしれません

3. 普通形 Past Tense Syntax 3. 「普通形 Past Tense＋みたいです」

For 普通形 Past Tense＋みたいです, you can express something happened in the past, guessing the speaker's thoughts and feelings from the information the person received.

「ダニエルさんは沖縄に行ったみたいです」 ("Daniel-san seems to have gone to Okinawa.")

Conversation Sample:

A:「このところ、ダニエルさんを見ないですね」

B:「ダニエルさんは沖縄に行ったみたいです」

Exercise: Change the sentences to 普通形Past ＋みたいです.

i.e.彼女はもう帰りました(She already went home)→	彼女はもう帰ったみたいです

先週の日曜日は雨でした(Last Sunday was rainy)→	先週の日曜日は雨だったみたいです
ダニエルさんはパーティーに行きませんでした (Daniel-san didn't go to the party)→	ダニエルさんはパーティーに行かなかったみたいです
バンドの演奏はかっこよかったです(The band's performance was cool)→	バンドの演奏はかっこよかったみたいです
先週はひまでした(It was slow last week)→	先週はひまだったみたいです
この辺に駅がありました(There was a station around here)→	この辺に駅があったみたいです
ファイルをメールしました(Emailed the file)→	ファイルをメールしたみたいです
あのカフェは月曜日休みでした(That café was closed on Monday)→	あのカフェは月曜日休みだったみたいです
ダニエルさんは学生の時、まじめでした (Daniel-san was diligent when he was a student) →	ダニエルさんは学生の時、まじめだったみたいです

Vocabulary List for Review

曲	Song
人気な	Popular
払う	Pay
雨が降る	Rain on
通じる	Be able to communicate
結婚する	Get married
美しい	Beautiful
素敵な	Nice
安い	Inexpensive
元気な	Healthy/Feeling well

大変な	Troublesome
静かな	Quiet
学生	Student
忙しい	Busy
体	Body
上手な	Good
危険な	Dangerous
映画	Movie
楽しい	Fun
彼	He
彼女	She
暑い	Hot (Weather)
試験に合格する	Pass a test
駅	Station
トイレ	Toilet
寒い	Cold (Weather)
もしかしたら	Might be
道	Road/Path/Way
混んだ	Packed/Crowded
雪	Snow
多い	A lot
引っ越す	Move
始める	Start

自転車 (じてんしゃ)	Bicycle
一周 (いっしゅう)	Circumnavigation
入口 (いりぐち)	Entrance
向こう (む)	Over there
苦手な (にがて)	Difficult/Weak
有名な (ゆうめい)	Famous
留学する (りゅうがく)	Study abroad
大学 (だいがく)	University
開く (ひら)	Open
日本茶 (にほんちゃ)	Japanese Green Tea
出る (で)	Out/Be Released
鍵 (かぎ)	Key
なくす	Lose
セーブする	Save
具合が悪い (ぐあい わる)	Not feeling well
かっこいい	Cool
ひま	Slow/Quiet
演奏 (えんそう)	Music Performance
先週 (せんしゅう)	Last Week
この辺 (へん)	Around Here
休み (やす)	Day-off/Closed
まじめ	Serious
添付する (てんぷ)	Attach
電話番号 (でんわばんごう)	Phone Number

間違える （まちが）	Mistake
天才児 （てんさいじ）	Prodigy

Take-home message

We covered the Plain Form of verbs and adjectives to express opinions, possibilities and guessing in this chapter, now your communication in Japanese is more elaborated and simply natural.

The first syntax is 「普通形＋と思います」. This is pretty simple to apply verbs and adjectives in the sentence. The only note you need to pay attention to is that not like English, "I don't think..." for that negative form, it's "I think that ...not."

「この曲はアメリカで人気が高いと思います」 ("I think this song is popular in the US.") →to negative form,

「この曲はアメリカで人気が高くないと思います」 (" I think this song is not popular in the US.")

The second one is to show possibilities with the form of 「普通形＋かもしれません」. 「明日は雨が降るかもしれません」 ("It might rain tomorrow.") And for the negative form, you can simply conjugate the verb or adjective to the negative form and add かもしれません.

The last syntax is similar to the second one in the context and tells information/thoughts/feelings based on your obtained information, 「普通形＋みたいです」 ("it seems..."). 「入口は向こうにあるみたいです」 ("The entrance seems over there.") And for the negative form, negate the verb or adjective and add 「みたいです」. 「入口は向こうじゃないみたいです」 ("It doesn't seem the entrance is over there.")

In addition, we covered three syntaxes in the past tense. In that context, you can express your opinions/thoughts/feelings by looking back to the event's occurrence or your memories. By changing the verb or adjective tense you can make the past tense of these syntaxes. 「雨は降ったと思います」 ("I think it rained.") For the negative form, 「「雨は降らなかったと思います」 ("I don't think it rained.")

For the second syntax in the past tense, 「木曜日だったかもしれません」 ("It might have been on Thursday"), for the negative form, 「木曜日じゃなかったかもしれません」 ("It might not have been on Thursday."). The last syntax goes like 「ソールドアウトだったみたいです」 ("It seemed sold-out") or 「ソールドアウトじゃなかったみたいです」 ("It didn't seem sold-out").

When you can express possibilities, guessing, opinions, and feelings, your communication in Japanese will be clarified and less confusing. And better communication builds better relationship, friendship, and rapport.

Exercises

1. Fill in the blank in the table.

U-verbs

ます形	Negative	普通形	Negative
行きます		行く	行かない
	座りません	座る	
払います	払いません		払わない

2. Fill in the blank in the table.

Irregular verbs

ます形	Negative	普通形	Negative
	しません	する	
来ます		来る	

3. Change them to 普通形

この町では英語が通じません→ *通じる(be able to communicate), 町: Town	
少し遅れます→	
もうすぐ結婚します→	

4. Change the です形 to 「普通形＋ "I think"」

ジョンさんは忙しいです(John-san is busy)	
あの映画はおもしろくない(That movie is not interesting)	
このゲームは楽しいです(This game is fun).	

5. Change the ます形 to 「普通形＋ "might"」

ダニエラさんはもうすぐ引っ越します(Daniela-san will move soon)	
ベサニーさんはビーガンです (Bethany is a Vegan)	
来月、沖縄に旅行に行きます(will travel to Okinawa next month)	
日本でビジネスを始めます(will start a Business in Japan)	
来年、京都に住みます(will live in Kyoto next year)	

6. Change the です形/ます形 to 「普通形＋ "seem"」

ダニエラさんは魚が苦手です(Daniela-san doesn't seem to like fish)	
ここのレストランには有名なシェフがいます (There is a well-known chef at this restaurant)	
ダニエルさんは人気のミュージシャンです (Daniel is a popular musician)	
ダニエラさんは日本の大学に留学しります (Daniela-san will study at a Japanese University)	
新しいデザインアプリが出ます(A new design app will be released.)	

7. Change the です形 to 普通形過去(Past Tense)

雨でした(It was rainy)→	
具合が悪かったです(Didn't feel well)→	
忙しくなかったです(It wasn't busy)→	
かっこよかったです (It was cool) →	

ひまでした(It was slow)→	

8. Change the sentence to 「思^{おも}います」 syntax.

バンドの演奏^{えんそう}はかっこよかったです(The band's performance was cool)→	
先週^{せんしゅう}はひまでした(It was slow last week)→	
この辺^{へん}に駅^{えき}がありました(There was a station around here)→	
ファイルを添付^{てんぷ}しました(Attached the file)→	
あのカフェは月曜日休^{げつようびやす}みです(That café was closed on Monday)→	

9. Change the sentence to 「かもしれません」 syntax.

ここにコンビニがありました(There was a convenience store here)→	
電話番号^{でんわばんごう}を間違^{まちが}えた(Mistook the phone number)→	
レストランは水曜日休^{すいようびやす}みでした(That restaurant was closed on Wednesday)→	
ダニエルさんは天才児^{てんさいじ}でした(Daniel-san was a prodigy)→	

10. Change the sentence to 「みたいです」 syntax.

先週^{せんしゅう}の試合^{しあい}で勝^かちました(Won the game last week)→	先週^{せんしゅう}の試合^{しあい}で勝^かったみたいです
ダニエラさんは試験^{しけん}に合格^{ごうかく}しました(Daniela-san passed the test)→	ダニエラさんは試験^{しけん}に合格^{ごうかく}したみたいです
バンドの演奏^{えんそう}はかっこよかったです(The band's performance was cool)→	バンドの演奏^{えんそう}はかっこよかったみたいです

209

先週（せんしゅう）は忙（いそが）しかったです(It was busy last week)→	先週（せんしゅう）は忙（いそが）しかったみたいです
この辺（へん）に駅（えき）がありました(There was a station around here)→	この辺（へん）に駅（えき）があったみたいです

Answer Keys

1.

ます形	Negative	普通形	Negative
行きます	行きません	行く	行かない
座ります	座りません	座る	座らない
払います	払いません	払う	払わない

2.

ます形	Negative	普通形	Negative
します	しません	する	しない
来ます	来ません	来る	来ない

3.

この町では英語が通じません→ *通じる(be able to communicate), 町: Town	この町では英語が通じない
少し遅れます→	少し遅れる
もうすぐ結婚します→	もうすぐ結婚する

4.

ジョンさんは忙しいです(John-san is busy)	ジョンさんは忙しいと思います
あの映画はおもしろくない(That movie is not interesting)	あの映画はおもしろくないと思います
このゲームは楽しいです(This game is fun).	このゲームは楽しいと思います

5.

ダニエラさんはもうすぐ引っ越します(Daniela-san will move soon)	ダニエラさんはもうすぐ引っ越しするかもしれません
ベサニーさんはビーガンです (Bethany is a Vegan)	ベサニーさんはビーガンかもしれません
来月、沖縄に旅行に行きます(will travel to Okinawa next month)	来月、沖縄に旅行に行くかもしれません

日本でビジネスを始めます(will start a Business in Japan)	日本でビジネスを始めるかもしれません
来年、京都に住みます(will live in Kyoto next year)	来年、京都に住むかもしれません

6.

ダニエラさんは魚が苦手です(Daniela-san doesn't seem to like fish)	ダニエラさんは魚が苦手みたいです
ここのレストランには有名なシェフがいます (There is a well-known chef at this restaurant)	ここのレストランには有名なシェフがいるみたいです
ダニエルさんは人気のミュージシャンです (Daniel is a popular musician)	ダニエルさんは人気のミュージシャンみたいです
ダニエラさんは日本の大学に留学しります (Daniela-san will study at a Japanese University)	ダニエラさんは日本の大学に留学するみたいです
新しいデザインアプリが出ます(A new design app will be released.)	新しいデザインアプリが出るみたいです

7.

雨でした(It was rainy)→	雨だった
具合が悪かったです(Didn't feel well)→	具合が悪かった
忙しくなかったです(It wasn't busy)→	忙しくなかった
かっこよかったです (It was cool) →	かっこよかった
ひまでした(It was slow)→	ひまだ

8.

バンドの演奏はかっこよかったです(The band's performance was cool)→	バンドの演奏はかっこよかったと思います
先週はひまでした(It was slow last week)→	先週はひまだったと思います
この辺に駅がありました(There was a station around here)→	この辺に駅があったと思います
ファイルを添付しました(Attached the file)→	ファイルを添付したと思います

あのカフェは月曜日休みです(That café was closed on Monday)→	あのカフェは月曜日休みだったと思います

9.

ここにコンビニがありました(There was a convenience store here)→	ここにコンビニがあったかもしれません
電話番号を間違えた(Mistook the phone number)→	電話番号を間違えたかもしれません
レストランは水曜日休みでした(That restaurant was closed on Wednesday)→	レストランは水曜日休みだったかもしれません
ダニエルさんは天才児でした(Daniel-san was a prodigy)→	ダニエルさんは天才児だったかもしれません

10.

先週の試合で勝ちました(Won the game last week)→	先週の試合で勝ったみたいです
ダニエラさんは試験に合格しました(Daniela-san passed the test)→	ダニエラさんは試験に合格したみたいです
バンドの演奏はかっこよかったです(The band's performance was cool)→	バンドの演奏はかっこよかったみたいです
先週は忙しかったです(It was busy last week)→	先週は忙しかったみたいです
この辺に駅がありました(There was a station around here)→	この辺に駅があったみたいです

Travel Japanese

「百聞_{ひゃくぶん}は一見_{いっけん}にしかず」 ("One eye-witness is better than many hearsays.")

- Japanese Proverb

What have you already accomplished? We finished all the grammar chapters and get ready to travel in Japan. What have you tried that worked or didn't work? If you forget, always you can go back to review. What's your strong point? What's your weak point? What events and decisions led you here?

We have learned the basic Japanese writing systems and grammar for communication. Now we're going to cover and practice travel Japanese you can use on the first trip. Firstly, here is the simple but right-on-target self-introduction you can use any occasion.

「はじめまして。ダニエルです。アメリカ出身です。どうぞよろしくお願いします」 ("Nice to meet you, [I] am Daniel. [I] am from America. Thank you in advance.")

Then, you can add additional information or your personal touch to the basic information, such as things you like in Japan that make it interesting. Here are some vocabularies you can use for your self-introduction.

職業 Occupation	趣味/日本に興味を抱いていること
学生 (Student)	マンガ (Manga)
先生/教師 (Teacher)	アニメ (Anime)
大学生 (College Student)	ゲーム (Video Game)
大学院生 (Graduate Student)	禅 (Zen)
エンジニア (Engineer)	空手 (Karate)
起業家 (Entrepreneur)	仏教 (Buddhism)
ビジネスマン	神道 (Shintoism)
ITエンジニア(IT Engineer)	ファッション (Fashion)

214

アーティスト (Artist)	日本食 (Japanese Food)
プログラマー (Programmer)	侍 (Samurai)
武道家 (Martial Artist)	歴史 (History)
デザイナー (Designer)	テクノロジー (Technology)
投資家 (Investor)	映画 (Movie)

For those vocabularies, you can put "I like…" syntax or "I'm interested in …" syntax.

「日本の＊＊が好きです」 ("I like ** in Japan.")

「＊＊に興味があります」 ("I'm interested in **")

Now, 「(どうぞ) よろしくお願いします」 is translated as "thank you in advance," but this is a very useful phrase you can use in everyday conversation and even in business situations. Even in a business meeting, a manager usually closes the meeting with this phrase. When you add （どうぞ） it's a more polite and formal way, you can say 「よろしく」 for much more casual occasions, just like Brit's "cheers."

Conversation Example 1.

A:「はじめまして」 ("Nice to meet you.")

B:「はじめまして。ダニエルです」 ("Nice to meet you. [I] am Daniel")

A:「ダニエルさん、私はミカです。どちらのご出身ですか」 ("Daniel-san, I'm Mika. Where are you from?")

B:「どこだと思いますか」 ("Where would you think I'm from?")

A:「カナダですか」 ("Canada?")

B: 「アメリカです。カリフォルニアから来ました。よろしくお願いします」 ("America. Come from California. Thank you in advance [pleasure to meet you]")

Conversation Example 2.

A:「はじめまして」 ("Nice to meet you.")

B:「はじめまして。ダニエラです」 ("Nice to meet you. [I] am Daniela")

A:「ダニエラさん、ヒロです。お国は?」 ("Daniela-san, [I'm] Hiro. Which country are you from?")

B:「アメリカです」("[I'm from] America")

A:「アメリカのどこですか」("Where in America are you from?")

B: 「マサチューセッツです。ボストンの近くです。よろしくお願いします」("From Massachusetts. It's near Boston. Thank you in advance [pleasure to meet you]")

Those samples are for one-on-one self-introduction. What if you're asked to introduce yourself in front of a group or at a meeting?

Conversation Example 3.

A:「ダニエラさん、自己紹介をお願いしていいですか?」("Daniela-san, can you introduce yourself?")

B: 「はい。ダニエラです。アメリカのマサチューセッツから来ました。大学生です。コミュニケーションを学んでいます。日本のアニメとカラオケが好きです。よろしくお願いします」("Yes. [I] am Daniela. [I] am from Massachusetts in th US. [I] am a college student. [I] am studying Communication. [I] like Japanese Anime and Karaoke. Nice to meet you.")

Conversation Example 4.

A:「ダニエルさん、みんなに自己紹介してもらっていいですか?」("Daniel-san, can you introduce yourself to us all?")

B: 「はい。ダニエルです。アメリカのカリフォルニアから来ました。プログラマーです。寿司と日本酒が好きです。よろしくお願いします」("Yes. [I] am Daniel. [I] am from California in the US. [I] am a programmer. [I] like Sushi and Sake. Nice to meet you.")

The Recognition of Age in Japanese Culture.

Even at the first encounter, Japanese people might ask your age. 「おいくつですか」("How old are you?") or 「失礼ですが、おいくつですか」("If I may, could I ask your age?").

They don't mean to be rude or judgmental. Age is something the Japanese try to relate to you. They would comment something like, 「わたしの息子はあなたより2歳年上ですが、まだ子供です。あなたはしっかりしていますね」"My son is older than you by two years, but he is still a baby. You look like you're your own man."

If you don't want to answer the how-old question, you could say, 「20代です」"twenty-something," 「30代前半です」" Early thirties." Or politely ask back 「いくつに見えますか」("How old do you think I am?"), then if you don't like their answers, show some upset facial expressions pleasantly, then they would change the subject.

Age has been the criteria for maintaining social and family order in Japan, and elderly people are supposed to be respected by the younger just like in other Confucius East Asian countries. In the family structure, the first son has been someone who carries the family name and takes over the family business traditionally, so it's important to know who is in charge among the brothers.

How to Describe Family

父/お父さん (formal, polite way/neutral way)	Father/Dad
母/お母さん	Mother/Mom
兄/お兄さん	Older Brother
姉/お姉さん	Older Sister
弟	Younger Brother
妹	Younger Sister
夫/主人	Husband
妻/奥さん	Wife
息子	Son
娘	Daughter

「あります」(There is/are...)「ありません」(There isn't/aren't...)Syntax

「（は）あります（か）」 is the sentence for "Is there...?" The good news is there is no singular/plural differences and no article in Japanese so no necessary for conjugations.

「すみません、近くにトイレはありますか」("Is there a restroom near here?" 近く: in the near distance)

Exercise: Ask if there is one by using the following places 近くに.

i.e. ATM（エーティーエム）	近くにATMはありますか
コンビニ (Convenience Store)	近くにコンビニはありますか
駅 (Station)	近くにATM駅はありますか

ネットカフェ (Internet Café)	近_{ちか}くにネットカフェはありますか
銀行_{ぎんこう} (Bank)	近_{ちか}くに銀行_{ぎんこう}はありますか

Location Demonstratives

Demonstrative	こ	そ	あ	ど
Thing	これ(This)	それ (It)	あれ(That)	どれ (Where/Which/What)
	この＋Noun i.e. This bag	その＋Noun i.e. Its bag	あの＋Noun i.e. This bag	どの＋Noun i.e. Which/What bag
Place	ここ(Here)	そこ(There)	あそこ（Over there）	どこ(Where)
Direction	こっち(This way)	そっち（Its way）	あっち（That way）	どっち（Which way）
Area	この辺(This area)	その辺((Its area)	あの辺(（That area）	どの辺(（Where)

「この辺_{へん}にはATMはありません。駅_{えき}まで行_いってください」 ("There is no ATM in this area. Please go to the station.")

Exercise: Ask a location with location demonstratives.

i.e. そこのコンビニ	ATM	そこのコンビニに ATMはありますか
この辺_{へん}	駅_{えき}	この辺_{へん}に駅_{えき}はありますか
あの辺_{へん}	バス停_{てい}(Bus stop)	あの辺_{へん}にバス停_{てい}はありますか
どこ	コンビニ	どこにコンビニはありますか
あそこの店_{みせ}(store)	駐車場_{ちゅうしゃじょう} (Parking lot)	あそこの店_{みせ}に駐車場_{ちゅうしゃじょう}はありますか

「（は）...どこですか」 (Where is the ...?)

We will go further on location questions. 「どこ」 is where and you can use 「ありますか」 (There is/are), or simply 「どこですか」 (Where is ...?).

Conversation Example:

A:「駅はどこですか」(Where is a station?)

B:「そこのコンビを右に曲がってまっすぐです」(Make a right at the convenience store and go straight.)

Exercise: Ask the following locations.

i.e. 階段 (Stairs)	階段はどこですか
トイレ(Toilet)	トイレはどこですか
レジ(Cashier)	レジはどこですか
出口(Exit)	出口はどこですか
受付(Reception)	受付はどこですか

Direction Vocabulary

日本語	英語	例
右	Right	「そこを右に曲がって」(Make a right there)
左	Left	「信号を左に曲がって」(Make a left a the lights)
上	Up	「もう少し上」(Go up a little)
下	Low	「一つ下」(One down)
右上、右下	Upper right Lower right	「ジョンは右上/右下の人」(John is the one on upper right/lower left)
左上、左下	Upper left Lower left	「左上/左下の本をください」(Give the book on upper left/lower left)
真ん中	in the center/in the middle of	「カンザスはアメリカの真ん中にあります」(Kansas is located in the center of the US)
の前	In front of	「病院の前」(In front of a Hospital)

の近く	near	「ガソリンスタンドの近く」(Near a gas station)
となり	next to	「交番のとなり」(Next to koban: police substation)
うしろ	behind	「学校のうしろ」(Behind a school)

Counting: One of the complicated elements in Japanese is unit. There are many unit names for nouns. The most common unit is 「つ」、「1つ、2つ、3つ…（One piece, Two pieces, Three pieces…）」. Here is the common units for locations.

階(Story)	1階、2階、3階、4階 (Remember 4, 7, and 9 are pronounced this way to avoid "bad luck")
つ(Piece)	1つ、2つ、3つ、4つ、5つ、6つ、7つ、8つ、9つ
つ目(showing order)	1つ目(1st)、2つ目(2nd)、3つ目(3rd)、4つ(4th)目、5つ目(5th)

「2つ目の信号を右」("Make a right turn at the second lights.")

「彼のオフィスは3つ目のドアです」("His office is at the third door.")

Exercise: Answer the questions in the table.

1F: メインフロア(Main Floor)

2F: 本屋(Book Store)

3F: コーヒーショップ(Coffee Shop)

4F: レストラン(Restaurant)

5F: ギフトショップ(Gift Store)

レストランは何階ですか	レストランは4階です
本屋はどこですか	本屋は2階です
コーヒーショップは何階ですか	コーヒーショップは3階です

Exercise: Here is the apartment building all the six people live in. Answer the questions in the table.

Daniel	John	Daniela

Michael	Sara	Michelle

ダニエラは何階に住んでいますか(Which floor does Daniela live?)	ダニエラは2階に住んでいます
サラの上には誰が住んでいますか(Who lives upstairs of Sara's apt?)	ジョンが住んでいます
ダニエルの下は誰ですか (Who is below Daniel?)	マイケルです

「東京ドームに行きたいんですが」("I'm trying to get to Tokyo Dome...") Syntax

「Place に行きたんですが」 is simply, "I'm trying to get to Place." 「ですが」 doesn't compile a sentence, "I'm trying to get to the place but..." This kind of incomplete sentences are used often in daily communication not to be aggressively speaking in Japanese to a stranger.

Conversation Example:

A:「すみません、国技館に行きたいんですが」(Excuse me, I'm trying to get to Kokugikan: National Sports Stadium.)

B: 「この道をまっすぐ行って、コンビニを右に曲がります。そこをまっすぐ5分ほど行くとあります」("Go straight on this street, make a right turn at the convenience store. Go straight, you will find it in five minutes.")

Exercise: Make a sentence of 「に行きたいんですが...」 with the places

i.e. 品川駅	品川駅に行きたいんですが
病院 (Hospital)	病院に行きたいんですが
海岸(Beach)	海岸に行きたいんですが
公園(Park)	公園に行きたいんですが
地下鉄の駅(Subway Station)	地下鉄の駅に行きたいんですが

Exercise: Choose the location of the hospital from the conversation among A, B, and C.

A: 「すみません、病院に行きたいんですが...」

B:「ここをまっすぐ行って、3つ目の信号を右です。ガソリンスタンドの前にあります」

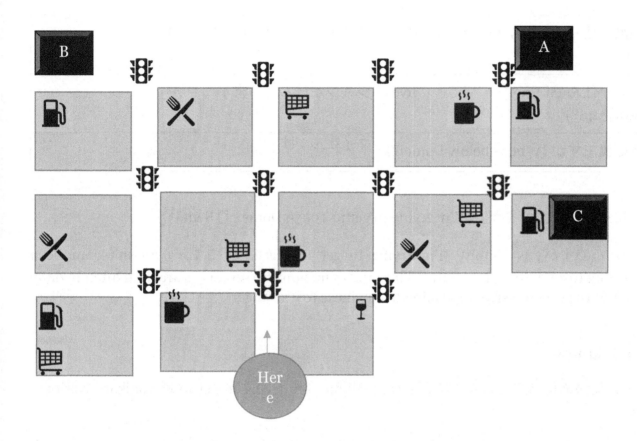

答え：A

Exercise: Here is a conversation between two people, and A-san is looking for some places. Look at the map below and fill the blanks in conversation. You're at the star near a bank facing 西(West).

A:「すみません」 ("Excuse me.")

B:「はい」 (Yes")

A:「病院に行きたいのですが」 ("I'm trying to get to a hospital.")

B:「えーと、まっすぐ行って、2つ目の信号を右に曲がります。そこをずっとまっすぐ行って、2つ信号を越えたところにあります」 ("Let me see, go straight and make a right at the 2nd lights. Go straight all the way. After two lights, there should be the hospital.")

A:「ありがとうございます。あ、それから、病院から駅に行くにはどう行ったらいいですか」 ("Thank you. Oh, then, from the hospital, how do I go to the station?")

B:「同じ道を戻って来て、1.＿＿＿＿の信号を2.＿＿＿に曲がって、まっすぐ行きます。一つ目の3.＿＿＿を左に曲がると駅があります」

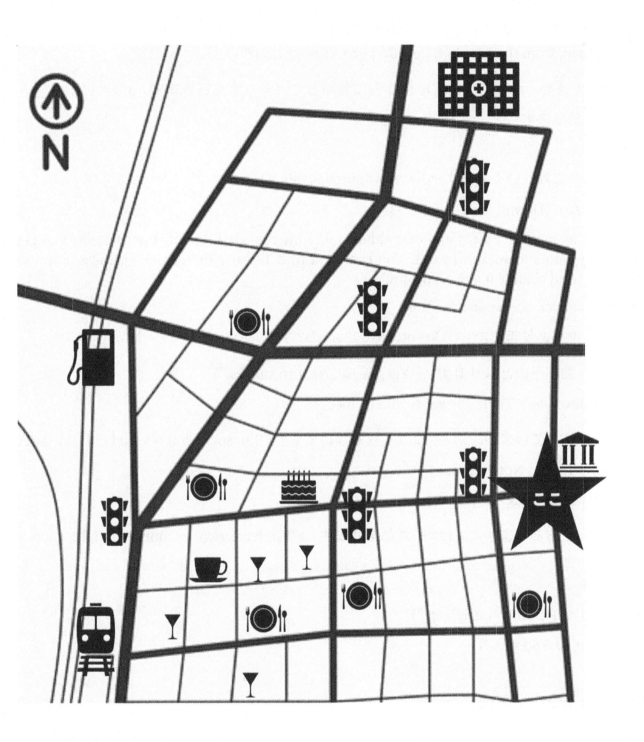

A: 「すみません」 ("Excuse me.")

B: 「はい」 (Yes")

A: 「病院に行きたいのですが」 ("I'm trying to get to a hospital.")

B: 「えーと、まっすぐ行って、2つ目の信号を右に曲がります。そこをずっとまっすぐ行って、2つ信号を越えたところにあります」 ("Let me see, go straight and make a right at the 2nd lights. Go straight all the way. After two lights, there should be the hospital.")

A:「ありがとうございます。あ、それから、病院から駅に行くにはどう行ったらいいですか」

("Thank you. Oh, then, from the hospital, how do I go to the station?")

B:「同じ道を戻って来て、1. 3つ目の信号を2. 右に曲がって、まっすぐ行きます。1つ目の3. 信号を左に曲がると駅があります」

Shopping Scenario 「これ、いくらですか」("How much is this?")

「Tシャツありますか」(Do you have T-shirts?)

Convenience stores in Japan are 24/7 and carry almost anything needed in daily life. Imagine you get caught in the heavy rain and soaked in wet. You can even find T-shirts or regular business shirts at convenience stores. And change it at a restroom.

In that situation, a conversation goes like this.

「すみません、Tシャツありますか」("Do you have T-shirts?")

「はい、あります。お菓子のとなりです」("Yes, we do. Next to snacks.")

What if they don't have one? Their answer would be like,

「すみません。売り切れています。Tシャツは1枚もないです」("I'm sorry, but it's sold out. We don't have any T-shirts.", 1枚も: Not even one)

They would suggest something else, though.

「普通のシャツでしたらありますよ。Lサイズがあります」("We have regular shirts though. There's an L-size.")

Then you would ask,

「それ、いくらですか」("How much is it?")

「1,800円です」("It's 1,800 yen.")

Higher Numbers and Counting

Here are numbers past 99.

日本語	百	千	万	億	兆
	100	1,000	10,000	100,000,000	1000,000,000,000

Numbers can be written in kanji as well.

1：一	6：六	11：十一	16：十六

2：二		7：七		12：十二		17：十七	
3：三		8：八		13：十三		18：十八	
4：四		9：九		14：十四		19：十九	
5：五		10：十		15：十五		20：二十	

Now you might find some numbers in first name such as 一郎 (いちろう)、二郎 (じろう)、三郎 (さぶろう) and you can tell how many older brothers they have, from the name. Ichiro is the first boy, Jiro is the second, Saburo is the third.

月 (つき) （Months）is pretty easy to remember. But the bad-luck numbers of 4,7, and 9 are pronounced in the way like the bad luck this time.

January	February	March	April	May	June
いちがつ 1月	にがつ 2月	さんがつ 3月	しがつ 4月	ごがつ 5月	ろくがつ 6月
July	August	September	October	November	December
しちがつ 7月	はちがつ 8月	くがつ 9月	じゅうがつ 10月	じゅういちがつ 11月	じゅうにがつ 12月

Now, days are tricky. The pronunciations might be confusing with other numbers.

	漢字 (かんじ)	読み方 (よみかた) (how to read)		漢字 (かんじ)	読み方 (よみかた) (how to read)
1st	一日	ついたち	16th	十六日	じゅうろくにち
2nd	二日	ふつか	17th	十七日	じゅうしちにち
3rd	三日	みっか	18th	十八日	じゅうはちにち
4th	四日	よっか	19th	十九日	じゅうくにち
5th	五日	いつか	20th	二十日	はつか
6th	六日	むいか	21st	二十一日	にじゅういちにち
7th	七日	なのか	22nd	二十二日	にじゅうににち

8th	八日	ようか	23rd	二十三日	にじゅうさんにち
9th	九日	ここのか	24th	二十四日	にじゅうよっか
10th	十日	とおか	25th	二十五日	にじゅうごにち
11th	十一日	じゅういちにち	26th	二十六日	にじゅうろくにち
12th	十二日	じゅうににち	27th	二十七日	にじゅうしちにち
13th	十三日	じゅうさんにち	28th	二十八日	にじゅうはちにち
14th	十四日	じゅうよっか	29th	二十九日	にじゅうくにち
15th	十五日	じゅうごにち	30th	三十日	さんじゅうにち
			31st	三十一日	さんじゅういちにち

Conversation Example:

A: 「このパンツをください」 ("Can I have this pair of pants?")

B: 「ありがとうございます」 ("Thank you.")

A: 「ええと、二つください」 ("Well, can I have two?")

A: 「かしこまりました」 ("Surely.")

B: 「カードでお願いします」 ("I'd like to pay by credit card.")

A: 「お支払い方法は」 ("How many payments would you like to make?")

B: 「一回でお願いします」 ("Once please.")

If you pay in cash, 「現金/キャッシュでお願いします」

Additional Important Counting Units

人（ひとり：one person、ふたり：two people 、N にん）	People
本（ほん）	Long things such as bottles, chopsticks, and umbrellas.
枚（まい）	Thin things such as paper or shirts
冊（さつ）	Bound things such as books
匹（ひき）	Animals like cats and dogs
歳（さい）	Age of living creatures
個（こ）	Small things
回（かい）	Number of times
力所（かしょ）	Locations

Conversation Example:

A:「このサンドイッチ、いくらですか」（" How much is this sandwich?"）

B:「250円です」（" ni-hyaku-go-ju-en desu"）

A:「この水はいくらですか」（ "How much is this water?"）

B:「100円です」（"hyaku-en-desu"）

A:「サンドイッチ二つと水をください」（"Can I have two sandwitches and water?"）

B:「合計で600円になります」（"The total will be roppyaku-en"）

Conversation Example 2:

A:「あのTシャツ、いくらですか」（ "How much is this T-shirt?"）

B:「1,980円です」（ "sen-kyu-hyaku-hachi-ju-en desu"）

A:「この帽子はいくらですか」（ "How much is this cap?"）

B:「1,200円です」（"sen-ni-hyaku-en desu"）

A:「Tシャツ2枚と帽子を一つください」（"Can I have two T-shirts and a cap?"）

B:「合計で4,160円になります」（"The total will be yon-sen-hyaku-roku-ju en"）

Exercise: Write the total number in Roman

i.e. 1,500+2,800	4,300 yon-sen-sann-byaku

50+35	85 hachi-ju-go
1,980+4,500	6,480 roku-sen-yon-hyaku-hachi-ju
27+56	83 hachi-ju-san
10,800+ 4,890	15,690 ichi-man-go-sen-roppyaku-kyu-ju

When you can't hear numbers clearly, you might ask,

「もう一度お願いします」（Say again）or 「ご・せん・よん・ひゃく?」（5,400 and ?），so a cashier would say「さん・じゅう・に・えん・です」(32 yen).

Vocabulary List for Review

出身 _{しゅっしん}	Place of origin
よろしくお願いします _{ねが}	Thank you in advance
趣味 _{しゅ み}	Hobby
興味 _{きょう み}	Interest
職業 _{しょくぎょう}	Occupation
大学院生 _{だいがくいんせい}	Graduate Student
起業家 _{き ぎょう か}	Entrepreneur
神道 _{しんとう}	Shinto
侍 _{さむらい}	Samurai
武道家 _{ぶ どう か}	Martial Artist
投資家 _{とう し か}	Investor
自己紹介 _{じ こ しょうかい}	Self-introduction
日本酒 _{に ほんしゅ}	Sake
失礼ですが _{しつれい}	If I may
おいつくですか	How old are you?
息子 _{むす こ}	Son

年上（としうえ）	Older
子供（こども）	Child/Children
しっかり	Firm/Steadfast
前半（ぜんはん）	first half
兄/お兄さん（あに/にい）	Older Brother
姉/お姉さん（あね/ねえ）	Older Sister
弟（おとうと）	younger brother
妹（いもうと）	younger sister
夫 /主人（おっと/しゅじん）	Husband
妻/奥さん（つま/おく）	Wife
娘（むすめ）	Daughter
近くに（ちか）	Near
駅（えき）	Station
ネットカフェ	Internet café
銀行（ぎんこう）	bank
これ	This
それ	That
あれ	That
どれ	Which
この	This
その	It
あの	That
どの	which
ここ	Here
そこ	There

あそこ	Over there
どこ	Where
こっち	This Way
そっち	There
あっち	That Way
どっち	Which
この辺	Around Here
その辺	Its Area
あの辺	That Area
どの辺	Which Area
バス停	Bus Stop
コンビニ	Convenience Store
店	Store
駐車場	Parking Lot
曲がる	Make a Turn
階段	Stairs
レジ	Cashier
出口	Exit
受付	Reception
右	Right
左	Left
上	Up
下	Low
右上	Top right
右下	Bottom right

<ruby>左<rt>ひだり</rt></ruby><ruby>上<rt>うえ</rt></ruby>	Top left
<ruby>左<rt>ひだり</rt></ruby><ruby>下<rt>した</rt></ruby>	lower left
の<ruby>前<rt>まえ</rt></ruby>	In Front of
の<ruby>近<rt>ちか</rt></ruby>く	Near

Take-home message

We're now little by little building vocabulary. Once you understand grammar and syntax, vocabulary and phrases are key to communicate. We first covered "Self-introduction." The essential phrase is 「（どうぞ）よろしくお<ruby>願<rt>ねが</rt></ruby>いします」 (Thank you in advance or nice to meet you, or pleasure to work with you, depending on situations). In formal occasions, add （どうぞ） in the beginning.

We also covered expressions related to locations. Kyoto is designed to be a grid pattern and is easy to navigate. However, Tokyo is very confusing if you only depend on the street number. Thanks to mobile map apps, things are so much easier now. However, if you can't get internet connection or batteries dies, all you can do is ask locals.... In that case, expressions like "make a turn on the second lights" "Turn left on the third intersection" are very common to communicate directions in Japan. Numbers, location related vocabulary are very important.

Numbers are also important for shopping. Just like the Japanese version of "99cent Shop" 「100円ショップ」 or casually 「ひゃっきん（Abbreviation of 「<ruby>百円均一<rt>ひゃくえんきんいつ</rt></ruby>(Everything is 100 yen)」, 「<ruby>百<rt>ひゃく</rt></ruby>」 (Hundred) 「<ruby>千<rt>せん</rt></ruby>」 (Thousand) 「<ruby>万<rt>まん</rt></ruby>」 (10 Thousand) are common monetary units you will hear in Japan. It's sometimes hard to hear all the numbers.

Exercises

1. Read the dialogue and find three mistakes.

A:「ダニエラさん、自己紹介をお願いしていいですか?」 ("Daniela-san, can you introduce yourself?")

B: 「はい。ダニエラです。アメリカのマサチューセッツから来ます。大学生です。政治学を学びます。私はクロサワの映画とラーメンを好きです。よろしくお願いします」 ("Yes. [I] am Daniela. [I] am from Massachusetts in the US. [I] am a college student. [I] am studying Politics. [I] like Kurosawa's movies and ramen. Nice to meet you.")

2. Choose ONE answer as B.

A:「ダニエラさん、ヒロです。お国は?」 ("Daniela-san, [I'm] Hiro. Which country are you from?")

B: 「＿＿＿＿＿＿＿＿」 ("[I'm from] London, UK")

1. わかりません

2. イギリスのロンドンです

3. オランダのハーグです

A:「趣味はなんですか」 ("What's your hobby?")

B: 「＿＿＿＿＿＿＿＿」 ("(It) is Karate. (I) have a Black Belt")

1. 空手です。白帯を持っています。

2. 空手が好きです。黒帯は持っていません

3. 空手です。黒帯を持っています

3. Read the passage and answer the question.

「三夏です。北海道の出身です。兄と札幌ラーメンの店を始めました。兄の名前は一郎と、二郎で、私は三夏なので、「一二三」という名前の店です」

三夏さんのお兄さんは、一人、二人、もしくは三人ですか。 ("Mika has one, two or three older brothers?")

232

4. Look at the map and choose ONE answer.

「エスカレーターはどこですか」

		Information Center				Elevator	
	Escalator						

Here

A. 「まっすぐ行ってインフォメーションセンターを右に曲がってください」

B. 「ここから左にずっとまっすぐ行ってください」

C. 「まっすぐ行ってインフォメーションセンターを左に曲がってください」

5. You're at a supermarket and looking for cereals. First, ask a staff if they have cereals. Then choose the right answer from the information from the staff.

_____ ("Do you have cereals?")

Staff: 「少々お待ちください。えーと、二番のフルーツのとなりにあります」

A: "That's isle two next to Fruits."

B: "That's isle two in that area."

C: "That's isle two in front of Fruits."

6. You're buying two shirts of 1,980 yen and one pair of Chino pants at 3,980 yen. The total amount will be

A: 「なな・せん・きゅう・ひゃく・よん・じゅう・

えん」

B: 「なな・まん・きゅう・せん・ご・ひゃく・えん」

C: 「なな・せん・はっぴゃく・よん・じゅう・えん」

7. Write in Hiragana

三月三日		四月八日	
五月五日		七月七日	
十一月二日		八月十五日	
十二月二十四日		九月九日	
四月七日		十月十日	

8. Fill the blank

日本語	百 (ひゃく)			億 (おく)	兆 (ちょう)
	100	1,000	10,000	100,000,000	1000,000,000,000

9. Here is Daniela's plan. First, go to an internet café and find the best ramen in the region and take a train from the station.

1. Speak to a local, "I'm trying to get to an internet café around here..."

「すみません、＿＿＿＿＿＿＿＿＿＿＿＿＿＿＿＿＿＿＿」

2. Ask how to get to the station from the internet café.

「それと(also)、＿＿＿＿＿＿＿＿＿＿＿＿＿＿＿＿＿＿＿」

10. Read the passage and choose the destination.

「ここからまっすぐこの道(みち)を西(にし)(West)に行(い)きます。信号(しんごう)を二(ふた)つ越(こ)えるとケーキ屋(や)があります。さらに(Further down)まっすぐ行(い)きます。レストランを越(こ)えて、3目(め)の信号(しんごう)があります。そこを右(みぎ)に曲(ま)がります。その道(みち)をまっすぐ行(い)くと左(ひだり)にあります」

A: レストラン

B: ケーキ屋

C: ガソリンスタンド

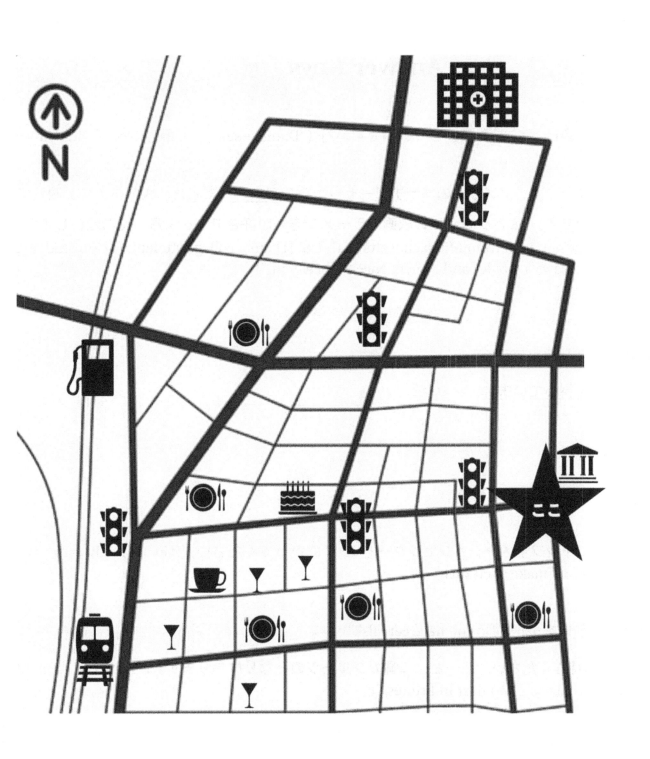

Answer Keys

1.

A:「ダニエラさん、自己紹介をお願いしていいですか?」 ("Daniela-san, can you introduce yourself?")

B: 「はい。ダニエラです。アメリカのマサチューセッツから来ます→ました。大学生です。政治学を学びます→んでいます。私はクロサワの映画とラーメンを→が好きです。よろしくお願いします」 ("Yes. [I] am Daniela. [I] am from Massachusetts in th US. [I] am a college student. [I] am studying Politics. [I] like Kurosawa's movies and ramen. Nice to meet you.")

2.

2. イギリスのロンドンです,

3. 空手です。黒帯を持っています

3. 二人 (two)

4.

C.「まっすぐ行ってインフォメーションセンターを左に曲がってください」 (Go straight to the Information Center and make a left turn)

5. 「シリアルはありますか」 ("Do you have cereals?")

Staff: 「少々お待ちください。えーと、二番のフルーツのとなりにあります」 ("Wait a second please. Let me see, that's isle two next to Fruites.")

A: "That's isle two next to Fruits."

6. A:「なな・せん・きゅう・ひゃく・よん・じゅう・えん」 (¥7,940)

7.

三月三日	さんがつ　みっか	四月八日	しがつ　ようか
五月五日	ごがつ　いつか	四月四日	しがつ　よっか

236

十一月二日	じゅういちがつ　ふつか	八月十五日	はちがつ　じゅうごにち
十二月二十四日	じゅうにがつ　にじゅうよっか	九月九日	くがつ　ここのか
四月七日	しがつ　なのか	十月十日	じゅうがく　とおか

8.

日本語	百 _{ひゃく} 百	千 _{せん} 千	万 _{まん} 万	億 _{おく} 億	兆 _{ちょう} 兆
	100	1,000	10,000	100,000,000	1000,000,000,000

9.1. Speak to a local, "I'm trying to get to an internet café around here..."

「すみません、ネットカフェに行きたいんですが...」

2. Ask how to get to the station from the internet café.

「それと(also)、そこから駅に行きたいんですが...」

10. C: ガソリンスタンド

237

Traveling Japan 2

"Expansion. That is the idea the novelist must cling to.

Not rounding off but opening out."

- E.M. Forster

This is final chapter in this book. What have you already accomplished? The Japanese language is not the easiest language on earth. And you're communicating in Japanese now.

One of the exciting experiences in Japan is local food. Even though Japan is a small country, you can enjoy different flavors and specialties. While Northern Japan, such as Hokkaido and Tohoku areas, can be very cold in winter, Okinawa is subtropical. And for food, let's see how ramen flavors are diverse.

From Hokkaido in the North, there are already three major ramen. Asahikawa (Soy sauce-based and mid-thin noodles), Kushiro (Chicken stock-based and thin noodles), and Sapporo (Thick miso-based and chewy noodles), in addition to Hakodate and Muroran ramen. Then, Tohoku area, Tokyo, Nagoya, then Osaka and Kyoto, then Fukuoka, and finally Okinawa Soba in Okinawa. There are so many different soups, flavors, toppings, noodles, and ramen masters.

When you find new flavors and enjoy tastes, all you want to do is to share your excitement with the restaurant staff and local people. How do you express the taste and food? Just 「おいしい」? All you can describe is "good," is that something you're expressing your priceless experiences? I was impressed to hear my American friend describes Japanese cuisine, "Japanese food is all about 歯応え(texture)." And the enjoyment of food comes from the experience of chewing/smelling /tasting.

At a restaurant, typical interaction with staff goes like the following.

A: 「いらっしゃいませ。何名様でいらっしゃいますか」 ("Hello, welcome. How many people are you?" 何名様: How many people in an honorific way, さまis an honorific word of さん, 名 is an honorific word of 人, 何人 is the plain form)

B: 「一人です」 ("One")

A: 「こちらへどうぞ」 ("This way please.")

Once you sit at table, many of restaurants have menus there, but in case there is not one,

「メニューお願いします」 ("Could I have a menu?")

Menus usually have pictures of the food so you can easily picture what to expect.

「お決まりですか」("Are you ready to order?")

「トンカツとアイスティーをお願いします」("I'll have Tonkatsu and Iced tea.")

Common 日本料理 Vocabulary

すき焼き	Beef and Vegetable Pot in Sweet Soy Sauce	しょうが焼き	Pork Ginger	うどん	Udon
しゃぶしゃぶ	Beef Tot Pot	鶏の照り焼き	Chicken Teriyaki	たぬきうどん	Udon with Tempura Batter
焼肉	Grilled Beef	おでん	Eggs, Fishcakes in Broth	きつねうどん	Udon with Deep-fried Tofu
焼き鳥	Grilled Chicken Skewers	親子丼	Chicken and Egg Rice Bowl	天ぷらそば	Buckwheat Noodles with Tempura
刺身	Sliced Raw Fish	牛丼	Beef Rice	ざるそば	Cold Soba with Dipping Sauce
てんぷら	Deep-fried Vegetable or Seafood	天丼	Tempura Rice Bowl	しょうゆらーめん	Soy Sauce Based Ramen
からあげ	Fried Chicken	寿司	Sushi	しおらーめん	Salt Based Ramen
たこ焼き	Octopus Ball	やきそば	Fried Noodle	みそらーめん	Miso Based Ramen
おにぎり	Rice Ball	お好み焼き	Meat, Vegetable, and Seafood Japanese Pancake	とんこつらーめん	Pork Born Based Ramen
トンカツ	Pork Cutlet	あげだしどうふ	Deep-fried Tofu with Broth	みそ汁	Miso Soup
餃子	Fried Dumpling	カレーライス	Curry with Rice	コロッケ	Croquette

えびフライ	Fried Prawn	チャーハン	Fried Rice	オムライス	Omelet Rice

Interaction Sample 1.

A:「ご注文、お決まりですか」("Are you ready to order?")

B: 「はい、からあげひとつとビールひとつをお願いします」("Yes, one Kara-age and one beer please.")

A: 「かしこまりました」("Right away.")

B: 「すみません、えだまめもひとつお願いします」("Excuse me, but one Edamame too.")

Interaction Sample 2.

A:「今日のランチスペシャルは何ですか」("What is the today's special?")

B: 「餃子定食です」("Fried dumpling set meal")

A: 「周りの白いのは何ですか」("What is the white stuff around it?")

B: 「炒めたもやしです。野菜です」("That's sauteed bean sprout. Vegetable.")

Exercise:

Here is a lunch menu. Please answer questions.

A. 今日のランチ 鶏のからあげ定食（ご飯、サラダ、みそ汁、ドリンク付き）850円	B. 餃子ランチ 餃子定食（ご飯、サラダ、みそ汁、ドリンク付き）800円
	C. ハンバーグランチ ハンバーグ定食（ご飯、ポテトサラダ、みそ汁、ドリンク付き）850円
ホットコーヒー、アイスコーヒー、アイスティー、コーラ、紅茶、ジンジャーエール	

1.「お決まりですか」

2.「ドリンクは何になさいますか」

3. ポテトサラダが付いているランチはどれですか?

Answer

1.「はい決まりました」 (Yes, I am.) or

「まだです」(Not yet.)「ちょっと待ってください」(Please wait a little.)

2.「＊＊（i.e., アイスコーヒー）をお願いします」

3. C （ハンバーグランチ）

Useful/Common Must Phrases/Questions

「＊＊ってなんですか」	"What is **?"
「＊＊、ご利用ですか」	"Will you be using **?" (i.e., coupons, parking, and payment methods)
「以上で」	"That's all." (You can answer to "what else would you like?" question.)
「＊＊はいかがですか」	"Would you like**?"
「どのくらい待ちますか」	"How long is the wait?" (They usually have the waiting list to fill at the reception.)
「これ、肉が入っていますか」	"Is there meat in this?"
「食券をお買いください」	"Please buy shokken (food ticket)." (Many ramen shops and diners have this food ticket system. And customers need to return the tray.)
並・大盛り/大・中・小 替え玉	Regular, Extra Large/Large, Regular and Small "Noodle refill"

Asking Permissions for shopping 1 「＊＊でいいですか」 (Is it okay with/by **?)

「＊＊でいいですか」 Syntax can be used to ask permission, " Is it okay for me to do **."

Interaction Sample 1.

A: 「お支払いはどうなさいますか」 ("How would you like to pay?")

B: 「カードでいいですか」 ("Can I pay by credit card?")

A: 「かしこまりました」 ("Certainly")

Ask permissions using the following vocabulary.

i.e. 予約なし (No Reservation)	予約なしでいいですか
カード (Credit Card)	カードでいいですか
ドル(Dollar)	ドルでいいですか
くつ (Shoes)	くつでいいですか(Can I keep my shoes on?)
ビットコイン (Bitcoin)	ビットコインでいいですか
ローマ字 (Roman)	ローマ字でいいですか

「こちらにご記入ください」 (Please fill out). If you're asked to write down your information, you might want to check if you can write in the alphabet. 「ローマ字でいいですか」

Asking Permissions for shopping 2 「＊＊てもいいですか」 (Is it okay to ＊＊?)

Interaction Sample 1.

A: 「こちらにご記入ください」 (Please fill out here.)

B: 「すみません。このペン借りてもいいですか」 (Can I borrow this pen?)

A: 「もちろんです」 (Surely)

B: 「ありがとうございます」 (Thank you)

Ask permission to do the following verbs.

i.e., 借りる (Borrow)	借りてもいいですか
見る (See/watch/look)	見てもいいですか
もらう (Have/receive)	もらってもいいですか

使<ruby>つか</ruby>う (Use)	使<ruby>つか</ruby>ってもいいですか
座<ruby>すわ</ruby>る (Sit)	座<ruby>すわ</ruby>ってもいいですか
食<ruby>た</ruby>べる(Eat)	食<ruby>た</ruby>べてもいいですか
飲<ruby>の</ruby>む （Drink）	飲<ruby>の</ruby>んでもいいですか
着<ruby>き</ruby>る (Wear)	着<ruby>き</ruby>てもいいですか
帰<ruby>かえ</ruby>る (Go home/return)	帰<ruby>かえ</ruby>ってもいいですか

Interaction Sample 2.

A: 「すみません。トイレ借りてもいいですか」 (Excuse me. Can I use the bathroom?)

B: 「はい、右手にあります」 (Yes, it's on the right hand side)

Interaction Sample 3.

A: 「すみません。ここ座ってもいいですか」 (Excuse me. Can I sit here?)

B: 「すみません。そちらは予約席です。こちらにお願いします」 (I'm sorry but it's reserved. Please come this way)

「それはちょっと」

「それはちょっと」 (That's a kind of ...) is a typical "no" in Japanese Business culture and a way not to offend customers. Or you would hear, 「今はちょっと」 (Now is not a good time). 「ちょっと」 is a little. And convenient word to say no indirectly. Another typical Japanese word is 「微妙」. The word means "subtle." But when you ask some opinions and if the answer is 微妙, usually means "not so good." It's similar in English when you ask someone's first impression, the answer is "interesting."

Grammar Review of conjugation: 普通形, ます形, and て形

The forms of verbs in Japanese determine tense and function in a sentence, and verbs come usually at the end. Three basic verb forms are 普通形 (Plain Form), which is known as 辞書形 (Dictionary Form), ます形, and て形.

普通形 is usually used in casual conversations with friends and is an effective way to learn conjugation before learning です形/ます形.

て形 makes a wide variety of grammatical expressions and doesn't not indicate tense.

Verbs are categorized to three groups, ru-verbs, u-verbs and irregular verbs. The difference is how verbs conjugate. Ru-verbs are the easiest conjugation form. U-verbs are the largest group of verbs. Irregular ones have three verbs.

Ru-verbs

普通形	英語	ます形	て形	て形「てもいいですか」(May I ...?)
i.e., 食べる	eat	食べます	食べて	食べてもいいですか
見る	see/look	見ます	見て	見てもいいですか

U-verbs

普通形	英語	ます形	て形	て形「てもいいですか」(May I ...?)
i.e., 座る	sit	座ります	座って	座ってもいいですか
使う	use	使います	使って	使ってもいいですか

Irregular verbs

普通形	英語	ます形	て形	て形「てもいいですか」(May I ...?)
i.e., する	do	します	して	してもいいですか
来る	come	来ます	来て	来てもいいですか

It's almost impossible to remember all the basic verbs and their conjugation in a short time. Please go back to Book 1 and review the exercise. Again, the key is "speaking aloud" just like Spanish conjugation, "me llamo, te llamas, and se llama." Sound memories will be your learning tutor.

Transportation expressions: 「これ、品川に行きますか」(Does this go to Shinagawa?)

ます形 of 「行く」is 「行きます」and for question, you need to add 「か」

「行きますか」then additional information is "this(train)" and "Shinagawa."

「これ、品川に行きますか」(Does this go to Shinagawa?)

Conversation Sample 1.

A:「すみません。これ、上野に行きますか」(Excuse me, does this go to Ueno?)

B:「いえ、行きません」(No, it doesn't.)

A:「３番線だと聞きました」(I hear Platform 3.)

B:「あそこに係員がいますから、聞いてみてください」(You should ask the station staff over there.)

Tokyo's train system is very complicated. There are Metro subways, Toei subways, JR lines, and many Private Train systems. And the fares vary depending on your destination. So, if you get lost, you need to find anyone in a uniform at the platform or station office. Also, you need to be careful with station names such as "Tokyo." "I want to go to Tokyo" is one thing, "I want to go to Tokyo Station" is another.

Conversation Sample 1.

A:「すみません。中華街に行きたいんですが」(Excuse me, I want to go to Chinatown...)

B:「横浜の?」(In Yokohama?)

A:「はい、これ、横浜に行きますか」(Yes, does this go to Yokohama?)

B:「ちがうホームだと思います」(I think you got a wrong platform.)

A:「ほんとうですか」(Really?)

B:「階段を降りて情報センターで聞いた方がいいと思います」(Go downstairs and ask someone at the information center.)

You will hear station announcements like this.

「まもなく1番線に京都行きのぞみ号が入ってまいります」(A Nozomi train bound for Kyoto is arriving at platform 1 soon.)

Ordinal Numbers

No.1 is 1番 and this unit is used for all the numbers. Now when you add 「目」literally "eye" it can indicate the order. 「1番目」is「1st」. In the same way, if you express "times" 回 will be used as a unit. 「これが5回目のチャレンジです」(This is the fifth challenge.) Another common unit is 人, for example,「彼女がこの質問をする3人目」(She is the third person who asked the question.)

For transportation, the common units are 線(せん) (Line/platform) and 車(しゃ) or 両(りょう) (Car): 3号車(ごうしゃ) (Car No. 3) or 3両目(りょうめ)(Third Car).

「東海道線(とうかいどうせん)は11番線(ばんせん)です」 （Tokaido Line stops at Platform 11.）

「トイレは7号車(ごうしゃ)と11号車(ごうしゃ)にあります」 (7th and 11th Car have restrooms.)

There are so many units for numbers that are even difficult for native Japanese to remember so if it's not so sure, try to use ＊＊番(ばん) to ask and confirm.

Conversation Sample 2.

A: 「すみません、トイレはどこですか」 （Excuse me, where is a restroom?）

B: 「５号車(ごうしゃ)と８号車(ごうしゃ)にあります」 （We have on fifth and eighth car.）

A: 「5と8ですか」 (Five and eight?)

B: 「そうです」 (That's correct.)

Directions: 「＊＊までどうやって行(い)けばいいですか」 (How do I get to **?)

「まで」 is "to" and 「どうやって」 is "how."

Conversation Sample 1.

Look at the train map. You're at Shinjuku station.

A: 「すみません。秋葉原(あきはばら)までどうやって行(い)けばいいですか」 （Excuse me, how do I get to Akihabara?）

B: 「総武線(そうぶせん)で一本(いっぽん)ですよ （You can go straight there by Sobu Line. : "Ippon" means the number of train line and no need to change train to use 2nd or 3rd train.）

A: 「中央線(ちゅうおうせん)ではだめですか」 (Not by Chuo Line?)

B: 「中央線(ちゅうおうせん)は東京駅(とうきょうえき)に行(い)きます」 (Chuo Line goes to Tokyo station)

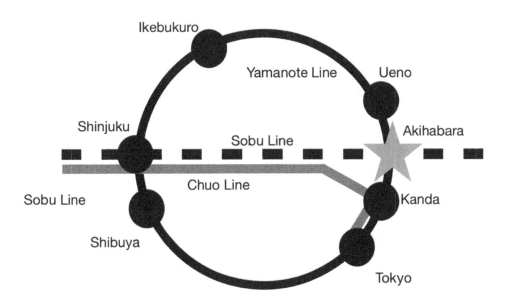

Conversation Sample 2.

Look at the train map. You're at Ikebukuro station.

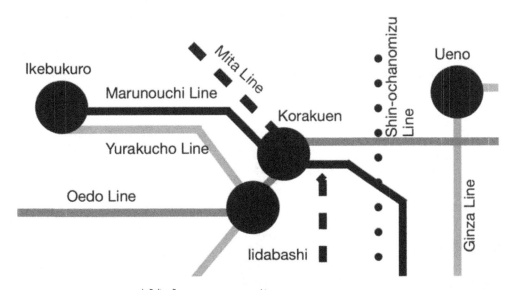

A: 「すみません。東京ドームまで行きたいのですが」 （Excuse me, how do I get to Tokyo Dome?）

B: 「丸の内線で一本ですよ （You can go straight there by Marunouchi Line.）

A: 「駅の名前は何ですか」 (What's the station name?)

B: 「後楽園です」 (It's Korakuen)

Conversation Sample 2.

247

A: 「ここから後楽園(こうらくえん)までどれくらいかかりますか」 (How long does it take to get Korakuen from here?)

B: 20分(ぶん)くらいです(It's about 20 minutes)

A: 「駅(えき)から東京(とうきょう)ドームまでどれくらいかかりますか」 (How long does it take to get Tokyo Dome from the station?)

B: 「5分(ふん)もかかりません」 (Should be less than five munities.)

Conversation Sample 2.

A: 「伊藤(いとう)さん、ニューヨークタイムズで盛岡(もりおか)の旅行記事(りょこうきじ)を見(み)ました。どうやって行(い)けばいいですか」 (Ito-san, I read a travel story about Morikoka on New York Times. How do I get there?)

B: 「新幹線(しんかんせん)だと2時間(じかん)ぐらいです」 (It's about 2 hours by Shinkansen)

A: 「いくらぐらいかかりますか」 (How much do you think it will cost?)

B: 「1万(まん)4,000円(えん)くらいだと思(おも)います」 (I think it's about 14,000 yen.)

A: 「盛岡(もりおか)でおいしいらーめんを食(た)べれますか」 (Do you think we can have delicious ramen in Morioka?)

B: 「盛岡(もりおか)は盛岡冷麺(もりおかれいめん)が有名(ゆうめい)です」 (Morioka is known for Morioka Cold Noodles.)

Expressions on Time and Hours

Time ＊時(じ)		Minutes ＊ 分(ふん/ぷん)	
1 AM/1 PM	午前(ごぜん)1時(じ)/午後(ごご)1時(じ)or13時(じ)	5	5分(ふん)
2 AM/2 PM	午前(ごぜん)2時(じ)/午後(ごご)2時(じ)or14時(じ)	10	１０分(じゅっぷん)
3 AM/3 PM	午前(ごぜん)3時(じ)/午後(ごご)3時(じ)or15時(じ)	15	15分(ふん)
4 AM/4 PM	午前(ごぜん)4時(じ)/午後(ごご)4時(じ)or16時(じ)	20	２０分(にじゅっぷん)
5 AM/5 PM	午前(ごぜん)5時(じ)/午後(ごご)5時(じ)or17時(じ)	25	25分(ふん)
6 AM/6 PM	午前(ごぜん)6時(じ)/午後(ごご)6時(じ)or18時(じ)	30	３０分(さんじゅっぷん) or 半(はん)(half)
7 AM/7 PM	午前(ごぜん)7時(じ)/午後(ごご)7時(じ)or19時(じ)	35	35分(ふん)

8 AM/8 PM	午前8時/午後8時or20時	40	４０分
9 AM/9 PM	午前9時/午後9時or21時	45	45分
10 AM/10 PM	午前10時/午後10時or20時	50	５０分
11 AM/10 PM	午前11時/午後11時or23時	55	55分
12 AM/12 PM	午前０時/ 正午	?	何分
About	ぐらい/約	Maybe	たぶん

Exercise: Choose the correct time.

1. にじゅうじにじゅっぷんです

A. 2:12

B. 20:20

C. 22:20

2. よじよんじゅうごふんです

A. 4:44

B. 14:14

C. 4:45

3. ごぜんはちじはん

A. 1:30 AM

B. 8:30 AM

C. 8: 15 AM

Three Important Syntax for Action to tell your plan, past action and your interests.

1. 「盛岡冷麺を食べに行きます」 (I'm going to have Morioka Cold Noodles.)

「＊に行きますor いきます」 indicates a purpose for going (action), 「食べに(to eat) 行きます(going)」

Conversation Sample 1.

A:「週末、どこに行きますか」（Where are you going this weekend?）

B:「盛岡に行きます」（I'm going to Morioka.）

A:「盛岡で何をしますか」（What are you going to do in Morika?）

B:「盛岡冷麺を食べに行きます」（I'm going to have Morioka Cold Noodles）

Conversation Sample 2.

A:「ダニエルさん、おつかれさまです」（Daniel-san, have a nice evening :「おつかれさまです」is generally used at work.）

B:「ヒロさん、おつかれさまです。これからどこに行きますか」（Hiro-san, have a nice evening too. Where are you going now?）

A:「今から新宿にレコードを買いに行きます。ダニエルさんは」（I'm going to Shinjuku to buy some records. How about you?）

B:「帰ります」（I'm going home）

A:「じゃ、駅まで一緒に行きましょう」（Okay, why don't we walk to the station.）

B:「はい、行きましょう」（Yes, let's do that.）

Syntax 2.「昨日はうちで料理をしました」（I cooked at home yesterday.）

「ました」is the past tense of「ます」. So if you describe the experience in the past,「ました」comes at the end of sentence.

The particle 「で」indicates the place where the action took place.「何をしましたか」is literally "What did you do?"

Conversation Sample 1.

A:「昨日は何をしましたか」（What did you do yesterday? ）

B:「家で料理をしました」（I cooked at home.）

A:「何を料理したんですか」（What did you cook?）

B:「ラザニアを作りました」（I made Lasagna.）

A:「おいしかったですか」（Was it good?）

B:「最高でした」（It was the best.）

Conversation Sample 1.

A:「日曜日は何をしましたか」（What did you do on Sunday?）

B:「曲を作りました」（I wrote a song.）

A:「どんな楽器を使うのですか」（What musical instrument do you use?）

B:「楽器は使いません」（I don't use any musical instrument.）

A:「じゃあ、どうやって作るんですか」（Then how do you write a song?）

B:「コンピューターを使います」（With a computer.）

Syntax 3.「陶器を見たいです」（I want to see Japanese ceramics.）

「＊＊たいです」is one of the most important syntaxes to build a conversation. Conjugation patterns are identical to て形.

Conversation Sample 1.:

A:「鎌倉で何をしたいですか」（What do you want to do in Kamakura?）

B:「陶器を見たいです」（I want to see Japanese ceramics.）

A:「お茶碗ですか」（Tea cups?）

B:「はい、父が集めているので、何か買って送りたいです」（Yes, my father collects them so I want to get something and send it.）

Lastly, it's important to express your impressions/feelings and opinions when you engage a conversation. No one wants to hear cliché. So, let's practice how to express yourself in Japanese.

Typical Question 1.「日本はどうですか?」（How do you like Japan?）

「どうですか」means "How is..." or "How do you like..." This simple question can be used conveniently in many situations such as「料理はどうですか」「天気はどうですか」「寝心地はどうですか(How comfortable is the bed?)」.

Conversation Sample 1.

A:「日本はどうですか?」（How's Japan?）

251

B:「楽しいです」(It's fun.)

Now, do you like this kind of answer? How does this sound like in English?

To communicate better and share your thoughts and feelings, your comments need to sound authentic and real.

1. Be specific.

2. Be real.

3. Be authentic.

A:「日本はどうですか?」(How's Japan?)

B:「コンビニはすごいですね」(Convenience stores are fantastic)

A:「どうしてですか」(Why is it?)

B:「美味しいものがたくさんあります。ソフトクリームのタイプがすごいたくさんあります。毎日食べています」(So many delicious foods. Many kinds of softy. I'm having every day.)

Here are some basic adjectives to describe your impressions/feelings.

楽しい	Fun	いい	Good/Great	むずかしい	Difficult
おもしろい	Interesting /Funny	かっこいい	Cool	高い	High/Expensive
おいしい	Delicious	便利な	Convenient	きちんとしている	Organized
きれい	Beautiful/Pretty	早い	Fast/Quick	親切な	Friendly

2.「盛岡旅行はどうでしたか?」(How was the trip to Morioka?)

Your answer needs to be past tense.

Conversation Sample 1.

A:「鎌倉はどうでしたか」(How was Kamakura?)

B:「素晴らしい茶碗を見つけました。父が喜びます」(Found a fantastic tea cup. My father would be happy.)

A:「高かったですか」(Was that expensive?)

B:「いいえ、高くなかったです」(Not so expensive)

Conversation Sample 2.

A: 「盛岡旅行はどうでしたか」(How was the trip to Morioka?)

B: 「らーめんがおいしかったです」(Ramen was so good.)

A: 「どうおいしかったのですか」(What did you like about the ramen?)

B: 「麺の硬さとスープがユニークでよかったです。人も親切でした」(The firm texture of noodles and soup was unique. People are friendly too.)

Here are basic tasting adjectives.

甘い	Sweet	からい	Spicy/Hot	すっぱい	Sour
しょっぱい	Salty	にがい	Bitter	油っこい	Oily
あまからい	Sweet and salty	さっぱりした	Refreshing	変わった	Unique

Conversation Sample 3.

A: 「この間、しいたけソフトを食べました」(I had shiitake softy the other day)

B: 「どうでしたか」(How was it?)

A: 「しいたけの匂いが少ししましたが、微妙でした」(I smelled a little bit of Shiitake mushroom, but it's hard to describe.)

B: 「じゃあ、今度食べてみます」(Well, I will give it a try next time.)

Vocabulary List for Review

何名様	How many people are you? (Polite way)
いらっしゃいませ	Welcome
人	Unit of People
さん/さま	Mr., Ms., Mrs., / Mr., Ms., Mrs. (Polite way)
こちらへどうぞ	Come this way please
すき焼き	Beef and Vegetable Pot in Sweet Soy Sauce
しゃぶしゃぶ	Beef Tot Pot

焼肉 (やきにく)	Grilled Beef
焼き鳥 (やきとり)	Grilled Chicken Skewers
刺身 (さしみ)	Sliced Raw Fish
てんぷら	Deep-fried Vegetable or Seafood
からあげ	Fried Chicken
しょうが焼き (しょうがやき)	Pork Ginger
鶏の照り焼き (とりのてりやき)	Chicken Teriyaki
おでん	Eggs, Fishcakes in Broth
親子丼 (おやこどん)	Chicken and Egg Rice Bowl
牛丼 (ぎゅうどん)	Beef Rice
天丼 (てんどん)	Tempura Rice Bowl
寿司 (すし)	Sushi
うどん	Udon
たぬきうどん	Udon with Tempura Batter
きつねうどん	Udon with Deep-fried Tofu
天ぷらそば (てんぷらそば)	Buckwheat Noodles with Tempura
ざるそば	Cold Soba with Dipping Sauce
しょうゆらーめん	Soy Sauce Based Ramen
しおらーめん	Salt Based Ramen
たこ焼き (たこやき)	Octopus Ball
おにぎり	Rice Ball
トンカツ	Pork Cutlet
餃子 (ぎょうざ)	Fried Dumpling
えびフライ	Fried Prawn
やきそば	Fried Noodle

お好み焼き	Meat, Vegetable, and Seafood Japanese Pancake
あげだしどうふ	Deep-fried Tofu with Broth
カレーライス	Curry with Rice
チャーハン	Fried Rice
みそらーめん	Miso Based Ramen
とんこつらーめん	Pork Born Based Ramen
みそ汁	Miso Soup
コロッケ	Croquette
オムライス	Omelet Rice
みそらーめん	Miso Based Ramen
とんこつらーめん	Pork Born Based Ramen
かしこまりました	Understood (polite way)
周り	Around
まだ	Not yet
利用	use
以上	That's all
食券	Food Ticket
並/大盛り	Regular/Extra Large
大/中/小	Large/Medium/Small
替え玉	Refill (Noodles)
予約	Reservation
ドル	Dollar
記入	Fill
もらう	Have/Receive
右手	Right hand

予約席 (よやくせき)	Reserved Seat
微妙 (びみょう)	Subtle
番・号 (ばん・ごう)(transportation)	Number
係員 (かかりいん)	Staff
中華街 (ちゅうかがい)	Chinatown
ホーム	Platform
情報センター (じょうほう)	Information Center
回 (かい)	A time
線 (せん)	A line
両/車 (りょう/しゃ)	A car
まで	to/until
旅行記事 (りょこうきじ)	Travel Story
くらい/ぐらい/約 (やく)	About
有名 (ゆうめい)	Famous
半 (はん)	Half
たぶん	Probably
おつかれさまでした	Have a good evening (at work)
最高 (さいこう)	Best
楽器 (がっき)	Musical Instrument
陶器 (とうき)	Ceramic
茶碗 (ちゃわん)	Teacup
寝心地 (ねごこち)	Sleeping Condition
すごい	Very/Great
楽しい (たの)	Fun

256

おもしろい	Interesting /Funny
おいしい	Delicious
きれい	Beautiful/Pretty
いい	Good/Great
かっこいい	Cool
便利な	Convenient
早い	Fast/Quick
むずかしい	Difficult
高い	High/Expensive
きちんとしている	Organized
親切な	Friendly
喜ぶ	Enjoy
硬い	Hard/Firm
硬さ	Hardness/Firmness
匂い	Smell

Take-home message

From the book 1, the intension to use kanji is to get familiar daily Japanese communication once you get here. Many experts would say it's not so recommended to be exposed with kanji from the beginning. But, even in the first trip in Japan, you will see many kanji in restraint menus.

Firstly, we covered how to communicate at a restaurant. How to ask a request, ask about the menu, and place an order.

Then, 「てもいいですか」 syntax allows you to ask a permission for shopping. Also, we learned to say no in the Japanese way.

We reviewed the polite style of 「です/ます」形 and 「て形」 with verb conjugations.

For transportation and direction sections, we practiced asking for stations and locations with ordinal numbers and units. Now you can understand time and minutes expressions as well.

For more advanced conversation, we covered to communicate plans/intensions, "want to," and express opinions/thought/feelings in the present and past tense.

Exercises

1. Read the dialogue and choose the right questions to ask what's in the yellow thing in the food.

A: 「今日のランチスペシャルは何ですか」 ("What is the today's special?")

B: 「オムライス定食です」 ("Omelet Rice set meal")

A: 「＿＿＿＿＿＿＿＿＿＿＿」 ("What is in this yellow stuff?")

1. 「その黄色いものはなんですか」

2. 「その黄色いものはいくらですか」

3. 「その黄色いものに何が入っていますか」

B: 「卵の下はケチャップライスです」 ("That's ketchup-flavored fried rice under the egg")

s movies and ramen. Nice to meet you.")

2. You decided to have the lunch special. Answer the question.

A: 「ランチスペシャルでございますね。ドリンクは何にしますか。アイスコーヒーとアイスティー、コーラが選べます」 (Sure, lunch special. What would you drink? We have Iced Coffee, Iced Tea and Cola.)

B: 「＿＿＿＿＿＿＿」 ("[I'd like] ....")

3. You're at a clothing store and wanted to try a sports jacket. Please choose the right request.

1. 「すみません、これください」

2. 「すみません、これいくらですか」

3. 「すみません、これ着てもいいですか」

4. How can you ask if you need to remove your shoes?

1. 「くつでいいですか」

2. 「くつはいいですか」

3. 「くつもいいですか」

5. You're at Iidabashi Station and trying to get to Ikebukuro. A station staff says you can go straight there on some line. Which subway line do you need to take?

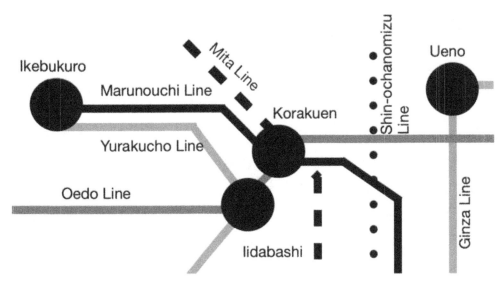

1. Oedo Line

2. Yurakucho Line

3. Marunouchi Line

6. It's 16:49 pm. You need to get to Tokyo Dome by 16:55 pm and are trying to get some information.

You: 「ここから東京ドームまでどれくらいかかりますか」

「地下鉄で7分くらい、歩いて、15分、タクシーで5分くらいです」

Which transportation do you need to make it to Tokyo Dome in time?

1. 地下鉄

2. 歩き

3. タクシー

7. Here is a Shinkansen Announcement. You're going to Atami for the short Onsen trip. Answer the two questions.

「お待たせいたしました。5番線は名古屋行き、10時22分発ひかり号です。自由席は1から6号車、13号車から15号車です。途中、新横浜、小田原、静岡、浜松に止まります」(発: departing, 自由席: non-reserved seats, 号車: Car No, 止まる: Stop).

You're waiting at 5号車 on the platform.

1. Are you waiting for the right car?
2. Are you on the right platform?

8. Choose the right time.

1. よじよんじゅうごふんです
A. 4:44
B. 14:14
C. 4:45

2. ごぜんはちじはん
A. 1:30 AM
B. 8:30 AM
C. 8: 15 AM

3. にじゅうじにじゅうにふん
A: 19:58
B: 20:22
C: 2:22

9. Choose the most appropriate answer for two questions.
1. 「週末、どこに行きますか」

A: 「秋葉原に行きます」

B: 「秋葉原に行きました」

C: 「秋葉原に行ったと思います」

2. 「熱海旅行はどうでしたか」

A: 「とてもリラックスしました」

B: 「とてもリラックスしたいです」

C: 「とてもリラックスすると思います」

10. Pick two things to do in Japan to answer to the question.

「日本で何がしたいですか」

_____

Answer Keys

1.

3.「その黄色いものに何が入っていますか」

2.

(アイスコーヒー, アイスティー, or コーラ)をお願いします。

3.

3.「すみません、これ着てもいいですか」

4.

3.「くつもいいですか」

5.

2. Yurakucho Line

6.

3. タクシー

7.

1. Are you waiting for the right car? Yes, you are.

2. Are you on the right platform? No, you're not (this train doesn't stop at Atami).

8.

1. C. 4:45

2. B. 8:30 AM

3. C: 2:22

9.

1. A:「秋葉原に行きます」

2. A:「とてもリラックスしました」

10.

(Answer Examples)

日本で桜を見たいです。

ラーメンを食べたいです。

新幹線に乗りたいです。

京都に行きたいです。

坐禅をしたいです。

熊野古道を歩きたいです。

CONCLUSION

"Everything in the world began with a yes."

- Clarice Lispector

PROCEEDING THE LEARNING JOURNEY

Congratulations on finishing the book2! It's now time to experience the Japanese culture yourself. Learning and understanding the different culture is so rewarding and inspiring. The way of thinking and feeling is no longer the same.

There are many YouTube channels, podcasts, and websites available to advance the language skill. For listening skills, check your favorite topics and keep listening to them. Listening is the king of communication. Once you feel ready, which is NOW, the best way we recommend is to travel in Japan and communicate with locals.

Communicating verbally is vital for your learning but also, Japan is a country that non-verbal communication has such an important role. That's something you can only learn in the country and while makes the culture so interesting. Showing and presenting are not always the impactful way of communication. Even Kimono, the best craft such as embroidery is sometimes hidden on the lining.

At this point, you have reached a basic knowledge of the Japanese language. You will be learning more of grammar, vocabulary, and expressions on the way to mastering Japanese. Verb conjugations and particles require constant practicing and learning. Logic helps you to understand but your intuition with open mind is such a powerful tool you can trust. The Japanese language doesn't have many offensive words compared to other language, but simple word can convey a strong message sometimes and show how much you respect or disrespect the person you're mentioning. Respect is the key element in Japanese communication.

LEARNING GRAMMAR/CULTURE

To improve your grammar, the best strategy is to work on simple books. Even manga. After finishing your favorite manga in English, you can pick the Japanese version. Story lines might not be the same, but you will understand the differences and how you feel about the story. Then, if they have Anime adaptation from the manga, watch it on computer. You will learn not only the grammar but also history and culture of Japan or how they see the future.

LEARNING VOCABULARY

To improve vocabulary, you can either watch Japanese content. One of the effective ways is dictation. Write down the word what you hear. Or the whole sentence. In that way, you will improve your listening skills drastically. Check with subtitle or English subtitle. When you write some words down, because of the combination of listening, processing, and writing, it stays in your brain clearly.

LEARNING PRONUNCIATION

To improve pronunciation, the most distinguished part from English is the rhythm. The Japanese language is closer to the Morse Code, not so much of intonation. It's flat. So it might be hard in the beginning to find where words and phrases end. However, pronunciation wise, there are not so many difficult sounds and the rhythm matters.

BOOK 3

Learn Japanese with Short Stories for Adult Beginners

Shortcut Your Japanese Fluency!
(Fun & Easy Reads)

Explore to Win

Introduction

"It's all a question of imagination.
Our responsibility begins with the power to imagine."
- Haruki Murakami

Welcome to the Japanese book3! Learning a language looks like a long and challenging journey, but when you reflect on what you've learned, time looks unreal, and the journey continues. This journey can make your life more colorful, full-flavored, and lively.

In book 3, we will experience the power of stories. We will do our best to make reading as pleasurable as possible, presenting you with intriguing stories written in simple Japanese that beginners can understand.

The authors of this book are native Japanese instructors who have successfully taught English-speaking students with no prior knowledge of Japanese, enabling them to work at Japanese corporations within a few months of training. The instructors understand the fundamental differences from English and can give you excellent tips on how to write and pronounce natural-sounding Japanese in this book. The cultural background behind communication also plays a vital role to understand the language.

Our collection of short stories consists of 8 selected tales, specifically written for readers who are not yet proficient in Japanese. Most of the stories take inspiration from popular tales from Japanese <u>folklore</u>, or the work of Japanese contemporary short stories. While learning the language, you'll have a chance to get to know more about Japanese culture and traditions.

Each story is followed by <u>comprehension exercises that</u> will help you test your general understanding of the stories. The vocabulary translation will be provided in tables right after the stories. So, this is what you will find in the following pages. But before getting to it, let's spend a minute discussing who can get the most benefits from this book and what strategies are best to achieve these results.

A. In the end, we'll all become stories. (Margaret Atwood)

This is a book for beginners, but it is pretty obvious that an absolute beginner cannot start by reading a book in the target language, as that is simply impossible without some sort of pre-existent knowledge.

Consequently, this book can be a great option for learners familiar with A1/A2-level Japanese and who want to learn Japanese culture. These selected Japanese old tales have not only a long history but also popularity in modern times. There are some reasons why they like those stories and can be a great hint to understanding the culture.

If you think that your level is not high enough to understand these stories, or if you realize that after starting the book, you can easily catch up with the basic knowledge by using our grammar book "Learn Japanese for Adult Beginners: Workbook!" and/or our phrasebook "Japanese Phrasebook for Adult Beginners: Speak Japanese in 30 Days!".

We did our best to create a collection of books for beginners that tackle Japanese from all sides and provide a thorough and all-inclusive approach to the language. The main reason we added this book to the collection is that reading is one of the best ways to <u>learn narrative and culture,</u> which is one of the target goals of this book.

The obvious downside to reading is that it doesn't help with pronunciation. This is true with any language, but it is a lesser problem with Japanese, as it is a phonetic language. You will need to check the meaning of Kanji (or a set of kanji) in a dictionary, but with furigana on top, you can read and learn the reading.

B. Learning Japanese by Reading

Because of the grammatical structure and word order, Japanese reading is relatively easier to master other communication skills such as listening/speaking and understanding the culture. Also, the Japanese language is phonetic, which makes Haiku and Tanka as you can easily work with syllables and rhymes along with building seasonal vocabularies. Haiku is a 5-7-5 syllable format short poem and Tanka is a 5-7-5-7-7 syllable format that requires a specific kigo (seasonal word such as plants, food, event and animal).

It was Haruki Murakami who revolutionized "" (author's voice and rhythm of writing) in Japanese literature. His plain writing style goes beyond thoughts and emotions and speaks to subconsciousness. Because of his plain writing, it's easier for translators to write in different languages, and readers worldwide appreciate the impact of his writing.

After Murakami, many female writers such as Mieko Kawakami ("Breasts and Eggs" considered one of the world's literary stars), Sayaka Murata("Convenience Store Woman" winner of the Akutagawa Prize in 2016, some critic says, "Not a single author on Earth sees, thinks, or writes like she does."), and Yoko Ogawa("Memory Police" shortlisted for International Booker Prize 2020) from Japan received recognition. They're all translated into English, but it's best to listen to their voice in their words directly. Now is a good time to spot great modern Japanese female writers. The world's first novel, "Tale of Genji," was also written by a Japanese female. Becoming proficient in reading Japanese will give you the keys to a whole new world of literary wonders, from the present and the past.

C. When the boundary disappears

Reading is deeply connected with listening and seeing. When you read in a foreign language, it is sometimes difficult to see the situation and people. You might try to understand the words and picture the scene. When the picture is not clear, you get lost in a fog.

There are keywords in each story that might stem from history or Buddhism. So try to understand the keywords or side stories that support the story's backbone. I understand that you don't want to stop on every word you don't know to look for the meaning. And it looks boring and time-consuming in the beginning. However, once the fog clears up and now you can see the whole new world, you might be able to understand mountaineers' bliss. Once the fog clears up and you don't have to have the "push" to understand, the boundary between you and the story is gone.

We recommend to read intuitively instead of analyzing grammar and structures. These strategies might not be useless, but that is not the most effective way to improve, especially in terms of effort VS results.

Once you get the flow and the boundary disappears, you're ready to enter (another world). Simply read the stories and enjoy them, that will do the trick. But if you want to study even harder, you can explore short stories by well known Japanese writers. The great part of reading is that you can take your own pace. Reading is just like mountaineering. You don't know the amazing part until the end.

Chapter 1: " Like" Monster

"Everything you can imagine is real."

-Pablo Picasso

There are so many "Yokai" or Monster in Japan. From ancient times to modern Pokemon (Pocket Monster), we now have the Yokai museum in Shodo island in western Japan.

One example of traditional Yokai culture is from Akita Prefecture, Northern Japan. "Namahage" is the new year festival in which village men in Yokai like costume (Mask with big eyes and mouth, straw jacket and long hair) visit kids in their house. They ask kids, "are you a bad kid?" "Do you listen to your parents?"

The funny part is that Yokai can be scary but at the same time can be friendly and funny. There is Yokai museum in a small island, Shodo Shima in western Japan and new Yokai has been invented in their annual contest. They're originated from our imagination and sometimes our obsessions. It's great to understand Japanese culture from Yokai culture.

「いいね」

*は*のなまはげです。きなにをしたで、につの*があります。なまはげはのようになった*のがてくるおり*です。*になると、なまはげはたちのにやってて「く*子はいないか」「*の言うことをかないはいないか」とし*にます。とてもいです。

From Oga Namahage Official

https://www.namahage-oga.akita.jp/ site

にはたくさんのがあって「ざしきわらし」や「かっぱ」や「てんぐ」が*です。ざしきわらしはのです。ですから、がさいです。たいていいいにんでいて、よくいたずら*をしたり、りった*りします。

271

かっぱはにいて、よくいでいます。が*です。のに*があって、のにはがあります。きゅうり*がきでよくべています。すしの「かっぱまき」はきゅうりのすしですが、かっぱからがつけられました。

てんぐはにいます。がいです。がとてもいです。それから、とのつめがいです。*の*をて、げた*をはいています。そして*をび*ます。スーパーパワーもっています。

というに*があります。、のコンテストがかれます。をったは、にいハート 🖤 がっている*だらけ*のいで、SNS（ソーシャルメディア）で「いいね」がき*ながいます。きすぎてになってしまいました。

にはえないにいろいろなをつけてしまうのがのおもしいところです。

*

: Photo	: Famous	:Sky
:Akita Prefecture	いたずら: Prank	ぶ:Fly
つの: Horn	りる:Run around	:Art Museum
: Village*です。	:Green	る:Shine
おり: Festival	:Plate	だらけ:Covered in hair
:New Year	きゅうり:Cucumber	き:Love
く: Cry	:Strolling Monk	
: Parent	: Kimono	
す: Find	げた: Geta Sandals	

Comprehension Exercises

1. Where does Namahage take place?

. Shodo Shima

. Akita

. Ariake

. Kyoto

. Osaka

2. What are Namahage(s) looking for?

. Good Kids

. Food

. Drink

. Bad Kids

. Toys

3. What's one of the most popular modern Yokai?

. Kappa

. Zashikiwarashi

. Tengu

. Pokemon

. Tamagocchi

4. Where do Zashikiwarasi live?

. River

. Tent

. Old House

. New House

. Mountains

5. What color is Kappa?

. Blue

. White

. Green

. Red

. Transparent

6. What's the Kappa's favorite food?

- Sushi
- Cucumber
- Rice
- Plate
- Water

7. What does Kappa do in a river?
- Walk
- Run
- Dance
- Fly
- Swim

8. What's special about Tengu's face?
- Green Eyes
- Blue Face
- No Eyeblows
- Big Nose
- Big Mouth

9. What does Tengu wear?
- Straw Jacket
- Armor
- Leather Jacket
- Kimono
- Rain Coat

10. What does Tengu do?
- Runs fast
- Talks fast
- Spins fast
- Swims
- Flies

11. Where is Yokai Museum located?
- Akita
- Kyoto

- Kappa Town
- Shodo Island
- Hokkaido

12. Which Yokai won one of the prizes at the museum?

- Kappa
- Pokemon
- Namahage
- "Like" Yokai
- Tengu

Answer Keys

1 → B

2 → D

3 → D

4 → C

5 → C

6 → B

7 → E

8 → D

9 → D

10 → E

11 → D

12 → D

Chapter 2: The Oldman and Sakura

"To lead the people, walk behind them."

– Lao Tzi

Our first story takes inspiration from a popular Japanese folk tale that has been handed down from generation to generation. The folk tale plays an important role in the Japanese culture, people, and community.

The story tells about a kind old couple and greed. Also, from this story, one of the most popular nicknames for dogs became "Pochi" which often represents loyalty and honesty. There is a movie called "Pochi" starring Richard Gere, in which his dog Pochi comes to pick up and wait for his master at the train station even after his master passed.

In Japanese stories just like Managa, there are a lot of onomatopoeic words and mimetic words that add so much rhythm, flavor, and feelings to stories. In order to understand the story and feelings, we will include some notes and side stories.

じいさん

おじいさんとおばあさん、そして*のポチがにんでいました。

ある、ポチがある*ところでえて*います。

「ここれ*、ワンワン*、ここれ、ワンワン」

おじいさんが*をると、ピカピカ*の*がてきます。

「おばあさん、*だよ」

「まあまあ、はごちそう*にしましょう」

おばあさんはでべをって、しい*ごをたくさんり*、のみんなにけて*あげました。みんなとてもびました。

「いいなあ*、うらやましい*」

*にむいじわる*じいさんがやってきて、*ポチをれて*いきました。

「さあ、くけ*」

ポチをき*ました。

ポチはくて*をげて「ワン」ときました。

いじわるじいさんはをると、

「これはなんだ」

そこには*や*がいっぱい*てきました。

この「たず*」といじわるじいさんはポチをり*ました。

ポチはんで*しまいました。

やさしいおじいさんとおばあさんはしみ*ました。

そして、ポチのお*をり、しく*ないようにとに*をえて*あげました。

はぐんぐん*ときくなりました。

ある、おじいさんとおばあさんはポチの*をました。

「あのを*にして、お*をって」

とポチがいます。

「そういえば、ポチはおがきだったね」と、はし、からをりました。

そして、ペッタン、ペッタンとおをりました。

すると、からがてきます。おがのにわって*いきます。

それをていたにむいじわるじいさんは「にらん*」と、をやし*てしまいました。

おじいさんとおばあさんはきながら*をめ*ました。すると、*でがんでいきます。がれた*につくと、そこにがきました。

おじいさんはれ*にをかせようと、にってをき*ました。あたり*がピンクのでいっぱいになります。

「なんてきれいなだ」

ちょうどりかかったお*はとてもんで、おじいさんとおばあさんにご*をあげました。

しく*なったいじわるじいさんがいました。

「をかせたのはです」

おはいじわるじいさんに「このつき*め」とまえました。

いじわるじいさんは*にれられました。

*

:Ground/Dirt	いじわる: Nasty/Mean	ぬ:Die
ピカピカ:Shiny	: By force	しむ: Mourn
:Gold Coin	れる: Take	お:Grave
:Big Time	く:Bark	しい:Missing

ごちそう:Fancy Meal	き:Hit	:Tree
しい:Tasteful	い:Painful	える:Plant
る:Make	:Snake	ぐんぐん:Rapid Progress
ける:Share	:Caterpillar	: Dream
いいなあ:Would be nice	いっぱい: Full of	: Rice Mortar
うらやましい: I wish I had	たず: Useless	お: Rice Cake
: Next to	り:Beat	わる: Change

Comprehension Exercises

1. Who did the old man live with?

    A. Alone

    B. With another old man

    C. With Pochi

    D. With the old woman and Pochi

    E. With his brothers

2. What color is the flower?

    A. Purple

    B. Red

    C. Pink

    D. White

    E. Yellow

3. How do you say "Bow Wow" in Japanese?

    A. Wao Wao

    B. Wani Wani

    C. Ware Ware

    D. Pyon Pyon

    E. Wan Wan

4. What was Pochi's favorite food?

    A. Hamburger

    B. Spaghetti

    C. Chocolate

    D. Rice Cake

    E. Cookie

5. What did the old man find from Mochi?

    A. Gold Coins

    B. Books

    C. Knives

    D. Diamonds

    E. Rocks

6. What did the mean old man find in the dirt?

A. Jewels

B. Wallets

C. Mirrors

D. Snakes and Insects

E. Towels

7. What did the mean old man do to the Usu made from the tree?

A. Cut into pieces

B. Burned

C. Ate

D. Put in a river

E. Made a bathtub

8. What did the old man do with the ash?

A. Put it into dead trees

B. Poured into the ocean

C. Put it into rice fields

D. Gave it to the mean old man

E. Gave it to the Prince

9. Who appreciated the cherry blossoms?

A. Princess

B. Villagers

C. Pochi

D. The mean old man

E. Prince

10. Where did the mean old man end up?

A. Townhall

B. Castle

C. River

D. Treehouse

E. Jail

11. How did the old couple come up with the Mochi idea?

A. From a dream

B. From a rumor

C. From an order from the prince

D. From a neighbor

E. From the mean old man

12. How did the old mean man end up in jail?

A. Stole flower

B. Cut trees

C. Lied to the prince

D. Hurt the prince

E. Sold trees

Answer Keys

$1 \rightarrow D$

$2 \rightarrow C$

$3 \rightarrow E$

$4 \rightarrow D$

$5 \rightarrow A$

$6 \rightarrow D$

$7 \rightarrow B$

$8 \rightarrow A$

$9 \rightarrow E$

$10 \rightarrow E$

$11 \rightarrow A$

$12 \rightarrow C$

Chapter 3: Mr. Fox

"Drop the idea of becoming someone, because you are already a masterpiece. You cannot be improved. You have only to come to it, to know it, to realize it."

-Osho

This is a Zen story about a young fox that is looking for food. Osho says Zen is about transformation. The story goes about how a young fox transforms or how a young fox remembers who he/she is.

All the characters are animal but this is how Zen basically sees in people. The fox found a lost baby bird. The baby bird is so innocent that it appreciates everything the fox does. The fox has all the opportunities to take advantage of all the encounters.

There is much paradoxicalness in zen stories and opportunities to discover the deeper layers of stories. It looks simple and nothing special at first time but when you get the deeper meaning you appreciate the story and apply it to your life.

*のおさん

のおさん*からいたです。

あるひよこ*が*から れ*てしまい、*になります。どんどん*とをいていくと、だんだん*とおもすいてきました。

すると、一のがひよこをつけます。は「の*だ」といました。しさいけど、になる。はひよこにづきます。そして、おう*としたときに、ひよこがりき*ます。

「あ、のおさん*」

はびっくり*して、てます*。すると、ひよこがいます。

「おさん、おがいて*いるんですけど、かべはありませんか」

はしばらく*えます。「まだこんなにさいひよこだから、にある*をえれば、もっときくなる。きくなってからべよう」といます。そしてかべをえます。

「ありがとう。な*のおさん」とひよこはいます。

なおさん...はそのにいい*になります。

の、ひよこはおもいっぱいになって「おさん、ちょっと*にってきます」とかけます。はにげられてはいけませんから、をつけます*。すると、はあひる*のがひよこにづいてきます。

「ひよこさん、とてもおがいているんですけど、なにかべるものはありませんか」

ひよこはいます。

「なのおさんをっているから、に*きましょう」

はろからていて「が二つになった。あひるのもきくしてらせ*てからべればいい」といます。そして、ひよことあひるにべをえます。

「ありがとう。でやさしい*のお兄さん」

あひるのでした。「やさしい」がわり*ました。はよりもいい*になりました。

の、あひるとひよこはにます。すると、はうさぎ*のにいます。

「あひるさんとひよこさん、とってもおがいているんだ。かべない?」

「*だよ。たち、でやさしいのおさんをっているから、にいにこう」

はそれをていて「が三つにえた*」といました。あひるとひよことうさぎはのでべをもらい*ます。

「ありがとう。やさしくて、で、のような*のおさん」

うさぎがお*をいます。「のような」とわれたはとてもいいになってしまいます。やさしくて、で、のようなおさんとわれて、とてもうれしいちになりました。の*がわっていきます。

の、たちは*へびにきます。はからついていきます。をしてはいけない、といううち*ではありませんでした。たちにかない*ことがこって*はいけない、たちをら*なければいけないとってついてきました。

すると、*がます。はたちをつけると、すぐにってきます。がたちにびかかろう*としたとき、はなにもえずに、たり*をします。そしてい*になります。はひどい*をしてぐったり*とれ*ます。はそのにたちへづきます。ったはをりして*にびかります。はげました。

たちはにづいて「おさん、おさん」とびます。しかし、はすでにんでいました。そのはとてもやか*で、した*、そしてうれしそう*なをしていました。

この、たちはしみましたが、おさんのお*をって、でをり*ました。そのおに*をてました。「やさしくて、で、のような*のおさんの」とかれていました。

: Fox	: Walk	: Protect
おさん:Abbot	あひる: Duck	びかかる:Jump to someone
ひよこ:Baby Bird	に: Together	たりする：Hurl oneself
:Mother Bird	らせる: Have them gain weight	い: Fight
れる: Leave	やさしい:Sweet	: Wolf
:Lost	わる: Add	: Injury
どんどん：By the second	うさぎ: Rabbit	ぐったり：Racked

だんだん:Gradually	: Okay	れる:Take down
:Food (for Animal)	える: Increase	りす:Squeeze up
う:Attack	もらい: Be given	とてもやか:Very Peaceful
おさん:Young man/Brother	のような: God-like	した:Relieved
てる:Panicked	お:Appreciation	うれしそう : Looks happy
お*がいて:Getting Hungry	:Mind and Heart	お: Grave
しばらく: A little while	: Outside	る:Bury
:Leftover	ち: Feeling	: Stupa/Monument
な:Kind	ない: Dangerous	
: Mood	こる : Happen	

Comprehension Exercises

1. Which one is faster, 「どんどん」 or 「だんだん」?

    A. Both

    B. 「どんどん」

    C. 「だんだん」

2. What was the fox's thought when he met the baby bird?

    A. Cute

    B. Food

    C. Friend

    D. Enemy

    E. Family

3. Why did the fox give his leftover to the baby bird?

    A. Because he can't eat the leftovers

    B. Because he wanted the baby bird to grow bigger

    C. Because he liked the baby bird

    D. Because he was told to do so by his parents

    E. Because the leftovers are delicious

4. What did the baby bird say about Mr. Fox?

    A. Strong

    B. Kind

    C. Big

    D. Cunning

    E. Ridiculous

5. What was the fox's idea when he met the baby duck ?

    A. Pretty

    B. Nice

    C. Another food

    D. Ugly

    E. Funny

6. What was the fox's thought when the two babies went for a walk?

    A. Have some fun

    B. Surprise them

C. Can't let them run away

D. Scare them

E. Let them go

7. How did the duck baby describe Mr. Fox?

    A. Cool

    B. Interesting

    C. Hungry

    D. Funny

    E. Sweet

8. How did Mr. fox feel when they call him "Kind and Sweet"?

    A. Pleasant

    B. Depressing

    C. Responsible

    D. Nothing

    E. Cheesy

9. How did the baby rabbit describe Mr. Fox?

    A. Elegant

    B. Stylish

    C. Intelligent

    D. God-like

    E. Weak

10. What was Mr. Fox's though when they went for a walk?

    A. Can't let them run away

    B. Have some fun

    C. Scare them

    D. Surprise them

    E. Protect them

11. Why Mr. Fox fought the wolf?

    A. Because he wanted to eat the wolf

    B. Because he wanted to eat the babies

    C. Because he was told to do so

    D. Because he wanted to protect the babies

E. Because he wanted to protect the territory

12. How did the grave describe Mr. Fox?

    A. Funny, interesting and pleasant

    B. Kind, sweet and God-like

    C. Stylish, cool and trendy

    D. Greedy, cunning and violent

    E. Strong, brave and independent

Answer Keys

1 → B

2 → B

3 → B

4 → B

5 → C

6 → C

7 → E

8 → A

9 → D

10 → E

11 → D

12 → B

Chapter 4: Fire-Crackle Mountain

"If you don't like something, change it. If you can't change it, change your attitude."

-Maya Angelou

This is one of the most popular Japanese folk tales and probably this is one of the educational/instructional stories for parents to tell their kids to behave.

Again, the power of the onomatopoeic words and mimetic words remains in the memories than storylines. When you hear "Kachi Kachi Yama (Fire-Crackle Mountain)" it even brings me physical sensations such as heat and pains. For that reason, all the onomatopoeic and mimetic words are closely connected to emotions and memories.

たぬき(Badger)and きつね(Fox)both represent cunningness in Japanese culture and they even deceit each other. Also those animals are believe to possess human spirits and 「きつねがつく」 meaning "Fox possesses you" when you encounter something strange and unusual. The funny thing is that we have noodles named after both of them for Udon noodles or Soba noodles. たぬき is the Tempura Flakes topping and きつねis the Fried Tofu Slice topping.

This fairly tale has different versions and some of them are crueller and more of a horror story. This is the soft version of the story and badger is often considered wicked animal in the meantime goofy and slow compared to fox.

かちかち

ある、おじいさんはいことをするたぬきをまえました。

「いつもをめちゃくちゃ*にしてしまって」

まったたぬきは「もうしないよ」としくしく*ときします。

たぬきのをほどいてはいけないとおじいさんにわれますが、たぬきは

おばあさんにたぬきのな*まんじゅう*をってあげるといます。

*べれば10きするとわれるまんじゅうです。

「おじいさんがき*しますよ」と、たぬきはおばあさんにいます。

おばあさんはをってあげると、たぬきはおばあさんに*でりかかり、してしまします。

「ばかなばばあだ」と、たぬきはびねてげていきました。

おじいさんがってきて、おばあさんがれているをていてしみます。そのおじいさんをたうさぎは

「がたぬきをらし*めてくる」

うさぎは*をい*、*でたぬきをちます。たぬきがやってくると、

「うさぎさん、ずいぶんたくさんのだな」

「ほしいなら*あげるよ」

たぬきはんで*をいました。うさぎは、たぬきのろでち*をうちます。

かち、かち、かちと音が出ます。

「さっきからかち、かちかちいうのはのなの?」

と、たぬきはねます。

「かちかち山のかちかちがいているの」

たぬきのにがつけられました。ボーボー*とがします。

「さっきから、ボーボーとがするけどのなの？」

「ボーボー山のボーボーがいているの」

「あちちちち、あちちちち」

たぬきは、やけど*をしました。うさぎはらないふり*をしていました。

「*をっているよ」

「それはかる。*にって*くれ」

うさぎは*りのみそをりました。

「ヒリヒリ*するよ」

「いいはいものだよ」と、うさぎはえました。

それから3。

「なんだかいことばかりだなあ」と、たぬきはうさぎにいます。

「それならにってしいになりましょう」と、うさぎはいます。

「くていの*と、くていの*、どっちがいい?」

たぬきは「もちろん、くていだよ」と、います。

は*でにります。うさぎのはスイスイ*とんできます。たぬきのはズンズン*んでいきます。

「うわー、けてくれ」

「とさをしないなら、けてあげるよ」と、うさぎはいます。

292

「*します。ごめんなさい」と、たぬきはいます。

それ*、たぬきはをれえ*、すっかり*さをしなくなりました。

まる:Capture	げる:Escape	る:Apply/Put
めちゃくちゃ : Horrible	らしめる:Punish	:Hot Pepper
しくしく : Softly	:Firewood	ヒリヒリ:Burning
:Rope	い : Shoulder(Verb)	:Lately
ほどいて : Loosen	:Mountain Path	くていの*:Light and Weak Woodend Boat
な:Special	ほしいなら : If you want	くていの*:Heavy and Strong Dirt Boat
まんじゅう:Bun	: Half	:Pond
:One Bite	ち:Flynt	スイスイ:Smoothly
き:Long Life	ボーボー:Furiously	ズンズン:Quickly
:Stick	やけど:Burn	:Promise
す : Kill	らないふりをする:Play dumb	それ:Since Then
ばか:Idiot	:Medicine	をれえ:Change one's mind
びねて:Jump around	:Back	すっかり:Completely

Comprehension Exercises

1. What trouble did the badger give to the old man?

    A. Messing his fields

    B. Stealing money

    C. Eating his rice

    D. Sleeping in his house

    E. Stealing his shoes

2. What did the badger offer to the old woman?

    A. Massage

    B. Special Sweets

    C. Tea

    D. Dance

    E. Fur

3. What's special about the sweet?

    A. Longevity

    B. Energy Booster

    C. Flavor

    D. Famous

    E. Expensive

4. What took the revenge for the old man?

    A. Rabbit

    B. Dog

    C. Bird

    D. Goat

    E. Monkey

5. What is the Fire-Crackle sound?

    A. Sword

    B. Campfire

    C. Noise from shoes

    D. Making Crackers

    E. Flint Striking

6. What happened to the badger's back?

294

    A. Back pain

    B. Burn

    C. Cut

    D. Itchiness

    E. Scars

7. How did the rabbit help with his burn?

    A. Water

    B. Hot Pepper Medicine

    C. Massage

    D. Patting

    E. Touching

8. How did the rabbit try to have the badger feel pleasant?

    A. Smiling

    B. Eating

    C. Walking

    D. Running

    E. Boat Ride

9. Which boat did the badger choose?

    A. Light wooden boat

    B. Heavy dirt boat

10. What happened to the badger's boat?

    A. Moved fast

    B. Sank

    C. Stayed in the pond

11. What's 「をれえる」?

    A. Stay in the heart

    B. Change one's food

    C. Change one's mind

    D. Promise the reward

    E. Replace the drink

12. How do you express "burning hard"?

    A. ばーばー

B. びりびり

C. ぼーぼー

D. ひりひり

E. ぽろぽろ

Answer Keys

$1 \rightarrow A$

$2 \rightarrow B$

$3 \rightarrow A$

$4 \rightarrow A$

$5 \rightarrow E$

$6 \rightarrow B$

$7 \rightarrow B$

$8 \rightarrow E$

$9 \rightarrow B$

$10 \rightarrow B$

$11 \rightarrow C$

$12 \rightarrow C$

Chapter 5: Echo in Mountains

"Nature is not a place to visit, it is home."

-Gary Snyder

We will read an essay this time. You will be able to experience and understand the person's inner world and how thinking and feeling function. There are many ways to relax from the daily busy life and the nature plays a big role in the modern world.

Shinto, the Japanese indigenous religion, is considered the Japanese native belief system and predates historical records. You probably know a little from many Anime stories. The word of Shinto means the way of Gods and there are about eight million of them. In Shinto, God is believed to exist in everything that creates the universe, including nature such as forests, mountains, and seas. From ancient times, Japanese people see deities in natural phenomenon and worship them.

びこ

は*がなくなるとへ行きます。にをいてもらいにきます。

にく*を「びこ」とびます。にかってきなをかけると、に*してがってきます。とでは、がしう*ようにこえます。のがいてこえるのは、に*がないからでしょうか。がとてもクリアにこえます。

「びこ」の*は「ヤマヒビキ（）」や「ヤマヒビクコエ（く）」などの*と、ののだとする*があります。「びこ」は「の」「の」などのでもわれ、「ヤマコ」とばれたり、「こだま」ともばれます。

「こだま」は*のでもわれていますが、くは「こたま」とばれ「の*」をす*でした。のはにく*が「の、の」がえてくれるものだとじて*いました。

をっていくと、だんだんと*が*くなります。にをれてんでいき、しずつ*がえ*られます。の*から、の*をじて、の*へとみます。がだんだんとくなります。のもわってきます。の*がするどく*なってきます。

これは、*でうことのないです。をとしないです。とくなれたようなです。

山の*にはでできた*がありました。いがに*がくなったになります。きくをみさないといけません。をれるに「よっこいしょ」とがます。

「よっこいしょ」は「どっこいしょ」からきたです。「どっこいしょ」はで*をし、、、、、*のきがれていると*にるにしいを行くことができないとされています。「よっこいしょ」をですと「Here we go」がいとされています。

「よっこいしょ」とをれながら、をっていきます。もうあきらめ*ようかなとうこともあります。そんなときも「よっこいしょ」のでい*がつきます。み、のへとみます。そんな*をのはかにって*います。

そして、ようやく*した*でる*はをしい*ちにしてくれます。のに向かってをかけたくなります。「ヤッホー」とのはびます。

「ヤッホー」のはドイツ*の「ヨッホー(Johoo)」だとわれています。あるドイツキリスト*がい*いをしていにった*に、ようやくいたでらしい*に*して、のの「ヤハフェ」をんだのがはじまりだというもあります。

い*いをしてりったのでは、にいてもらいたかったのことなど、すっかり*れてしまいました。

:Energy	:Muscle	い:Momentum
く:Reflect	える:Tone up	:Aspect
:Reflection	:Bottom	る:Behold
う:Different	:Energy	:Peak
:Leaf	:Back	:View
:Meaning	:Senses	しい:Refreshing
:Theory	するどく:Sharp	ドイツ:German
:Bullet Trains	:Work	キリスト: Christian Missionaries
:Nymph	:Foot of a mountain	:When
す:Indicate	に:Gradually	らしい:Amazing
じる : Believe	:Purifying of the six roots of perception	:Sensation
:Breath	、、、、:Eyes, Nose, Tongue, Body and Thoughts	い : Difficult/Bitter
く:Hard	: Spiritual Mountains	すっかり : Completely

Comprehension Exercises

1. Why this person goes to mountains?

    A. Because he/she likes to drive

    B. Because he/she lives in mountains

    C. Because he/she works in mountains

    D. Because he/she likes to talk to mountains

    E. Because he/she likes hiking

2. What is "Yamabiko"?

    A. Spiritual Message

    B. Echo in mountains

    C. Ghosts

    D. Meditation

    E. Mountain Trails

3. What is "Kodama"?

    A. Local Trains

    B. Fast Cars

    C. Sprits of Woods

    D. Sprits of Mountains

    E. Spirits of Sun

4. How does this person feel in the deeper mountains?

    A. Scared

    B. Happy

    C. Sense of belonging to the mountain

    D. Sense of responsibility to the environment

    E. Sad

5. In Buddhism, what needs to be clean? Eyes, Ears, Nose, Tongue, Body and?

    A. Shoes

    B. Hair

    C. Bag

    D. Thoughts

    E. Stomach

6. Why those six need to be cleaned?

A. Ruled by law

B. To be happy

C. Buddhist Tradition

D. To walk on the right path

E. To get a free pass

7. What does "Yokkoisho" help?

A. Keep you going

B. Relax

C. Focus

D. Calm down

E. Make you sleep

8. What did "Yahho" come from?

A. German

B. Swiss

C. Chinese

D. English

E. American

9. What does this person find on top of the mountain?

A. Flower

B. Spectacular View

C. Rocks

D. Shrine

E. Monument

10. This person felt something from the bottom of their foot. What is Ki?

A. Electricity

B. Water

C. Energy

D. Message

E. Ghost

11. What did this person say about the feeling in the mountains?

A.   Sleepy

B.   No words needed

C.   Intense

D.   Humble

E.   Needy

12. What did this person talk about to mountains?

1.   Food

2.   Money

3.   Marriage

4.   Health

5.   Nothing

Answer Keys

1 → D

2 → B

3 → C

4 → C

5 → D

6 → D

7 → A

8 → A

9 → B

10 → C

11 → B

12 → E

Chapter 6: What is Kaizen？

"One can choose to go back toward safety or forward toward growth. Growth must be chosen again and again; fear must be overcome again and again."

- Abraham Maslow

In Business, Kaizen has been a practical way to approach to improve functions, especially in the manufacturing industry. In Zen, and among Yoga enthusiasts, the concept of "Here, Now" from Ram Das, impacted tremendously in the west.

This is a story about the Zen master, Shunryu Suzuki, who taught Zen in the US in 1960's. It's interesting to know after the glorious American culture of the 1950's, with the outbreak of Vietnam War, young Americans started asking questions about politics, religions, economy, and life.

"Status Quo" is not always considered positive in the west and east as well. But it's interesting to know that Zen has the premise of "nothing stays the same." And Sakura, cherry blossom reminded you of the concept vividly. The cherry blossom season only last two weeks or so. And they live fully in such a short time of period and give viewers the opportunity to celebrate the beauty and preciousness of life in this ever-changing world.

とは?

*は1960*にアメリカでをめた*おさんです。

の本「は、ここ。-Zen is Right Here」がです。

1960のアメリカでカウンターカルチャーがきました。アメリカは*では*になりましたが、*のでかな*になったのでしょうか。そんなに「かがう*」とじている*たちが、*やヨガを学んだり、*やLSDに*をちます。そののつがカルチャーで、にくのがまり*ました。

「かがう」とじているたちはをしていたのでしょうか。ベトナム*にしての*もらのでは*でした。は*の*から*をろうとしたのでしょう。

そのような、たちにとってキーワードとなったが「*である」(Spontaneous)であっとわれています。「である」とはどういうことなのか、しい*をしました。*とされる1950のアメリカはではなかったのでしょうか。どこかに*をしていたのでしょうか。

1950のアメリカは、や、ライフスタイルでのあこがれ*となりました。すべてがかにえました。のはアメリカのロックやジャズにあこがれました。

はある、*のにいをしました。

「みんなそのままで*である、でもほんのし*することができる」

をぶのくはにけている*ものを*によってたそう*とします。のようにになりたいとえているがくいました。しかし、「であろう」とするともうそこで、ではなくなってしまいます。「ありのまま*」でいいわけでもない。ではどうしたらいいのでしょうか。

にんだ*によると、は*をって、*にすれば、の*がにって*くるとっている。その「」というものをしれて*みる。のためにかする、のではなく、ただってみてはどうだろうか。がし*になるかもしれない。

「いまのは*であるが、ほんの少し*することができる」

: Master	: Protest	けている:Missing
: Era	:Important	:Efforts
める: Spread	:Government	たす:Fill
: Economy	:Communism	ありのまま: As it really is
:Best in the World	: Threats	: Purpose
に:Really	: Democracy	: Effective
かな: Rich	:Nature	: Accomplishments
かがう:Something is wrong	しい:Discussion	:Perfect
: Young People	:Glory	:Monk
: Eastern Thought	: Against Reason	る：Return
: Spirituality	あこがれ：Icon	れる：Forget
: Interests	そのまま: As it is	：Freedom
まる: Gather	:Perfect	
: War	:Progress	

Comprehension Exercises

1. Which country is the richest in 1960s?

    A. Japan

    B. UK

    C. USA

    D. Germany

    E. China

2. What's the question many young American had in 60's ?

    A. Why USA won WW2?

    B. Something is wrong

    C. Why Vietnam is strong

    D. Why China is rich

    E. Communism is powerful

3. What did young American discuss?

    A. Spontaneity

    B. Freedom

    C. Equality

    D. Peace

    E. Business

4. What kind of American music did Japanese people like in 60's?

    A. Country

    B. Bluegrass

    C. Heavy Metal

    D. Rock and Jazz

    E. Hip Hop

5. Which war impacted young American in 60's?

    A.   Vietnam War

    B.   Korean War

    C.   WWII

    D.   American Civil War

    E.   Gulf War

6. Who was the first Zen master who taught in the US

A.   Budhhda

B.   Yogananda

C.   Shunryu Suzuki

D.   Ram Dass

E.   Bruce Lee

7. What is 「ありのまま」?

A.   On Demand

B.   Peacefulness

C.   Stillness

D.   As you are

E.   As you learn

8. What do most people try to get something from their efforts?

A.   Money

B.   Time

C.   Bonus

D.   Result

E.   Strategy

9. How do you improve from 「ありのまま」?

A.   Meditate

B.   Ask

C.   Not to think too much about oneself and improve

D.   Patience

E.   Repeat

10. What is 「自然である」?

A.   Being spontaneous

B.   Being in the nature

C.   Being eco-friendly

D.   Being Vegan

E.   Being selfless

11. What do you need to have for Zazen?

A.   Purpose

B.   Timeline

C. Mantra

D. Bell

E. Nothing

12. In this method, how do you do Kaizen?

A. Big Challenge

B. Small Improvement

C. Manager Acknowledgement

D. Huge Improvement

E. Break

Answer Keys

$1 \rightarrow C$

$2 \rightarrow B$

$3 \rightarrow A$

$4 \rightarrow D$

$5 \rightarrow A$

$6 \rightarrow C$

$7 \rightarrow D$

$8 \rightarrow D$

$9 \rightarrow C$

$10 \rightarrow A$

$11 \rightarrow E$

$12 \rightarrow B$

Chapter 7: The Game

"I have to get stronger – like a stray crow" from Kafka on the shore"

-Haruki Murakami

This is a short story about "Naimono Nedari," "Something Missing" or "Asking Something You don't have" in English. Some dictionary says "Crying for the Moon" or "Asking for the Impossible." The translation is not exactly conveying the essence of "Naimono Nedari" and I wanted to write about it because we all spend so much time on this in our limited time of life.

One of the most famous contemporary Japanese writers is Yoko Ogawa. Her stories are mystical and transformational in everyday life. Some say you can travel to a different dimension from the ordinary everyday life settings. It is a kind of magic realism in Japanese language and her story telling is close to human memories.

"When we face a difficult reality that looks impossible for us to accept, I think we always work on creating a story and mold the reality to fit into our shape of heart so we can leave it in our memories."

Like her stories and Haruki's stories, many readers worldwide pointed out their therapeutic effects in their story telling. The voice of their stories often reflects our voice and when you feel heard, something magical can happen in our heart.

ないものねだり

あきらは*だとわれてった。どこにっても、*だった。でもそううことがよくあった。みんなからかれるタイプではない。をやっても、にしても、も*しないがいた。

*を*して、*のわれるままにえばいいをいくつかした。しばらくつと、リストラ*でを失った*。のを見つけても、*がよくなくないとリストラにう。にうらみ*をつわけではないが、く**がどんどんとなくなっていった。

30になるしに*になろうとった。フランチャイズのチェーンをつことができる。トレーニングに3*したが、よくわからない*とのわからない*システムに、やる*がなくなった。*にサインをさせられて、*してみようとったが、がらなかった。*のファンだけが、*をもらっていた。

をんで、のをでった。がつく*との*にっていた。サラダボールをさま*にしたようなにづくときな*があった。*なのだという。

310

サラダボールのにあるさな*にをめた。さな*があって、そこが*になっていた。*は500円だった。をってにった。

*の*にをれる*はあきらだけだった。さな*をもらい、*がかれているのへっていく。ひんやり*とした*にっていくと、こげ*をした*にところどころ*がかれていた。*のような*や、*などもかれている。*のには*のようなものがかれていた。

「それで?」

と、がこえた。ののなのだろうか。

のへとむと、またがする。

「うん、それで?」

「*?」と*をげた*。

「をそんなに、わからないといこんでるの*」とはった。

「がですか?」

は*をしない。このを*していいのか、どうなのか、わからなくなってしまう。このえたはいつしか*、かくなり、*とはう**でるく*なっていた。はではなく、からけている*ように見えるが、これはのせいだろうか。

「*にえてもらってよ」

はいます。

「を?」

「*について」

あきらはますます*わからなくなっていきます。

「のこと」とはけえます。

「あなたは*ですか?」

「の*」

「なんですか?」

「のっていうの」

「そうなんですね」と、あきらはった。のことだかさっぱり*わからない。

のは、ゆっくりとあきらにをめた。*がにるとえなくなることがいくつかある。

わからないことなど、はもない。りない*ものなどなにもない。*はにある。そしては「ないものねだり」のゲームをけるがほとんどだということ。

あきらはをいて、はっきりと*できたわけではなかったが、かとても*なことをにした*と*をつことができた。そしてをえたかおおきなものの*をした。

「がんでくるものはがえてくれる」

あきらはにり、をりてった。

にしかり、*をった。やがてになったをした。いつもとはかうスタートだった。があっても、やっていけるがした。

*

:Hoodoo	:Ancient Grave	いつしか:Without noticing
育つ:Grow up	:Admission	: Lighting
:Trouble	:Weekdays	:Light
:Expectation	:Parking	るく:Bright
:College	:Hut	ける:Come out
:Graduation	:Reception	:Bird
:Boss	: AM	える:Teach
リストラ:Downsizing	れる:Visit	:Wind
失う:Lose	:Leaflet	ますます:More and more
:Economic Climate	:Stone Coffin	: at all
: Company	ひんやり:Cold	の: Tree of Life
うらみ: Hatred	:Cave	さっぱり:Completely
く: Work	こげ:Dark Brown	:Soul
: Willingness	: Wall	りない:Lacking
:Shiatsu Masseur	: Painting	:Security
:Participate	:Animal	りげている*
理念: Corporate Identity	:Pattern	はっきり: Clearly
のわからない:Unclear	:Flower	: Understanding
やる:Motivation	:Big Tree	にする:Hear
:Contract	:I (Male)	:Confirmation
:Independence	:Neck	:Existence
:President	げる: Tilt	:Intersection

:Customers	いこむ:Presume	しかる:Get close to
がつく:Notice	:Reply	:Red Light
:Signage	:Trust	

Comprehension Exercises

1. What type of person Akira was when he was growing up?

    A.   Trouble

    B.   Happy Role Model

    C.   Positive Energy Ball

    D.   Invisible

    E.   Bullied

2. Did you find passion at work?

    A.   Yes

    B.   No

    C.   More or less

3. He lost jobs because of?

    A.   Downsizing

    B.   Talents

    C.   Family Situations

    D.   Communication Skills

    E.   Peronality

4. What did he try before becoming 30 years old?

    A.   Acting

    B.   Dancing

    C.   Singing

    D.   Skateboarding

    E.   Shiatsu Massage Training

5. Did he get along with the president of the Shiatsu Massage Company ?

    A.   Yes

    B.   No

6. What did he go when he took an unexpected absence?

    A.   River

    B.   Waterfall

    C.   See

    D.   Mountains

    E.   Lake

7. What did he find in the mountain?

    A.   Camping Place

    B.   Restaurant

    C.   Cafe

    D.   Salad Bowl

    E.   Ancient Tomb

8. What happened to Akira in the cave?

    A.   Fire

    B.   Got lost

    C.   Heard some voice

    D.   Ghost showed up

    E.   Attached by snakes

9. How did the voice identify oneself?

    A.   Tree of Light

    B.   Tree of Life

    C.   Tree of Letter

    D.   Ancient King

    E.   Princess

10. Where did the voice say security is located?

    A.   Weapons

    B.   Guns

    C.   Heart/Mind

    D.   Legs

    E.   Bag

11. What message can you find from birds?

    A.   Water and Relaxation

    B.   Fire and Inspiration

    C.   Winds and Directions

    D.   Earth and Stability

    E.   Tree and Growth

12. What did the voice give Akira ?

    A.   Some Assurance

B. Some Happiness

C. Some Money

D. Some gift

E. Some story

Answer Keys

$1 \rightarrow A$

$2 \rightarrow B$

$3 \rightarrow A$

$4 \rightarrow E$

$5 \rightarrow B$

$6 \rightarrow D$

$7 \rightarrow E$

$8 \rightarrow C$

$9 \rightarrow A$

$10 \rightarrow C$

$11 \rightarrow C$

$12 \rightarrow B$

Chapter 8: Sounds of Water

"It's the simple things in life that are the most extraordinary."

-Paul Coehlo

This is a short essay about water. In Feng Shui, Water plays such an important role because water is the element that collects energy in. Feng Shui's Shui is Water, Mizu or Sui in Japanese. The main concept of Feng Shui is Ying Yang, "In Yoh" in Japanese and five energy elements of water, fire, metal, earth and wood. And as you see the system on earth, water is important and will be important for not only humans but all the living on earth because we are not able to manufacture water even, we invented robots, computers and chat GPT.

When you go to Shinto shrines in Japan, you might find what types of deity the shrine represents. There are fire deities, water deities, local community deities, Sun deities, and animal deities. Shinto is Japanese animism from ancient times, and we imported Buddhism in 6th century. The interesting part of Shinto shrines share space and deities with Buddhist temples and many of Shinto shrines are located next or in the same location as temples.

When Buddhism was imported from China via Korea, there are other technologies, culture and people are integrated in Japan as well. I personally believed the culture of water was imported around this period form China. Water is considered most powerful, resilient, and generous element in nature as Lao Zi says.

"Water is fluid, soft, and yielding. But water will wear away rock, which is rigid and cannot yield. As a rule, whatever is fluid, soft, and yielding will overcome whatever is rigid and hard. This is another paradox: what is soft is strong."

の

はにくとず*、のをします。さなやき*や*などにいます。

のはしく*、えめ*で、をちかせて*くれます。まるでのにれて*いると*しているようです。

らはいったいどこからて、そしてどこにれていくのでしょうか。ののも、どこからてどこへくのでしょうか。

のにをすませると、はいところへといて*くれます。*のがれにって*ゆっくりとり*をんでいきます。ただそこにいればいいのに、どうしてはれていくのでしょうか。

*のをけて、しいところへり*ます。のはのだといますか。にたったり、とがぶつかったり*するではありません。、のなのです。

をしているかっていますか。

たちとまったくじです。が*たちとをしています。おい*をべたり*、*ったり*することもあります。いろいろなみ*もあります。

*なをとり、い*いをしたり、*で*してされ*たりします。しかし、そこにじっと*しているわけにはいきません。*にたからにはくところがあるのです。

*から、へとれ、*をった*り、の*をります。*でみとして*するや、で*をてる*につくもてきます。

にると、*されたたちとって*をしました。にれとされ*ました。

そして、らからいろいろなをきました。ないをしてになったのです。*をくとじからやってたというではありませんか。らのをゆっくり*といてあげました。すると、だんだんと*のきれいなのにわっていきました。

きなを*に、はどんどんときくなっていきます。れ*はゆったりとしていて、いろいろなたちがいます。うからた、*としてちて*きた、からた、*からになってれてきたなどがみんなにじへんでいます。

やがて*がえてきます。そのこうにはきな*がいくつもあります。そこはもう*です。いろいろな*がじって*います。どこまでい*のかもここからではえません。もう「」というはありませんでした。しい*というちもありません。ただ、ってきた、というちでいっぱいです。どこかで「おかえりなさい」とがしているようでほっとしました。

*

ず:Defenite	:Company	
き:Spring Water	おい:Each Other	:Farm Crop
: Waterfall	べる:Compare	:Pollution
う:Encounter	う:Compete	:Fight
しく:Gentle	む : Have a conflict	にる : Join
えめ:Humbly	な:Heavy	す:Threaten
をちかせて:Calming	い: Scary	:One's Origin
れる: Flow	: Lake	ゆっくり:Slowly
:Interaction	: Break	:Clear and Colorless
をすませる:Listen carefully	される : Healing	で:From the tail of one's eye
いく:Lead	じっと:Fixedly	: Rain
:One Drop	:The Earth	ちる:Drop
って:Along with	:Fields	: Snow
り:Path Way	る:Cross	: Port

:Rock	:Residential Area	: Sea
る:Slide	:Reservor	じる: Mix
ぶつかる:Clash	み:Drinking Water	い: Deep
じ:Same	:Getting a job	しい: Lonely

Comprehension Exercises

1. What does the author try to find in the mountains?

   A.   Water Bottle

   B.   Sounds of Water

   C.   Water Bugs

   D.   Water Colors

   E.   Smell of Water

2. How does the author describe the sound of water?

   A.   Strong and clear

   B.   Calming and humble

   C.   Pleasant and happy

   D.   Loud and confusing

   E.   Noisy and annoying

3. Which word did the author use for the sound of water?

   A.   Light

   B.   Singing

   C.   Voice

   D.   Laughing

   E.   Sleeping

4. What did water do in a lake?

   A.   Party

   B.   Dancing

   C.   Resting

   D.   Singing

   E.   Talking

5. What types of jobs can water get?

   A.   Tour Guide

   B.   Police

   C.   Drinking Water

   D.   Singer

   E.   Entertainer

6. Who did the water fight within a river?

A.   Polluted Water

B.   Muddy Water

C.   Drinking Water

D.   Cold Water

E.   Mineral Water

7. What happened to polluted water after a long talk?

A.   Became mineral water

B.   Became muddy water

C.   Became drinking water

D.   Became multi-color water

E.   Became purified water

8. How did the polluted water intimidate the water?

A.   To join the polluted water group

B.   To go to the other river

C.   To go back to the mountains

D.   To go talk to humans

E.   To pay the fees

9. What did the water see after the river?

A.   Surfers

B.   Fish

C.   Cats

D.   Swimmers

E.   Port

10. What did the water see in the sea?

A.   Waves

B.   Moon

C.   Sun

D.   Camera

E.   Mixed colors

11. How did the water feel in the sea?

A.   Not scared

B.   Not happy

C.   Not lonely

D.   Not depressed

E.   Not panicked

12. What did the water hear in the sea?

A.   Voice

B.   Laugh

C.   Beep

D.   Gong

E.   Whistle

Answer Keys

1 → B

2 → B

3 → C

4 → C

5 → C

6 → A

7 → E

8 → A

9 → E

10 → E

11 → C

12 → A

Conclusion

"It's not as if our lives are divided simply into light and dark. There's shadowy middle ground. Recognizing and understanding the shadows is what a healthy intelligence does. And to acquire a healthy intelligence takes a certain amount of time and effort."

After Dark

- Haruki Murakami

Congratulations on completing the Japanese Book 1, Book 2, and Book 3! Throughout this journey, we hope you have enjoyed the stories and discovered not only the language but also something valuable about yourself.. And we hope you continue this journey.

An example of the profound impact of language and cultural exploration is Dr. Robert Campbell, a Japanese literature professor at Tokyo University. He discovered the world's oldest novel, 'The Tale of Genji,' written by a female writer in 11th century Japan, which sparked his passion for Japanese art and culture. Dr. Campbell who is from the Bronx, NYC, and was not interested in Japan or the language until his college days. His language skills are not only fascinating but his ability to communicate politics to art history in perfect Japanese word choice on television.

"Remember, this was when postmodernism was rampant and people were confidently announcing the "end of literature." I sensed something in classical Japanese literature that seemed to offer a way of breaking away from that way of thinking."

And he started taking classes in Japanese art. He was captured by screen paintings from the 16th century depicting bird's-eye views of scenes. He said he felt a tremendous energy emanating from the paintings. Then his professor advised him to learn the language first. He took a two-month intensive immersion course in Vermont, then he came to study more in Japan and now he is an expert on 19th century Edo period culture. Because of the woodblock printing in the period (Japan was isolated in the period), he was fascinated not only by high culture but also low culture because it sometimes contains serious messages and hints on how to live.

Through Dr. Campbell's experience, we can see how learning a foreign language and immersing ourselves in a different culture can have a profound impact on our lives. Now is the perfect moment to reflect on your progress, evaluate your fluency, and plan your next steps to continue this journey of exploration and discovery."

Made in the USA
Las Vegas, NV
25 January 2024